T0326300

Additional praise for *Mourning and Modernity*

"In this collection of essays, many previously unpublished, Isaac Balbus elaborates a psychoanalytically informed theory of cultural mourning that enables him to shed light on an extremely diverse set of topics, among them feminism, Marxism, the 60's counterculture, reparations for racism, deep ecology and the 12-step recovery movement. At once imaginatively conceived and rigorously argued, *Mourning and Modernity* is free of jargon; here, intellectual sophistication is combined with consistent readability. This volume confirms Balbus's standing as one of the leading American critical social and political theorists."

—Sandra Lee Bartky, Professor Emerita,
University of Illinois at Chicago

"Few essay collections fit together as well as this one. The years over which they were written reveals a subtext almost as fascinating as the main text, a story of emotional as well as theoretical development. Few works of theory are as personal without feeling confessional. Balbus does more than hold the reader's attention, however. He insists on an unpopular thesis in the era of postmodern play and display: that it is issues of rage and mourning that must be worked through again and again in almost every aspect of our culture, from childrearing to racial relations, if we are to come to terms with our hatred and loss. This is a brave book and an important one."

—C. Fred Alford, Professor of Government and Distinguished
Scholar-Teacher, University of Maryland, College Park

"Reading *Mourning and Modernity* as a clinician, I was reminded once more that in order to keep psychoanalysis healthy, we should not forget that besides providing therapy for individuals, it has broader applications to human affairs. Isaac Balbus, a political theorist, primarily utilizing Kleinian theories, explores a wide range of topics—from the influence of coparenting on the developing psyche of children, to America's reparation for slavery and racism, to a comparison between modernity and a narcissistic individual's 'grandiose self.' To follow Balbus as he links clinical phenomena with social and political theory is intellectually rewarding in itself, but more important, this kind of work also has practical applications for making the world we live in a better place."

—Vamik D. Volkan, M.D., Senior Erik Erikson Scholar,
The Austen Riggs Center, Stockbridge, MA

"*Mourning and Modernity* is a book about how we become who we are, how to mourn who we cannot be, and why we must not give up on ourselves. It reflects Isaac Balbus's persistent, ground-level engagement with the theories of Melanie Klein and Dorothy Dinnerstein, and shows once again how much their use provides light and guidance for these difficult times."

—E. Victor Wolfenstein, Professor of Political Science, UCLA

MOURNING
AND
MODERNITY
Essays in the Psychoanalysis of Contemporary Society

Isaac D. Balbus

OTHER

Other Press
New York

Permission to reprint excerpts from the following (some with minor alterations) is gratefully acknowledged:
Chapter 1–*Theory and Society* 21:817-835, © 1992 Isaac Balbus, Kluwer Academic Publishers, with kind permission of Springer Science and Business Media.
Chapter 3–*Emotional Rescue*, by Isaac Balbus, pp. 259-269. Reproduced by permission of Routledge/Taylor & Francis Books, Inc.
Chapter 4–*Political Theory* 31(6), by Isaac Balbus. Reprinted by permission of Sage Publications.
Chapter 7–*Soundings* 14:39-52, Spring 2000, "Mourning the Movement" by Isaac Balbus. Reprinted by permission of Lawrence & Wishart.
Chapter 8–*Journal of Psychoanalysis, Culture and Society* 9 (2), August 2004, "The PsychoDynamics of Racial Reparations" by Isaac Balbus. Reproduced with permission of Palgrave Macmillan.

Production Editor: Robert D. Hack

This book was set in 11 pt. Berkeley by Alpha Graphics of Pittsfield, NH.

10 9 8 7 6 5 4 3 2 1

Library of Congress Cataloging-in-Publication Data

Balbus, Isaac D.
  Mourning and modernity : essays in the psychoanalysis of contemporary society / Isaac D. Balbus.
    p. cm.
  Includes bibliographical references and index.
  ISBN 1-59051-155-7 (pbk. : alk. paper) 1. Psychoanalysis and culture.
2. Dominance (Psychology) I. Title.
  BF175.4.C84B35 2005
  150.19'5–dc22
                          2004021692

For Mary

Contents

Acknowledgments

Like any project that spans a good part of two decades, this one has accumulated a great many intellectual debts. Judith Feher-Gurewich, publisher of Other Press, Sandy Thatcher, editor-in-chief of Penn State Press, and Stanley Fish, former dean of the College of Liberal Arts and Sciences at the University of Illinois at Chicago, were each kind enough to read, and evaluate, the entire manuscript prior to its publication. A number of chapters benefited from the characteristically close reading of my comrade-in-theoretical-arms, Stephen Engelmann, who also helped me maintain my equanimity during turbulent academic times. As usual, my dear friends Ron Bayer and Rob Crawford provided similar—and much appreciated—intellectual and emotional support.

Many other colleagues were kind enough to comment on the original versions of individual chapters. They include Sandra Bartky, Simon Clarke, Phil Cushman, Christine DiStefano, Miriam Dixson, Judith Gardiner, Jim Hall, Bonnie Honig, David Ingram, Steve Jones, Lynne Layton, Charles Mills, Danny Postel, Michael Rustin, John Sanbonmatsu, Donnel Stern, and Ryan Van Meter.

A number of institutions and groups also deserve credit. A fellowship at the Institute for the Humanities at the University of Illinois at Chicago in academic year 1998–99 enabled me to write the article that became Chapter 7 of this book, and a sabbatical leave from UIC in fall 2003 gave me the time and energy to write its introduction and concluding chapter. The essay that became Chapter 8 was first presented in fall 2001 at a meeting of the Dean's Seminar at UIC and then at a conference organized by the Chicago Political Theory Group in spring 2002. What is now Chapter 2 was initially prepared for the Feminist Political Theory Conference of the Western Political Science Association in spring 1999, and an excerpt from that paper was also presented at the Conference on Dorothy Dinnerstein at the New School for Social Research in April 2000. A preliminary version of Chapter 9 was initially prepared for the Annual Conference on Cultural Studies at Kansas State University in March 2002, and subsequently presented at a seminar organized by the Department of Communications at UIC. A version of Chapter 3 was read at a colloquium of the Department of Philosophy at UIC in September 2000. Finally, Chapter 10 was presented at the 100th Anniversary Conference of the American Political Science Association in Chicago in September 2004.

I would also like to thank Marilyn Getzov, James Knell, and—especially—Volker Kleinschmidt for invaluable assistance in the preparation of this manuscript. Volker's generously offered expertise helped me to avert and overcome a number of technically induced traumas from which I might otherwise have never recovered.

All of these important contributions, however, are dwarfed by those of my wife, Mary Holmquist, to whom this book is dedicated. Mary read almost all the chapters in their original form, listened with unfailing patience to trial runs of their oral presentations, and encouraged my decision to edit and assemble them into the manuscript that became this book. Our life together has been a consistent source of personal light shining though the political darkness of the past two decades. The third time really *has* been a charm.

Introduction

This book is a collection of essays written over the past twelve years. But to call it a collection is rather to underestimate the closeness of the connections among its various parts and thus the coherence of the work as a whole. All the essays in this volume are psychoanalytically informed explorations of the psychological foundations of modern domination that are motivated by the political commitment to eliminate it.

This is a project to which I have devoted the better part of the last twenty-five years. In 1979 I began work on a book that critically evaluated Marxist and neo-Marxist theories of sexual, political, and technological domination and culminated in an alternative account of those forms of domination that borrowed from, but significantly modified, the feminist psychoanalysis of Dorothy Dinnerstein, Nancy Chodorow, and other so-called "feminist mothering theorists." The argument of the concluding part of *Marxism and Domination*, published in 1982,[1] was that different forms of patriarchy, the state, and the relationship between human and nonhuman nature are emotionally anchored in different forms of mother-dominated child rearing, and that the overcoming of those forms of domination therefore demands (among other things) that what I have since decided to call the maternal mode of child rearing be replaced by early parenting that is shared equally by women and men.

In 1984 the birth of my daughter gave me the opportunity to put my theoretically informed commitment to coparenting into practice. This effort proved to be much more problematical than I had planned. I discovered to my chagrin that there were problems in my parenting and that these problems could not be explained by the feminist mothering theory I was, in effect, trying to put into practice. From the assumption that boys need to define themselves in opposition to their (m)others, one would (I thought) predict that fathers would privilege the independence over the dependence of their children, that, in other words, they would be threatened more by their child's merger with them than by their separation from them. But in my case it was exactly the reverse: my delight in my deep attachment to my daughter during her first year was more than matched by a growing anxiety that this attachment would be lost in the years that immediately followed. This anxiety provoked an encounter with nonfeminist psychoanalytic theories of narcissism which, I learned, were able to account for my difficulties in ways that feminist mothering theory could not. Whereas feminist mothering theory argues that there are gender-based differences in object relations that owe their existence to the (mother-monopolized) *structure* of parenting, narcissism theory treats differences in the object relations of individuals as the ungendered result of differences in the quality of the parenting *practice* that occurs within that (taken-for-granted) structure. It predicts, more specifically, that both girls *and* boys who were raised by mothers who subverted their separation would grow up to become parents who were threatened by the independence of their children. In short, narcissism theory helped me explain—and ultimately transform—my parenting practice. Thus in the course of my effort to put one theory into practice I became a partisan of another theory whose assumptions were not only different from but also in some ways opposed to the theory to which I remained committed. The stage for a theoretical synthesis was set.

Emotional Rescue: The Theory and Practice of a Feminist Father[2] tells the story of the personal practice that made that theoretical synthesis both necessary and possible and goes some distance toward working it out. The partial synthesis of feminist mothering theory and psychoanalytic theories of narcissism that I elaborate in that volume incorporates some, while repudiating other, central assumptions of feminist mothering theory. In particular it retains the assumptions (1) that the maternal mode of child rearing necessarily engenders unintegrated, split-off rage against the mother that is projected onto women; (2) that rage against women cannot but poison our relationships with our natural and political counterparts; and (3) that coparenting is necessary (if not sufficient) to establish relationships with gender, natural, and political counterparts that are free from the drive to dominate.

Part I of this volume is devoted to the defense of these as well as other related assumptions against a number of different criticisms that derive from a number of different theoretical directions. Chapter 1, "De-Kleining Feminist Mothering Theory?"[3] assesses the argument of C. Fred Alford in his important *Melanie Klein and Critical Social Theory*,[4] that Dinnerstein's derivation of patriarchy from mother-dominated child rearing—and thus the overcoming of patriarchy from coparenting—suffers from an unwarranted privileging of reality over phantasy that is inconsistent with Klein's own understanding of that relationship. I demonstrate that Dinnerstein's so-called revisionism is entirely consistent with the revision of Klein for which Alford argues elsewhere in his book, and that there are in fact no good Kleinian reasons for rejecting Dinnerstein's deductions. My conclusion, then, is that the Dinnersteinian assumptions I have adopted and adapted in my own work can well withstand a challenge mounted from a nonfeminist Kleinian theoretical position.

Chapter 2, "Patriarchal 'Production' in Marx,"[5] summarizes the critique of Marx and Marxism I derived from those assumptions in *Marxism and Domination* and then reviews and evaluates critiques of those assumptions, as well as my anti-Marxist derivation from them, that proceed from a variety of different nonpsychoanalytic theoretical positions. Here I encounter Marxist, broadly social constructionist, and Wittgensteinian objections to my argument that the domination of nature is an historically specific form of male domination that owes its existence to a peculiarly punitive form of mother-dominated child rearing, and that Marx's commitment to the domination of nature is therefore not only counter-ecological but counter-feminist as well. In the course of this encounter I defend at length the thesis of (what I call) the determining power of the mode of child rearing that I first set forth in *Marxism and Domination*. I also summarize briefly my effort in *Emotional Rescue* to reconcile this claim of its determining power with the fact of its historicity—to reconcile synchrony and diachrony—with what I dubbed in that volume a *gender-struggle* theory of changes in the mode of child rearing. That theory, as I have already intimated, derived a gender-based opposition in parenting interests from the defining assumptions of feminist mothering theory and conceived this opposition as the necessary (but not sufficient) source of major changes in child-rearing practices. In brief, I conceptualized the mode of child rearing as a contradictory structure that contains the seeds of its own transformation. Speaking grandiosely, I tried to do for child rearing what Marx tried to do for production.

This theoretical effort relied, among other things, on the concept of "core gender identity." My gender-struggle theory was based, in other words, on the assumption that "a cognitive sense of gendered self, the sense that one is [either] male or female"[6] that corresponds to one's anatomical sex is, in fact, a culturally universal sense. This assumption has been called into question by Judith Butler, first in her enormously influential *Gender Trouble* and somewhat later in her *Bodies That Matter.*[7] In Chapter 3, "The Butler Didn't Do It," I outline Butler's deconstruction of the psychoanalytic concept of gender identity as well as her alternative, performative account thereof, and I contest both her claim that the psychoanalytic concept normalizes heterosexuality and the coherence of her alternative account. In short, I argue that Butler's postmodernist objections to feminist mothering theory entirely miss their mark.

In Chapter 4, "Against the Idealism of the Affects"[8] I consider four recent feminist works—by Nel Noddings, Kelly Oliver, Cynthia Willett, and Sonia Kruks—whose laudable search for the sensuous sources of sociality is unfortunately unaccompanied by any sustained reflection on the sensuous sources of what subverts it. Their common neglect of the origins of aggression in the formation of the self, in other words, prevents them from clarifying the conditions under which their ideal of solidarity might in fact be realized. I argue that a feminist appropriation of Kleinian psychoanalytic theory is the most attractive alternative to their common "affective idealism." Klein's assumptions that both love and hate are inherent in the child's relationship to the mother, and that his or her emotional development depends on the extent of integration of those opposing passions, enable us to grasp not only the permanence of aggression but also the conditions under which it will find benign as compared to malignant expression. Realistic optimism, then, is what Klein has to offer.

This gift is also celebrated in Chapter 5, "Remembering Melanie Klein," which begins by locating Klein within the history of the psychoanalytic movement and goes on to consider the ways in which her account of the role of reparations in individual development can be extended to embrace the development of groups.[9] Both the individual and the group accounts, I conclude, underscore the inevitability of doing damage as well as the possibility of repairing the damage being done. Thus Klein gives us reason to hope (even) in hard times.

Hope in hard times is, in a way, the subject of Part II of this volume. The darkness of recent decades makes this topic all too timely. The subversive spirit of the Sixties and the new social movements that followed in the wake of that era have long since succumbed to the very system they once appeared—briefly—to have so thoroughly discredited. Indeed, it increasingly appears as though the only alternative to the madness of modernity is a fundamentalism that is, if anything, much worse. Thus we have lived through a transition from a period when everything seemed possible to a time that seems bereft of any progressive political possibilities at all. In short, we have lost the hope we once had.

To regain it we need to mourn its loss. When the present is so bleak we must try, in the words of Walter Benjamin, to find "hope in the past." So in Chapter 6, "Working Through Benjamin: Walter Benjamin and the Work of (Counter) Cultural Mourning,"[10] I turn to his merciless critique of modernity and his commitment to radical remembrance as the way to break its chains. Benjamin is perhaps the only Marxist—if he was a Marxist—to understand that we can only give ourselves a future if we pay our debts to the past. Thus he prescribes an "anamnestic solidarity" with our "oppressed ancestors"—the effort to make good in the present on the failed liberation struggles of the past—as an antidote to a modernity that murders both metaphor and memory. There is, I argue, much to be learned from Benjamin, but in the end his project suffers from a conceptual split between a (capitalist) modernity that is rendered "all-bad" and (proletarian) struggles against it that are figured as "all-good." This split prevents him from identifying both the distinctively modern sources of remembrance on which those struggles must rely and the way in which domination necessarily infects even these ostensibly emancipatory efforts.

"Working Through Benjamin" thus culminates in a call for a theory of political mourning for which such splitting is a problem to be overcome rather than a supposed solution. Chapter 7 responds to this call by applying Melanie Klein's account of the mourning of individual losses to the problem of "Mourning the Movement."[11] Although Freud was the first to suggest that lost ideals must be mourned along with the lost loved ones (he assumed) they represent, his model of successful mourning as a "detachment of libido" from what has been lost, I argue at the outset of this chapter, is much too modernist to serve as the basis for a theory of political mourning that seeks not to break with, but rather to build on, the past. Klein argues, in contrast, that successful mourning is a process that transforms loss into growth through a selective identification with what has been lost that requires that the mourner work through his inevitable admixture of love and hate for that object. Thus an enduring idealization or demonization of the lost object is a sign that mourning has gone awry.

In the second half of this chapter I apply this model of mourning to our relationship to (what we used to call) the Movement. I suggest that the persistent pattern of nostalgia for and denigration of the Sixties on the Left is an indication that we have yet to recover from their loss, and that this unmourned loss is a significant source of the profound political pessimism from which we currently suffer. Mourning that loss—working through our ambivalence for a Movement that both lit us up and burnt us out—might enable us selectively to identify with the spirit of the Sixties and thus help us find the hope in the past we need to open up the future.

Klein also teaches us that the losses of real objects suffered by adults necessarily evoke the losses of the internal objects they suffered as children, and thus that their ability to mourn the later losses depends on whether they have ever been able to mourn the earlier ones. The child, she argues, will only be able to integrate his love and hate for the mother and thus to achieve healthy object relations if he has been able both to grieve the loss of the "all-good" mother of phantasy and to make reparations to the real mother—thus overcoming his anxiety and guilt—for his aggressive assaults on her "all-bad" phantasy counterpart. Thus Klein makes the process of mourning central to the very formation of the self and makes reparations central to the process of mourning.

In Chapter 8, "The Psychodynamics of Racial Reparations,"[12] I apply Klein's account of the role of reparations in the development of the individual to the problem of the development of the relationship between white Americans and African Americans. I argue that proposals for reparations for racism—for slavery and its sequelae—are likely to engender the unconscious resistance of the very whites who would most benefit from them. This argument is based on the assumption that demonizing and idealizing white racial fantasies are fueled by the split-off aggression and libido—hatred and love—that racist whites have projected into blacks. On the one hand, a proper program of racial reparations might enable those whites simultaneously to reclaim those rejected parts of themselves and to develop more realistic relationships with blacks. On the other hand, proposals for reparations are likely to trigger their anxiety and guilt over the harm they have done—or fantasized doing—to blacks, and to encourage them to defend against that anxiety and guilt by denying responsibility for the suffering of blacks. Thus the Kleinian message is that (manic) racial denial reproduces the very racism that reparations might reduce.

The relationship between modernity and manic denial is the subject of the last two chapters of this volume. More specifically, they describe the way in which modernity mobilizes manic defenses against mourning that militate against cultural and individual maturity. Maturity mandates that we mourn the loss of a world that initially appeared to obey our every wish. The distinction between fantasy and reality, self and world, in other words, is only won in a struggle against infantile omnipotence. But modernity incites omnipotence and thus militates against maturity. In Chapter 9 I contend that computer-mediated communication re-creates the infantile condition of a world without spatial and temporal limits and thus powerfully promotes and reinforces the grandiose fantasies of omnipotence that mark the "Infancy of Modernity."[13] In Chapter 10, "Toward Green Recovery,"[14] I pursue in greater depth and in more detail the way in which omnipotence both fuels and is fueled by the modern cycle of (what I call) compulsive production and compulsive consumption, but I also argue that the pathologies produced by that cycle engender compensatory movements of mourning that are dedicated to the overcoming of omnipotence. More specifically, I interpret contemporary deep ecology and twelve-step recovery movements as devoted respectively to the mourning of omnipotent production and omnipotent consumption, and thus to the development of a more reparative and realistic relationship to the world. This interpretation allows me to conclude that the realization of this world requires the unification of, or at least an alliance between, these two movements which have hitherto gone their separate ways. Thus hope is recovered in the form of "Green Recovery."

****

Coparenting and cultural mourning are, then, the two (related) hopeful practices that follow from the neo-Kleinian theory that I elaborate and defend in this volume.[15] Coparenting helps to defeat domination by ensuring that subsequent generations of children are less susceptible to its impulses than the generation of parents who raised them. As I have already indicated, the theoretical assumptions that serve to ground this practical commitment are defended in Part I of this volume.

In contrast to coparenting, the cultural mourning to which Part II is devoted challenges domination by promising to transform the impulses of the current generation itself. But the possibility of cultural mourning can be, and in fact has been, called into question. I want to close this introduction by responding to that question.

At least at first glance it might appear that my own account of modernity as a cultural defense *against* mourning contests its very possibility. If, as I argue in the second half of this volume, modernity militates against mourning the many losses that it mandates, why should we expect people to participate in what would be, under any circumstances, a painful and precarious psycho-political process? What might motivate modern individuals to take up this difficult counter-modern task? It is true, as I have already suggested, that modern defenses against mourning produce many of the persistent pathologies from which modern individuals suffer, and we might reasonably assume that these individuals have an interest in reducing that suffering and recovering from those pathologies. But there is no reason to anticipate that they would identify *mourning* as the road to their recovery from those pathologies unless they were aware of their source—unless, in other words, they were familiar with, and took seriously, the claim of (post-Freudian) psychoanalysis that locates the origins of modern suffering in the inability to mourn.[16] Thus the cultural diffusion of psychoanalysis would appear to be necessary for a common commitment to overcome that inability. The popularization of psychoanalysis makes it possible—for the first time—for large numbers of people to grieve the losses against which their culturally reinforced compulsions defend.

Psychoanalysis is, of course, *as much a product of modernity as are the defenses that it contests.* It follows that modernity must be grasped dialectically as a culture that enables us to defeat the very defenses that it deploys. If, in other words, we want to understand how mourning is possible even in a culture that manically denies its necessity, we need to conceptualize modernity as a culture that reveals the remedy for its own dis-ease. Anything less would either deny the dis-ease or make it impossible to account for efforts—including this one—to remedy it.

But to conceptualize psychoanalysis as a modern remedy for modern cultural diseases is not to demonstrate that all or even most of the many people who suffer from them could ever rely on this remedy. Indeed, one might be tempted to argue that psychoanalytically informed movements of mourning can *never* be as ubiquitous as the cultural defenses they contest. In *The Ability to Mourn*, Peter Homans insists, for example, that "analytic access always exists at the margins of a common culture" and that "what flourishes at the margins (depth-psychological self-understanding) cannot exist at the center (the common culture) without being itself destroyed."[17] Homans points here to the very real risk that a culturally central psychoanalysis would have to sacrifice critical depth for institutional adjustment and thus would no longer really be a psychoanalysis at all.[18] Philip Rieff also claims that psychoanalysis and a common culture are mutually exclusive, but unlike Homans worries that the contest between them culminates in the death not of the former but rather of the latter: psychoanalysis necessarily calls faith into question, and "faith is the compulsive dynamic of culture, channeling obedience to, trust in, and dependence upon authority." Thus for Rieff the "triumph of the therapeutic" undermines any "commitment to communal purpose" in favor of a purely and "intensely private sense of well-being."[19] But both Rieff and Homans assume that the "tension between analytic access and a common culture" cannot be overcome because "a common culture . . . by definition, does not allow the unconscious to be recognized."[20]

It is precisely this assumption that I would like to call into question. In fact it has already been called into question by Homans himself, who occasionally points to the possibility of a very different—in fact mutually reinforcing—relationship, between "analytic access" and a "common culture" than the one I have just outlined. Against his own assumption of the inherently cultural marginality of analytic access, Homans acknowledges that "analytic access [has] gradually . . . become a shared sociological reality, at least among the middle class."[21] And, against Rieff, Homans argues that this increasingly common analytic access need not portend the end of a common culture:

> Whenever a person comes to recognize how psychological are his commitments to the common cultures of the past, he will also come to recognize how psychological all culture is. Through this recognition he can then come to "own" in a more conscious way the character of his participation in culture and his commitments to its imperatives and consolations. *But this is not the end or death of culture . . . it is, rather . . . a new beginning of cultural activity.* . . . [W]hen psychological understanding prevails, the products of culture do not "die" simply because their psychological significance is known; rather they "return" to the person in the form of powerful illusions which the ego-self then uses as the raw material for the construction of new meaning and of a new relationship to the past.[22]

Here Homans suggests that what might be called a culture of common analytic access is not an oxymoron after all. Such a culture would support the struggles of its members to become aware of and work through the unconscious ties that bind them to it. But awareness of those ties would *not* end them: although the "psychological recovery of the products of one's cultural past does rob them of their absolutistic power," it preserves them as "necessary illusions" that serve as the raw materials for renewed cultural creativity.[23] In short, the products of a culture of common analytic access would function as *transitional objects* rather than *fetishes.*[24] Otherwise put, cultural reproduction would lose its *compulsive* character and become more like *play.*

There are, it seems to me, two problems with Homans's otherwise instructive analysis. First, his account fails adequately to distinguish between (initially "absolutistic") cultural products that are worth "recovering" and those that are not. I have already suggested that the cultural omnipotence of modernity defends against necessary mourning and thus must itself be mourned before a richer, more realistic relationship to the world can be forged. Mourning culturally destructive defenses is, I will argue in the pages that follow, an inescapably painful process. Homans does not appear to understand that an increase in (directly experienced) *suffering* is an inevitable concomitant of the decline in compulsive cultural reproduction to which he is committed. The irony of Homans's admirable emphasis on the "ability to mourn" is that, in the end, he drastically underestimates the magnitude of the task of modern mourning. For modern adults, in other words, there can be no cultural *play* without a great deal of cultural *grief.*

Second, and relatedly, Homans's account of cultural creativity is rather too individualistic to assuage Rieff's anxiety about the (psychoanalytically induced) decline of "communal purpose." In that account, it is always "the person" or "the ego-self" who confronts the "realm of cultural symbols," and whose psychological understanding leads him or her to recognize these symbols as "powerful illusions" or transitional objects, which he or she then uses to create "new meaning and . . . a new relationship to the past." Although Homans's psychological self draws on what he or she understands to be a socially shared stock of cultural traditions, the appropriation and/or transformation of those traditions—the actual creation of new meanings—is conceptualized as a solitary activity. Thus, Rieff could conclude that in Homans's culture of common analytic access, "communal purpose" is lost to as many "new meanings" and "new relationships to the past" as there happen to be individuals in that culture.

To avoid this conclusion we need to emphasize what Homans does not: namely, the *shared* nature of the suffering that would accompany the mourning of modern cultural defenses. Common cultural losses encourage the grieving of those losses in the company of others who suffer from them—misery loves company. Grieving in the company of others, in turn, is likely to intensify our dependence on and identification with those whose company we keep. This was, at any rate, the insight of Rousseau, who argues in his *Emile* that

> It is man's weakness which makes him sociable; it is our common miseries which turn our hearts to humanity . . . we are attached to our fellows less by the sentiment of their pleasures than by the sentiment of their pains, for we see far better in the latter the identity of our natures with theirs and the guarantees of their attachment to us. If our common needs unite us by interest, our common miseries unite us by affection.[25]

If Rousseau is right, then we should expect that the "common misery" accompanying the shared mourning of necessary cultural losses would "unite us by affection" with all those who suffer from them. This increase in *solidarity*, in turn, could sustain projects of cultural renewal—of "new meanings"—designed to diminish the *unnecessary* losses from which we continue to suffer. This, I should think, would be communal purpose enough.

Part I

In Defense of Dinnerstein

1 De-Kleining Feminist Mothering Theory?

Introduction

For more than seventy years, leftists whose commitment to the struggle against domination has been matched by the conviction that domination has an inescapably psychological dimension have wrestled with the problem of the integration of psychoanalysis and critical social theory. From the late 1920s through the mid-1970s—from Wilhelm Reich to Herbert Marcuse—this problem was posed as a marriage of Marx and Freud. But this couple could not survive the combination of its internal tensions and the attacks launched against each of its members by Second Wave feminists.[1] By the early 1980s a new cohort of critical theorists had turned to what came to be called "feminist mothering theory" for the persuasive psychoanalytic account of domination that Freudo-Marxism promised, but failed, to deliver.[2]

To speak of a single feminist mothering theory is actually to use something of a misnomer. There were important differences, both in the scope of and in the psychoanalytic assumptions underlying the accounts of its two principal proponents, Nancy Chodorow and Dorothy Dinnerstein. As to differences in scope, Dinnerstein claimed not only that male domination but also political domination and the domination of nature were psychologically rooted in the soil of the maternal monopoly of early child care. Chodorow also argued that mother-dominated child rearing engendered the psychology of male domination, but left it to other social theorists to account for these other forms of domination. Dinnerstein effectively subsumed critical theory under feminist theory, while Chodorow made a much more modest case for an equal partnership between the two. But their common political message was that the feminist movement was central to the Left and that coparenting was essential to the success of the feminist movement.

As to differences in psychoanalytic assumptions, Chodorow relied on object-relations theorists like Fairbairn who assume that the infant's first and most fundamental experience of the world is merger with a mother on whom it is totally dependent.[3] She argued that men devalue women because boys must deny this dependence on, and identification with, their mothers in order to become men. Dinnerstein did not neglect the boy's need to dis-identify with his mother, but placed this problem within the context of Melanie Klein's assumption that infancy is a state of intensely ambivalent feelings for, rather than perfect fusion with, the mother.[4] For Dinnerstein, the domination of men over women reflects the rage that both boys and girls feel for the first, and most important, woman they encounter.

Since the publication of Dinnerstein's *The Mermaid and The Minotaur* in 1976 there has been a remarkable upsurge of interest in Klein on the part of Left social theorists. Until very recently this interest was centered in England, where Klein's "influence on . . . psychoanalysis is today arguably second only to Freud."[5] In 1982, the *New Left Review* published Michael Rustin's appreciative "A Socialist Consideration of Kleinian Psychoanalysis," and a number of the contributors to Barry Richards's 1984 collection *Capitalism and Infancy* used Kleinian categories critically to comprehend crucial features of contemporary capitalism.[6] The publication of Juliet Mitchell's *The Selected Melanie Klein* in 1986 marked the beginning of an ongoing English feminist encounter with her work that was punctuated a few years later by the publication of an entire issue of *Women: A Cultural Review* devoted to Klein.[7] In the United States Christopher Lasch made limited use of Klein in *The Culture of Narcissism* and *The Minimal Self,* but it was not until the publication of C. Fred Alford's *Melanie Klein and Critical Social Theory* in 1989 that a sustained case was made for the integration of critical theory and Kleinian psychoanalysis.[8]

Alford argues that the principal problems posed by the Frankfurt School of critical theory can only be solved by a shift from Freud to Klein. This had, in effect, also been the argument of Dinnerstein. But here the similarity ends. *Melanie Klein and Critical Social Theory* opens with a case for

Kleinian critical theory but closes with a Kleinian case *against* feminist mothering theory, including the work of Dinnerstein, Chodorow, and Jessica Benjamin. Alford's critique of Chodorow and Benjamin entails a straightforward rejection of their reliance on post-Kleinian object relations rather than Kleinian assumptions. Since Dinnerstein, in contrast, claims to rely on Klein, Alford's critique of her account is necessarily more nuanced. He acknowledges that this account is based on "Kleinian assumptions" but contends that it "deviates in unacknowledged [and unacceptable] ways from Kleinian thought."[9] The correction of this "deviation" culminates in the conclusion that a properly Kleinian connection cannot, in fact, be established between male domination and mother-dominated child care. Thus Alford's Klein is at one and the same time indispensable to critical theory and unavailable for feminism. Whereas Dinnerstein had relied on Klein (among others) to unite critical theory and feminism, Alford uses Klein to drive a wedge between them.

In the next section of this chapter, I summarize and evaluate Alford's critique of Dinnerstein's position. This "Kleinian" critique, I show, is undermined by Alford's own critique of Klein. The "revisionism" for which he takes Dinnerstein to task at the end of his *Melanie Klein and Critical Social Theory* is, in fact, in no way inconsistent with the (insufficiently developed) revision of Klein for which he argues at the beginning of that book. Thus Alford suggests, against himself, that there are no good Kleinian reasons for dismissing the hypothesis linking male domination and mother-monopolized child rearing.

In the third section, I take up the task of developing further Alford's critique of Klein. The modification of Klein that results from this critique is not only compatible with, but offers strong support for, the position of Dinnerstein. Thus I conclude that there are, *pace* Alford, good Kleinian reasons for proposing coparenting as a solution to the problem of patriarchy.

Coparenting practice is, of course, the ultimate test of coparenting theory. But Alford's critique discourages us from taking this test in the first place. Although he claims that coparenting can be supported for other reasons, these reasons, as I argue in the fourth and final section of this essay, are not likely to be persuasive to anyone who does not already accept the psychoanalytic reason he rejects. The effect, if not the intent, of his critique of Dinnerstein's theory is to minimize the likelihood of putting coparenting into practice. Hence the political importance of the critique of his critique.

Dinnerstein, Alford, and Klein

Dinnerstein's Argument

Dinnerstein follows Klein in arguing that the mother, as the "source of [the infant's] ultimate distress as well as ultimate joy,"[10] is at once the object of the infant's intense, worshipful longing and the target of the infant's overwhelming, murderous rage. Like Klein, she also argues that the young child handles this otherwise explosive, intolerable mixture of love and hate for the mother by splitting her in two: "the menacing, vengeful aspects of the mother . . . are walled off from her comforting, providing aspects," and the child comes to feel that both a "bad mother" and a "good mother" exist.[11] The price that the child pays to keep its connection to a loving and lovable object is the creation of a terrifying, hostile object against which it must defend. Thus Dinnerstein agrees with Klein's assumption that the "paranoid-schizoid" position is both the foundation for, and the chief obstacle to, the child's further emotional development.[12]

According to Klein, this development demands that the child experience the guilt that inevitably results from the realization that the mother whom one hates is also the mother whom one loves. The splitting of the paranoid-schizoid position is transcended by the integration of what Klein calls the "depressive position" when the child comes to terms with this guilt by making emotional reparations to a mother who is recognized as neither all good nor all bad, that is, as a separate and whole person, a subject rather than an object. Thus love triumphs over fear when the child masters the depressive position.[13]

Klein recognizes, but according to Dinnerstein drastically underestimates, the barriers to this emotional position. On the one hand, Klein emphasizes that "depressive anxiety"—the child's fear that his or her hate has irreparably damaged the very being on whom his or her life is now recognized to depend—is an obstacle to the achievement of the depressive position, and that the child may defend against this anxiety either by "splitting the mother once again into good and bad" or by a "manic" denial of any dependence on her that takes the form of omnipotent fantasies of "triumph or contempt."[14] On the other hand, Klein argues that most children will eventually negotiate the depressive position with success.[15] This is what Dinnerstein denies. The fact that the father (or substitute father) of the mother-raised child is "innocent of the association with the inevitable griefs of infancy," and is therefore available as a "blameless" refuge from

the mother, enables both the boy and the girl to "dodge the work of healing the split between good and bad feelings toward the first parent."[16]

The dodge differs depending on the gender of the child. The boy's depressive anxiety is compounded by his anxiety over the difference between
his mother's gender and his own. He not only fears that he has permanently
destroyed the mother he so desperately needs but is also unable to acknowledge that he needs her without feeling like a girl. Ordinarily the boy re-
lieves both his depressive and his gender anxiety by "dis-identifying" from
his mother and identifying with his father—that is, by simultaneously denying his dependence on her and affirming that he is a "man" like him. This
paternal identification prepares the boy for participation in a masculine world
within which his still intensely ambivalent feelings toward his mother can
be kept safely under control. Thus the emotional stage is set for his treatment of the women who come to represent her as objects from which he
will attempt to establish a "principled . . . more or less derogatory distance."[17]
Maintaining this distance typically requires the exclusion of women from
positions of public power and prestige. Thus do men seek to ensure that
they will never again have to encounter the female authority they so painfully experienced as children within the family. Manic denial (of their dependence on women) is, in other words, the path of retreat from the
depressive position taken by most mother-raised men.

The mother-raised girl will also find it difficult, if not impossible, to
attain this position. *Her* depressive anxiety is exacerbated by problems
resulting from the *identity* between her gender and the gender of her
mother. Because the girl's preoedipal identification with her mother is
experienced as the source of, rather than an obstacle to, her sense of herself as female, that identification will normally be both more intense and
more persistent than her brother's. The difficulty for the girl is precisely
that—unlike the boy—she cannot rely on any obvious difference to help
disentangle herself from a relationship with her mother that is even more
overwhelming than his. What she *can* and usually does do is "transfer to
the father . . . much of the weight of [her] positive feelings [toward her
mother], while leaving the negative ones mainly attached to their original object."[18] By transforming the split between the good mother and the
bad mother into the split between the bad mother and the good father,
the girl "gains a less equivocal focus for her feelings of pure love, and feels
freer to experience her grievances against her mother without fear of being
cut off altogether from . . . a magic, animally loved, parental being." But
the price she eventually pays for falling in love with her father is a "worshipful, dependent stance toward men" to whom she will sacrifice her

agency in order to repudiate her mother's.[19] Thus are women psychologically prepared to submit to the very men who are emotionally committed to their domination.

It follows from Dinnerstein's diagnosis of the "traditional symbiotic emotional equilibrium"[20] between women and men that coparenting is the only possible treatment for this problem. When men come to participate with women as equal partners in the process of gratifying and frustrating the vital needs of their infants and young children, fathers will join mothers as the object of both their love and their hate. With mothers no longer the exclusive target of infantile rage, women would "stop serving as scapegoats . . . for human resentment of the human condition."[21] With fathers no longer available as an "apparently blameless category of person" to whom children can turn to evade their intense ambivalence, "split-off feelings of love and anger . . . would have to be integrated within each individual person."[22] Thus coparenting would open the door to Klein's "depressive position" and enable "our infantilism [to] be more easily outgrown."[23] Having truly grown up, men would no longer need to dominate women and women would no longer need to be dominated by men.

Alford's Critique of Dinnerstein

Alford does not contest Dinnerstein's claim that coparenting might "distribute the burden of hatred and aggression more fairly" but denies that "it would force the type of psychic integration [of hatred and love] that Dinnerstein has in mind." "What reason is there to think," he asks, "that dual parenting, in which the good object is actually two, would lead to greater integration, rather than simply reinforcing paranoid-schizoid defenses associated with splitting and idealization-devaluation?"[24] Alford is able to pose this question rhetorically because he neglects even to mention Dinnerstein's answer, namely that coparented children could no longer rely on an identification with an "uncontaminated" father permanently to postpone their confrontation with their own ambivalence. Although Alford chooses to ignore this particular part of Dinnerstein's argument, we can infer from his overall critique of that argument why he would reject it.

According to Alford, Dinnerstein's entire argument "assumes that the fundamental plane along which splitting occurs is the male-female axis."[25] But this assumption contradicts Klein's teaching that "splitting is subtle, complex, fluid and manifold. To treat it as fundamentally channeled along the male-female axis, because the first object that we loved and hated was female, the second male, is too concrete, too literal."[26]

The argument that it is too concrete or literal to assume that the form of the child's splitting is determined by the gender-based differences in the roles of his or her parents implies that the child's fantasies are not shaped by these real differences. Alford makes this explicit when he confronts (what he takes to be) the logic underlying Dinnerstein's case for the elimination of those differences:

> The actuality of two objects in the external world performing a single function (dual parenting) leads in an unmediated fashion to the integration of the mental representation of these two objects in the psychic world. It is as though we could make the internal object world less fragmented simply by functionally integrating the external counterparts of these objects in real life.[27]

This privileging of the external world over the internal world, Alford concludes, "is not truly psychoanalytic thinking. It overemphasizes the external world at the expense of the internal, and reverses the [actual] direction of the influence."[28]

Alford's Critique of Klein

Thus Alford's critique of Dinnerstein rests on the assumption that "psychoanalytic thinking" necessarily and properly attributes priority to the internal over the external world. But this is precisely the assumption that Alford *rejects* in his earlier critique of Klein. Klein assumes that the infant's earliest fantasies of a good and bad breast are the inevitable "mental expression of the activity of both the life and death instincts" and that its actual experience of oral gratification and frustration can only serve to reinforce these fantasies.[29] Thus even the most favorable real ratio of gratification to frustration cannot protect the infant from the terror of attack by a breast that is nothing other than a projection of its own internally generated rage. And nothing the mother does can prevent the infant from forming new fantasies—involving splitting, projective identification, and idealization—designed to defend against the intense anxiety associated with the original one. These defenses, moreover, necessarily engender new anxieties against which the infant must defend. Thus the infant in the paranoid-schizoid position is trapped in a self-created cycle of hatred and fear.

Klein grants that a "good relation to its mother and to the external world helps the baby to overcome its early paranoid anxieties" (and thus eventually to enter the depressive position). But this "external factor," she insists, is only "so important" because of its impact on these preexisting anxieties.[30] Thus external reality can modify internal experience, "but it is not itself the source of [that] experience."[31] That source, as we have seen, is the loving and hateful fantasies that are themselves but "the mental corollaries" of the instincts of life and death.[32] Hence Donald Meltzer's conclusion that, for Klein, "psychic reality [is] a place where the meaning of life [is] generated for deployment to the outside world."[33]

This is precisely the position against which Alford protests. "Psychic reality," he tells us, is "real and important," but not "paramount." To treat it as paramount entails "an exaggerated emphasis on internal phantasy at the expense of external reality." To overcome this problem "any social theory based on Kleinian principles" would have to pay more attention to "the interchange between internal and external worlds," including "real parents and their reactions to the infant."[34]

By now the contradiction between Alford's critique of Klein and his "Kleinian" critique of Dinnerstein should be clear. His claim that Dinnerstein "overemphasizes the external world at the expense of the internal" is based on the assumption that the actual "direction of influence" runs from the inner to the outer world. His claim that Klein is guilty of an "exaggerated emphasis on internal phantasy at the expense of external reality" is based on the assumption that there is an "interchange"—or a reciprocal relationship—between the inner and the outer worlds. These two assumptions are mutually exclusive. Forced to choose between them, Alford, I presume, would abandon the orthodox ("inner to outer") Kleinian assumption that underlies his brief critique of Dinnerstein in favor of the modified ("interchange") Kleinian assumption on which (or so he claims) the rest of his book is based. But this would mean that he could no longer rule out the possibility that splitting *is* "fundamentally channeled along the male-female axis." The interchange assumption, as we have seen, directs us to "pay more attention" to the impact that "real parents and their reactions to the infant" have on his or her fantasies. Real parents are *gendered*. To pay more attention to the impact of real parents on their infants' fantasies requires that we be open to—rather than rule out—the possibility that these fantasies are influenced by the fact that "the first object that we love and hate is female." Thus Dinnerstein's hypothesis that splitting is "fundamentally channeled along the male-female axis" appears perfectly consistent with Alford's interchange assumption.

But perhaps we have too hastily come to this conclusion. Alford could (but does not) argue that although Dinnerstein's hypothesis might be consistent with some interchange assumptions, it is not in fact consistent with the specific version of the interchange assumption to which he is committed. The closest he comes to specifying his interchange assumption is his claim that unconscious phantasy

> is a reflection of our experiences of external objects, as mediated by conflicts of ambivalence on the one hand and psychological defenses against these conflicts on the other. Such a perspective restores the connection between the internal world and external reality without rendering the former the mirror image of the latter.[35]

But this specification could easily stand as a description of precisely the process that Dinnerstein describes. According to her account, the misogynist unconscious fantasies of exclusively mother-raised children are "a reflection of [their] experience of" a mixture of maternal gratification and frustration, "as mediated by conflicts of ambivalence [over the mother] on the one hand" and a turn to the father that is the psychological defense against these conflicts on the other. Similarly, the nonmisogynist unconscious fantasies of coparented children would be a "reflection of [their] experience of "a mixture of maternal gratification and frustration *and* paternal gratification and frustration, "as mediated by conflicts of ambivalence [over both the mother and the father] on the one hand" and the overcoming of "psychological defenses against these conflicts on the other."[36] Thus Dinnerstein's account is entirely compatible with the only specification of his interchange assumption that Alford supplies.

There is, however, one additional Kleinian objection that Alford does not make but with which a defense of Dinnerstein must nonetheless contend. According to Klein, the infant starts life in the paranoid-schizoid position and enters into the depressive position as early as its third or fourth month.[37] According to at least some Kleinians, by the end of his or her first year the normal child no longer splits.[38] We know from the work of Robert Stoller, however, that "core gender identity" only begins to develop during the second year of the child's life and is not "irreversibly established [until] the time a child is around three."[39] It is not until they are at least 18 months old, in other words, that female children start to understand that they are girls like their mothers and unlike their fathers and that male children begin to realize that they are boys unlike their mothers and like their fathers. Thus splitting cannot be "fundamentally channeled along the male-female axis" because (1) children are not even aware of this axis until the second year of their life, and (2) splitting begins and ends while they are still in their first year.

But this objection presupposes the accuracy of the Kleinian schedule for the beginning and end of splitting. The objection would lose its force if this schedule turned out to be inconsistent with what we have learned about child development since Klein. This is precisely what I argue in the next section. The lessons from the literature I review will require major modifications in the Kleinian emotional timetable. These modifications, in turn, significantly strengthen Dinnerstein's case.

Dinnerstein and Child Development

We have already seen that the privilege that Klein extends to internal fantasy over external reality is connected to her assumption that "phantasy is the mental corollary, the psychic representative of instinct." Because she assumes that "there is no impulse [or] instinctual urge that is not experienced as unconscious phantasy"—that, for example, the infant's oral impulses are necessarily accompanied by fantasies of a "good breast" that can satisfy them—she dates the formation of fantasy from the beginning of life and is thus able to argue that fantasy is the necessary condition for, rather than the result of, the infant's experience of the world.[40] But this presupposes that the neonate is *cognitively capable* of forming fantasies. Alford recognizes this when he writes that "the Kleinian approach to phantasy ... is bound to the view that the infant possesses sufficient ego at birth to establish primitive object relationships and to employ primitive versions of such defense mechanisms as projection, introjection, and splitting,"[41] but his critique of that approach fails to include an explicit consideration of this view. The completion of his critique requires that we overcome this omission.

Recent and systematic observations of newborns have revealed that they are active participants in the interaction that takes place between them and their primary caregivers. But even those scholars who have most consistently stressed the activity of the neonate would contest Klein's claim that this activity includes the formation of fantasies. Both Beatrice Beebe and Daniel Stern argue that it is only after "thousands of experiences of . . . each changing with the other" that the "infant begins to schematize . . . this process of mutual adjustment [with the mother]."[42] It is not, in fact, until the infant is 3 or 4 months old that he or she is able to form an internal image of any part of his or her interaction with anything, or anyone, in his or her environment. Thus the idea of a breast that is "good" because it is given and a breast that is "bad" because it is withheld—the split definitive of the paranoid-schizoid position—cannot develop until this point. Whereas Klein dates the paranoid-schizoid position from the birth of the infant, the cognitive preconditions for this position are not established until the end of the first quarter or third of the infant's first year of life.

This is precisely the point at which the infant, according to Klein, reaches the depressive position. This position, you will recall, entails the recognition that the mother of gratification and the mother of frustration are one and the same person. This recognition presupposes the cognitive capacity to form a permanent internal representation of the mother in the face of her temporary absence, that is, it presupposes the development of what has been called "object permanence" by Piaget and his followers. Their studies suggest that object permanence is usually not solidified until the middle of the second year of life,[43] and thus that the cognitive preconditions for the depressive position are not established until more than *a year after* the Kleinian timetable. This conclusion, however, is based on the assumption that the schedule for the development of a permanent internal representation of the mother corresponds to the schedule for the development of a permanent internal representation of the "inanimate, transiently cathected, physical objects" which were the focus of Piaget's studies.

Pine has speculated that "the heightened learning and recording of memories that may take place under conditions of optimal arousal . . . and under conditions of repeated encounter may solidify aspects of the internal representation of the libidinal object [the mother] even before 18 to 20 months."[44] Stern maintains, in fact, that "some degree of object permanence [vis-à-vis the mother] is in evidence . . . toward the end of the first year of life."[45] But even this earlier date would make it impossible for the infant to enter the depressive position until *6 to 9 months after* the Kleinian date.

Object permanence, moreover, is a necessary but not sufficient condition for the successful negotiation of the depressive position. The child must not only be cognitively capable of representing the mother in spite of her absence but also *emotionally* capable of loving the mother in spite of her "badness." What Margaret Mahler and her colleagues call "object constancy" requires that "the internalized representation of the love object . . . continues to be libidinally cathected in the face of both absence of the object and anger toward the object."[46] But object constancy—the unification of the good and bad object into a single, "ambivalently regarded" object—develops much later than Piaget's object permanence.

Until the child is at least 3 years old, "the mental representation of the mother may be so buffeted by violent and angry feelings that the stability of this image, at least from the libidinal as opposed to the cognitive side, is disrupted."[47] These "violent and angry feelings" are particularly likely during the second half of the second year of the child's life.

This is the time when the child undergoes what Mahler and her associates have labeled his or her "rapprochement crisis," during which the child simultaneously experiences a heightened need for, and fear of, both the independence and the dependence on which his or her further development depends. The increasingly mobile "junior toddler" increasingly encounters maternally imposed limits to his or her mobility that threaten to undermine the feeling of omnipotence that resulted from the more consistent maternal gratification of his or her wishes at an earlier age. This threat only intensifies the child's already growing need to assert his or her will in the face of his or her mother's disciplinary demands. This intensified need to establish independence from the mother, however, dramatically increases the fear of losing her that has already begun to haunt the child's previously pleasurable autonomous efforts. This heightened awareness of dependence on the mother, in turn, threatens the child's sense of independence from her and is therefore experienced as a fear of engulfment from which the child must flee. Of course, this only serves to heighten the terror of maternal abandonment. And so on. The child of rapprochement is caught in a double-bind from which there is no apparent escape and for which he or she holds the mother responsible. Thus the child's grievances against the mother are likely to be at their peak during this period.[48]

So too, therefore, is the child's "depressive anxiety." The temptation to defend against this anxiety by denying that the mother of gratification and frustration are one and the same—by regressing from the depressive to the paranoid-schizoid position—is correspondingly great as well. Thus Mahler and her colleagues argue that "splitting [enables the child] to protect the good mother image from his [or her] destructive rage," which develops during rapprochement, and they interpret the "rapidly alternating clinging and negativistic behaviors" of the toddler—what all parents recognize as the sorry signs of the "terrible twos"—as behavioral manifestations of the splitting that takes place at this time.[49] The tightness of the temporal tie between splitting and rapprochement is reflected in the "glossary of terms" with which *The Psychological Birth of the Human Infant* concludes, in which splitting is *defined* as "a defense mechanism often found during the rapprochement subphase."[50]

The same authors report that their "observation of mother–child pairs . . . in an essentially naturalistic setting" revealed that "the child's discovery of the anatomical sex difference . . . occurred sometimes during the 16 to 17 month period or even earlier, but more often in the twentieth or twenty-first month."[51] This corroborates Stoller's claim that "core gender identity" normally develops during the second half of the second year of the child's life—that is, during the rapprochement period. *Thus splitting is most likely precisely at that point when the child becomes preoccupied with the problem of determining his or her gender.* The height of children's depressive anxiety over the fate of their mother coincides with the onset of their concern about whether they are either the same as or different from her. Does it not seem probable that the way in which they come to defend against that anxiety will depend decisively on their answer to this question? Would it not be strange if splitting were not "fundamentally channeled along the male-female axis" at this point in time?

In fact, Mahler and her colleagues report gender differences during rapprochement that are consistent with the gender differences in defenses described by Dinnerstein. The boys they observed during rapprochement "were more motor-minded than girls and more stiffly resistant to hugging and kissing." They "showed a tendency to disengage themselves from mother" and "seemed to find it more expedient than girls to function separately." They were "better able to turn to the outside world [and] to father as someone with whom to identify."[52] "Manic" denial of dependence thus appeared to be the boys' characteristic defense against both their depressive and their gender anxiety.

This defense was apparently not available to the girls. Just when the boys were beginning "to enjoy their functioning in the widening world," the girls "seemed to become more engrossed with mother . . . and were more persistently enmeshed in the ambivalent aspects of the relationship." The girls, "upon the discovery of [their gender identity], tended to turn back to mother, to blame her, to demand from her, to be disappointed in her, and still be ambivalently tied to her." Thus "the task of becoming a separate individual seemed . . . to be generally more difficult for girls than for boys."[53] Dinnerstein's claim, you will recall, is that the girl's more intense and prolonged tie to the mother can only be broken by a subsequent turn to a father who becomes her (over)idealized object. Although the observations of Mahler and her associates ended prior to the period when this oedipal turn to the father is supposed to take place, their description of the girl's preoedipal identification with her mother corroborates Dinnerstein's explanation of why that turn would be necessary.[54]

Conclusion

Alford claims that his critique of Dinnerstein's case for coparenting is not
an argument against coparenting, which would "no doubt . . . carry with
it a number of benefits." He tells us that "perhaps . . . the best argument"
[and the only one he mentions] is that it would "certainly [be] more
fair."[55] Since Alford does not elaborate further, we are in no position to
evaluate the precise fairness argument that he has in mind. But I think it
can be demonstrated that any fairness argument is an unlikely basis for a
convincing case on behalf of coparenting.

It is not, to begin with, self-evident to all or even most men that
coparenting is fair. Men who believe that they should or must contribute
more than women outside the home will (and do) certainly contest the
claim that they are morally obliged to contribute equally to child care
within it. Thus only those men who are already committed to equal female participation in the public sphere will find that equal male participation within the domestic sphere is fair.

There is no reason to believe, moreover, that these men would necessarily conclude that coparenting is fairer than other alternatives to mother-
monopolized child care within the home, such as nannies and privately or
publicly funded day care. These alternatives seem (at least to those unfa-
miliar with or uncommitted to Dinnerstein's argument) as consistent with
equal female participation in work and politics as coparenting. Both appear
to eliminate the unfair burden of the mother's exclusive responsibility for
early child care. Thus only those men (and women) who consider child care
a benefit, rather than a burden to them are likely to conclude that an arrangement that enables them to share that responsibility is fairer than an
arrangement that enables them to evade it.

Moreover, even those men who *are* convinced that coparenting is the
fairest possible arrangement are likely (if Dinnerstein and other feminist
mothering theorists are correct) to be afraid of it. If masculinity is defined
by the denial of dependence, then even politically committed male
coparents will be emotionally ambivalent about an intimate relationship
with an almost entirely dependent infant. The message of feminist mothering theory is that most "mothering" men will be torn between their need
to be, and their fear of being, coparents. Thus there is every reason to expect that they will backslide unless they believe that their participation is
not only a benefit to them but also to their children.[56]

Many women are also unlikely to be persuaded that coparenting is fairer
than traditional arrangements. Most obviously, those women who iden-

tify more strongly with their child-rearing role than any other and believe that their monopoly on that role is in the interest of their children will not conclude that it would be fairer to break up this monopoly. But even women who are as committed to the public sphere as they are to the private may be reluctant to share child-rearing power with men unless men share economic and political power with women.[57] Is it fair to ask women to give up control of one of the few realms they have been able to control, virtually the only one where they are recognized as being more competent than men? Finally, even those women who would answer "yes" to this question—who believe in the principle of coparenting—are likely to be ambivalent about putting this principle into practice. Coparenting requires a willingness on the part of women to relinquish the preeminent place they have always had in the hearts of their children. Thus women are likely to be as afraid of it as men.[58]

This is why Dinnerstein's theory is politically indispensable. By persuading men and women that coparenting is *necessary for their children*, it encourages them to act out of love rather than fear. This is, perhaps, the most important sense in which Dinnerstein remains consistent with Klein.

2 Patriarchal "Production" in Marx

Introduction

In *Marxism and Domination* I argue that Marxism is part of the problem of patriarchy rather than the basis for its solution. More specifically, my claims are (1) that the category of "production" entails a counter-ecological commitment to the domination of nature, and (2) that the domination of nature is a culturally and historically specific form of the domination of men over women. Thus the interrelated struggles for (what I call) a post-instrumental relationship between humans and (nonhuman) nature and a post-patriarchal relationship between women and men must be waged not with, but *against* Marx. In short, an ecofeminist Marxism is simply, and necessarily, a contradiction in terms.

In this chapter I reconsider this argument in the light of the rejoinders it has received. In the following section I consider critiques of my claim that Marx's commitment to an instrumental relationship with nature is both culturally specific and necessarily counter-ecological in favor of the claims that it is neither possible nor necessary to overcome an instrumental relationship with nature. None of these critiques, I conclude, effectively calls into question the possibility or the desirability of a post-instrumental relationship between humans and the natural surround.

In the third section I consider arguments that challenge my understanding of the connection between the domination of nature and the domination of men over women. I summarize my effort in *Marxism and Domination* to historicize Dorothy Dinnerstein's psychodynamic account of this connection in order to specify the precise conditions under which a culturally universal fear and loathing of the female assumes the form of a modern Western assault on the earth she represents. Then I defend this theoretical account from critics who either contest Dinnerstein's depth-psychological explanation of male domination or my effort to historicize her account of its connection with the domination of nature. Although I conclude that none of the critics successfully undermines my theoretical account, I acknowledge that this account could benefit from additional historical support. This is exactly what I offer in the fourth and final section of this essay.

"Production" as Domination

In *Marxism and Domination* I showed that Marx treats nature as but a constituent element of the process of production, as either the raw material for or the product of human labor. As raw material it is an object that people have yet to make, and as product it is an object that people have already made. In either case, nature is accorded no significance apart from the cycle of human making, or objectification, to which Marx subordinates it. Thus for Marx nature figures as a mere object that exists for the sake of the human subject, a pure means for the realization of human ends. We should not be surprised, then, to hear him herald communism as "the advent of real mastery over . . . the forces of nature."[1]

To emancipate these "forces" it is therefore necessary to contest Marx's exclusively instrumental conception of the relationship between humans and their natural surround. *Pace* Marx, I argued that objectification is not an ontological category—not a universal condition of human existence—but rather a culturally and historically contingent mode of symbolizing nature that must be transcended in favor of what I called a *post-instrumental* mode of symbolizing nature as an end-in-itself. As a step in this direction I undertook the task of doing to/for Marx's constitutive concept of objectification exactly what Marx did to/for the central concepts of the bourgeois thinkers he confronts: explain its origins in order to contribute to its overcoming.

My critics claim that this task is neither possible nor necessary. The claim that it is not possible entails a reiteration of Marx's insistence on the ontological status of objectification. Thus Judith Burton and Douglas Kellner call into question my "equa[tion of] objectification with a historically contingent mode of behavior that is in principle transcendable" in favor of the possibility that "some forms of objectification are a distinctive human trait intrinsic to production."[2] Less cautiously, Lawrence Simon writes that "I cannot imagine any human culture that survives by not adopting some form or other of an instrumental relationship to nature."[3] Similarly, Wolf Heydebrand concludes that "a noninstrumental attitude [cannot] be implemented vis-à-vis nature" without inviting "collective suicide."[4]

The logic of Simon's and Heydebrand's argument is revealed in their references to human survival. Major premise: human survival requires that humans make use of nature. Minor premise: "making use" of nature entails an instrumental relationship with nature. Conclusion: a noninstrumental relationship with nature is inconsistent with human survival, and therefore impossible. Q.E.D. But not so fast. It is precisely the equation of "making use of" with "instrumental" that is in question. This equation, it seems to me, obscures the fact that there are radically different ways of making use of nature. It is of course true that humans will always be obliged to interact with nature in order to satisfy their needs and thus that they will, in that sense, inevitably make use of nature. However, what is at issue is precisely whether in the course of interacting with nature in order to satisfy their needs humans acknowledge or deny that nature has needs that must also be satisfied. A "noninstrumental" relationship with (or "making use" of) nature entails the affirmation of those needs that an instrumental relationship with nature would negate. On this meaning of noninstrumental it is by no means self-evident—and in fact I believe that it is counterintuitive to argue—that a noninstrumental relationship with nature is inconsistent with human survival. Unless the critics can explain why humans cannot simultaneously satisfy their needs and the needs they find in nature, they cannot make their case for the impossibility of overcoming objectification.

Of course at this point the critics are likely to respond by calling into question what I have described as the "needs of nature." Their claim would be that the needs that the post-instrumental partisans purport to find in nature are in fact nothing other than their own needs *projected into* nature. For example, Tim Luke argues that the "deep ecological" conception of

> nature appears to be a projection of an idealized humanity onto the natural
> world . . . no more than the individual ecosphere's identification of his/her
> self with those particular aspects of Nature that idiosyncratically express
> their peculiarly personal human liberation. . . . The emphasis still falls on
> people and their needs.[5]

In short, the *perception* of post-instrumentalists that they are simultaneously satisfying their needs and the needs of nature obscures the *reality*
that they are in fact exclusively preoccupied with their own. Thus their
relationship with nature is every bit as instrumental as the relationship
they reject. The only difference is that they are *falsely conscious* of their
inevitably instrumental relationship with nature while their avowedly
instrumental opponents are not.[6]

The first point that I would make in response is that the projections
humans make inevitably inform *any* relationship they can have with nature. The objectifying assumption that nature *is* a mute object that awaits
the intervention of the uniquely human subject is every bit as much a
human projection as is the post-objectifying assumption that nature *is* a
(certain kind of) subject with which human subjects can collaborate. The
former assumption projects the human need for control, while the latter
projects the human need for communication, onto nature. Thus the contest between an instrumental and a post-instrumental mode of symbolizing nature is not a contest between "reality" and "projection" (or fantasy)
but rather between two different projections that enable two radically different real relationships with nature.[7] We can, if we wish, redefine both
relationships as instrumental, but this terminological maneuver (1) leaves
unanswered the crucial question of the different sources of (what now
might be described as) the "dominative" and "communicative" species of
the genus "instrumental relationship with nature" and (2) discourages the
search for an answer to this question by obscuring the dramatic difference between them. Exactly what human wish, we might ask, is satisfied
by this terminological conflation?

Notice that this terminological tactic perfectly parallels the semantical
stance of the "possessive individualist" critics of the Marxist commitment
to the possibility of noninstrumental relationships among human beings.
The partisans of egoism have always contested that possibility on the
grounds that even the altruist helps himself by helping others. Marxists
(as well as other "social" critics of egoism) have replied, correctly, that there
is a world of difference between taking pleasure from actions that contribute to the welfare of others and taking pleasure from actions that are
indifferent to and/or deleterious to their welfare, and that the redescrip-
tion of both forms of action as self-interested or instrumental obfuscates
a difference that is worth fighting for. If we substitute the word "nature"
for the word "others" exactly the same can be said about the Marxist terminological transformation of an ostensibly noninstrumental into an essentially instrumental relationship.

Of course it is just this substitution (of nature for humans) to which the now thoroughly exasperated Marxist will inevitably object: the claim that the ontology of objectification is the ecological analogue of the ontology of self-interest founders on the fundamental, irreducible difference between humans and nature. Thus Heydebrand is able to argue in his review of *Marxism and Domination* that "Balbus' critique of objectification . . . is appropriate where humans use other humans as means rather than as ends (or as subjects)" but *in*appropriate where humans exploit nature because he seems to take for granted what, for example, Habermas explicitly asserts, namely that "nature does not conform to the categories under which the subject apprehends it in the unresisting way in which a subject can conform to the understanding of another subject on the basis of reciprocal recognition."[8] Humans, in short, *are* subjects but nature *is* not. A noninstrumental relationship is therefore possible with the former but not with the latter.

But it is precisely this ontological difference that the egoist is unwilling to concede. Individuals who "feel they have a right to control and possess others and to exploit them without guilt feelings,"[9] and who are therefore emotionally incapable of "reciprocal recognition," are scarcely likely to recognize the essential reality that other individuals are subjects like themselves. Instead their aggressive projections will predispose them to experience others as dangerous "objects" *not* fundamentally different from (the rest of) nature. Conversely, the capacity of individuals to empathize with others, and thus to experience their subjectivity as equally real as their own, arguably depends on projective identifications by means of which their own feeling-states are attributed to them.[10] The point is that projections inform our relationships with other human beings every bit as much as they inform our relationship with nature. Thus the subjectivity of human beings is no more objective than the (supposed) objectivity of nature.

Count on the defender of ontological difference to continue to contest this conclusion. He or she will concede the point that our projections inevitably inform both our relationships with other people and our relationship with nature but will also insist that this concession does not oblige us to give up the essential difference between them. That (alleged) difference consists in the fact that other people can object to our projections, and thus help us correct them, while nature cannot. People who are treated as objects can and do insist on their subjectivity whereas nature has no way of protesting against its objectification. Nature, in short, lacks the *communicative competence* that humans possess.

To this rejoinder I would raise two objections. First, human communicative competence is a two-way street. The speaking subject has only as much power to correct the projections of others as they have the ability to *listen* to what the subject says. The projections of people who are psychologically unprepared to treat other people as interlocutors will be impervious to even their most eloquent objections. If human communicative competence includes the capacity for reciprocal recognition, then the *norm* of communicative competence is not, *pace* Habermas, inscribed in the *fact* of human speech itself.[11] In short, the assertion that humans possess communicative competence is open to question.

So too—and this is my second point—is the assertion that (some kind of) communicative competence is lacking in nature. In fact I would argue that the plausibility of this assertion rests entirely on an illicit equation of communication with verbal language or speech. Once this equation is called into question in favor of a broader concept of communication it is perfectly obvious that nature has myriad ways—from the suffering of animals to the mutations of plants—to communicate to people its response to their projections and its "objections" to its objectification.[12] Of course these objections will only be heeded by people who are emotionally inclined to learn, and listen to, the various languages of nature. But the assumption that nature has nothing to say scarcely nourishes that inclination. Thus the privileging of speech and the objectification of nature are merely two sides of the same (non)communicative coin.

So much for the argument on behalf of the impossibility of a noninstrumental relationship with nature. Now I would like to take up the argument that a noninstrumental relationship is unnecessary. It is unnecessary, the critics of my position argue, because the ubiquitous ecological problems of contemporary capitalist and (the few remaining) "actually existing" socialist societies are the result not of an inherently instrumental relationship with nature but rather of what might be called an *insufficiently enlightened* instrumental relationship with nature. According to Heydebrand, it is the interests of capitalists and bureaucrats who currently control the objectification of nature and not the objectification of nature *tout court* that preclude the "conscious policy of maintaining the ecosystem" that human survival demands.[13] It follows that human survival and the ecological policy on which it depends require not the end of objectification but rather merely the elimination of those social structures that are inconsistent with that ultimate "collective human good."[14] Thus, for Simon, "it is a problem of better understanding human interests and the social structures in which they can be satisfied, not a problem of better understanding the interests of nature in itself."[15]

The assumption underlying these arguments, then, is that a *properly* instrumental relationship with nature is not only not inconsistent with, but in fact requires, that nature be protected. This is made explicit by Simon when he claims that "we need to respect the structure and resources of nature, not because nature is and should be treated as a subject, but rather because by not taking these into account we risk the real possibility of species suicide."[16] This claim is echoed by Richard Watson's insistence that "there is a very good reason for thinking ecologically, and for encouraging human beings to act in such a way as to preserve a rich and balanced planetary ecology: human survival depends on it."[17] It is, in short, precisely because nature really *is* a means to the (ultimate) human end that nature must be protected. Thus a noninstrumental relationship with nature is simply not necessary in order to reach ecologically desirable results.

I remain unconvinced. The message of the "enlightened instrumentalists" is that harming nature harms human beings. But this is a proposition that those who are inclined to harm nature are likely to contest. It will not be easy to make the case against any given predatory practice, because that case will always rest on a contestable empirical claim, namely that the practice does, *in fact*, threaten human survival. Consider, for example, the case of clubbing baby seals to death in order to sell their skins to make fur coats. Is there any obvious sense in which this practice threatens human survival? Unless this sense could be made obvious, there would be no instrumentalist grounds on which to protest the practice. The point is that an (always in principle) contestable empirical argument is too weak a weapon with which to defend nature against the predatory practices of human beings. That defense requires, instead, that nature be seen as an end in itself.[18]

It is worth pointing out that Marxists (among others) have consistently contested instrumentalist arguments designed to protect people from other people. The assumption that rationally self-interested individuals will decide that it is in their interest to treat other individuals as equals because it is the only way they can avoid the equally "evil choices [of] isolation, anarchy, subjection or despotism"[19]—that is, to ensure their long-run social survival, is clearly counter-factual in the light of the persistent and pervasive efforts of "possessive individualists" to survive by subordinating others to their wills. The point is that at any given point the self-interested individual may in fact conclude that the benefits of a strategy of cooperation are outweighed by its costs and thus decide to pursue an alternative (hostile) strategy.[20] And, if we cannot rely on individual self-interest to prevent human beings from preying on other members of their own species, it is scarcely plausible to propose (what might be called) *human-species* self-interest as a stable source of protection for members of other species against the predatory practices of human beings.

Finally, instrumentalism no more serves the needs of human beings than it serves the needs of nature. Human beings who seek *solidarity* with the other beings of nature will find no comfort in the claim that the best they can hope for is a relationship in which these beings are protected as the necessary means to the end of human survival. What they want—and what some of them already have—is a deep feeling of kinship with non-human (as well as human) life. But this need for a noninstrumental relationship with nature is the one human need that an instrumentalism that otherwise privileges human needs is unwilling to grant. It is unwilling to grant this need, we have seen, because it considers *false* any need to transcend what cannot be transcended. But this claim, we have also seen, is as weak as the impossibility arguments on which it is based.

I will assume that by now the reader agrees that my argument that an instrumental relationship with nature is both culturally specific and counter-ecological has survived the assaults of its critics. I will therefore turn to a summary of my effort in *Marxism and Domination* to account for the origins of that relationship and then take up the objections that have been raised to that account.

"Production" as Patriarchal Domination

In *Marxism and Domination* I argue that objectification (and the domination of nature that it entails) is a culturally and historically specific form of male domination. This argument adopts—and adapts—Dinnerstein's psychodynamic account of the way in which both forms of domination are emotionally engendered by what might be called the maternal mode of child rearing. In all cultures mothers (or female mother-substitutes) have been far more responsible than fathers (or male father substitutes) for the care of infants and very young children. If we assume, with Dinnerstein, that the object relations of individuals are established during their first years of life, it follows that the subsequent nature of their relationships with others will be determined by the nature of their early relationship with their mothers.

As we saw in the previous chapter, this relationship is inevitably a deeply difficult one: the mother cannot but become the target of both the love *and* rage of the infant she both satisfies and denies. Since the mother is the infant's first representative of the natural world—both the source of his or her being and the other in relationship to which this being is defined—it follows that nature will inevitably inherit this explosive mixture of feelings for the mother. *She* becomes both the giving mother whom we love and on whom we wish to remain dependent and the begrudging mother whom we hate because that wish cannot be fulfilled. Thus our love–hate relationship with our mother becomes a love–hate relationship with nature: nature will be symbolized both as the loving woman to whom we owe our life and as the dreaded, dangerous woman who must be dominated or even destroyed. Dinnerstein acknowledges that the balance between "respect, concern, awe" and "hostility and rapacity" varies "from culture to culture" and that "it need not always be tipped in the same direction for woman and for nature."[21] But she does not attempt to explain the changing character of that balance, and why, in particular, it has been tipped dramatically in the direction of hostility and rapacity toward nature since the early modern era in the West.

This is what I tried to explain in *Marxism and Domination*. My hypothesis was that child-rearing practices that are considerably harsher in modern than in traditional societies are responsible for the peculiarly pernicious modern Western conception of nature. A cross-cultural comparison revealed that Western mothers not only typically touch their children much less but also frustrate them much more, and much earlier, than non-Western mothers. The Western (or westernized) child has normally been nursed for a much shorter period, sometimes on schedule rather than on demand, has been toilet trained earlier, and probably more severely, and has been genitally more repressed.[22] He or she—especially he—is therefore likely to experience a much less intense primary identification with the mother than the traditional child. At the same time, the resentments that inevitably accompany separation from the mother will necessarily accumulate much sooner within the Western than the traditional child, since separations from her have likewise been imposed much earlier on the former than on the latter.

Thus we can assume that the Western child's symbolization of nature, in contrast to his or her traditional counterpart, is established during a period of intensely ambivalent feelings toward the mother, with the mother serving as an object of both love and hate. This balance will tilt more toward hate in the case of the male child, whose normal masculine development demands that he define himself in active opposition to this mother. Since his masculinity also demands that he define himself against the world that represents her, his emotional balance will be tipped even more than his sister's in the direction of "hostile and rapacious" feelings toward nature. We should expect that his unconscious desire to unite with mother-nature will be combined with an even more powerful, unconscious desire to defeat her.

Thus my hypothesis in *Marxism and Domination* was that the instrumental (or objectifying) mode of symbolizing nature is emotionally fueled by child-rearing practices that entail rather more maternal frustration than gratification during the earliest years of life of the child. This hypothesis has been directly called into question by reviewers of *Marxism and Domination* and indirectly called into question by critics of the Dinnersteinian assumptions on which it is based. Let me first summarize and respond to the claims of Dinnerstein's critics and then address the criticisms of my effort to extend or historicize her account.

Dinnerstein's Critics

Almost all of the critics have challenged the preeminence that Dinnerstein attributes to the preoedipal period. The fantasies that result from the infant's earliest interactions with the mother, they have argued, are less determinative of the way in which either women or nature is treated by adults than are the "real," extra-familial factors that these fantasies are supposed to, but do not in fact, explain.[23] There are a number of variations on this theme.

(1) The universality of these fantasies has been called into question. Thus Patricia Elliot complains that, for Dinnerstein, "The phantasy of maternal omnipotence is not one among others, nor is it a phantasy that some have and others do not. . . . [T]he problem with this assumption is . . . that it does not recognize other possibilities. To assert the universality of this particular phantasy presupposes a homogeneous phantasy life and precludes multiplicity and personal variation."[24]

I must confess that I do not understand why the universality of "this particular phantasy" precludes "multiplicity" and "personal variation." To assert that all infants and young children assume that the mother is all-powerful, that she is therefore seen as responsible for their frustrations, and that she thus becomes the target for the rage that results from those frustrations is not to deny either that there will be individual variations on this omnipotent theme or that other fantasy-themes can coexist with this omnipotent one. Commonality and difference can and do go hand in hand. Thus Dinnerstein can justifiably plead not guilty to Elliot's political charge of suppressing differences in the individual fantasy-lives of mother-raised women and men.

But Elliot's objections are conceptual as well as political. In the context of a comparison of Juliet Mitchell's and Jacqueline Rose's treatment of the fantasy of castration and Dinnerstein's treatment of the fantasy of maternal omnipotence she questions the evidentiary basis for Dinnerstein's claim on behalf of the universality of the latter: "while the 'castration' fantasy taken up by Mitchell and Rose refers to social and symbolic significations of gender, Dinnerstein's support for the fantasy of omnipotence refers to the actual experience of mothering."[25] It is difficult to know what to make of this claim. If, on the one hand, Elliot means to say that Dinnerstein infers the fantasy of maternal omnipotence exclusively from the *fact* that the mother exercises power over the infant, then her claim is clearly incorrect. Dinnerstein's text is replete with references to misogynistic myths of dangerously powerful women that have widespread, cross-cultural currency[26] and that lend symbolic support for her psychoanalytic account. Thus Elliot is simply wrong to suggest that Dinnerstein's treatment of the fantasy of omnipotence does *not* "refer to social and symbolic significations of gender." If, on the other hand, Elliot's critical reference to "the actual experience of mothering" implies that there is no such universal experience—which is what she seems to claim when, in her very next sentence, she argues that Dinnerstein's assumption of a "mothering experience . . . unmediated by the social context in which it takes place is a problem that renders [her] theorization highly questionable"[27]—then it would seem that the burden would be on Elliot to offer a plausible explanation of the universality of misogynistic myths that is not based on the assumption of the universality of the mothering experience. But she offers no such explanation.

Much the same can be said about Chodorow's and Contratto's critique of Dinnerstein's treatment of the fantasy of maternal omnipotence. Like Elliot, they argue that she "confuses infantile fantasy with the actuality of maternal behavior. Thus, even as Dinnerstein describes the infantile fantasies that emerge from female-dominated child care, she also asserts that mothers are in fact all-powerful, fearsome creatures. She emphasizes the *'absolute power'* of the *'mother's life-and-death control over help-less infancy.'*"[28]

Thus their argument appears to be that Dinnerstein cannot possibly *explain* the fantasy of absolute maternal power as the result of actual maternal behavior because her description of that behavior *reads into* that behavior the very omnipotent fantasy that it is supposed to explain. Since "maternal behavior" cannot explain this fantasy, we need to look elsewhere for an explanation. Chodorow and Contratto find it in the "mother–child isolated unit that nineteenth-century industrial development produced" and the "cultural ideology about motherhood" that legitimated that unit, as well as in a "post-Freudian psychological theory" that takes that unit and this ideology for granted and therefore "blame[s] mothers for any failings in their children."[29] In short, the fantasy of maternal omnipotence is not a cultural universal but rather the psychic product of a particular mode of mothering within the context of a particular kind of culture. Presumably Chodorow and Contratto would argue that it is only within this cultural context that the *actual* power of the mother over her child is sufficiently great to evoke the fantasy of maternal omnipotence.[30] If we start from the psychoanalytic assumption that cultural myths have their origins in infantile fantasies, it follows from their argument that we should only find maternal-monster myths in nineteenth- and twentieth-century Western (or westernizing) societies. But in fact we find them everywhere. This suggests either that their argument about the cultural specificity of the fantasy of maternal omnipotence is wrong or that there must be an alternative, nonpsychoanalytic explanation for the universality of those myths. What that explanation might be Chodorow and Contratto do not say.

Finally, Roger Gottlieb proposes a thought experiment that purports to demonstrate the "highly questionable" nature of Dinnerstein's "reading of infant and early childhood experience."[31] The fact that we can easily imagine that an infant might experience its mother as "the one part of the environment over which [he or she] has any control at all" rather than as an "all-powerful figure" who resists his or her will and "against whom she or he must [therefore] rebel," reveals that it is not exclusive mothering but rather "the rest of the culture which is the problem." It is the encounter of children with the "misogyny of the wider culture" and not "the way mothers deprive" them that "poisons their relationship with the mothering figure" and dramatically exacerbates what otherwise "might be a merely passing [hostile] emotion." In the absence of "the rest of society's misogyny," we should expect the fact that the mother is "amenable to manipulations by the infant–small child" to lead not to rage but to "a feeling of dependence, emotional closeness, and safety with the mother."[32]

Gottlieb is apparently unaware that his supposedly alternative emphasis on the mother's responsiveness to the infant is already incorporated into—and is in fact central to—Dinnerstein's account. According to that account, it is precisely because the mother *is* initially so responsive to the needs of the newborn that her subsequent frustration of those needs is so painful. Here I can do no better than to quote Dinnerstein:

> The fact that human infants receive such nearly perfect care seduces them into fantasies . . . of a world that automatically obeys, even anticipates, their wishes. The loss of this infant illusion of omnipotence—the discovery that circumstance is incompletely controllable, and that there exist centers of subjectivity . . . opposed to or indifferent to one's own—is an original and basic human grief.[33]

Thus it is not the mere fact that the mother frustrates the young child, but rather the fact that this frustration undermines his or her grandiose illusions that accounts for the rage against her. Once we understand that the mother typically takes the blame for this terrible wound to our narcissism—for this "original and basic human grief"—we can more easily imagine why that rage is both so persistent and so intense. The irony of Gottlieb's critique of Dinnerstein, then, is that his premise of the manipulable mother actually *strengthens* Dinnerstein's case.

My argument against Gottlieb to this point is that there is no need to refer to the "misogyny of the wider culture" to account for the infant's rage against his or her "omnipotent" mother. I also want to argue that there is something intrinsically problematical about that reference itself. But this brings me to a second category of criticisms of Dinnerstein's position.

(2) Critics have also argued that, whether the infantile fantasies formed within the family are culturally universal or not, these fantasies are simply less determinative of male domination than the extra-familial *realities* on which Dinnerstein (supposedly) fails to focus. Thus Gottlieb argues that "exclusive female mothering will [only] reproduce patriarchy in a society [in which] women . . . are [already] politically, culturally, and economically devalued,"[34] and Elliot claims that the "devaluation of femininity [and the accompanying] idealization of masculinity are a consequence of patriarchal valuations and not attributable to exclusive female mothering."[35]

Gottlieb complains that Dinnerstein's admittedly "ingenious" argument to the contrary

> ignores the fact that children learn at a very young age the source of real power in family life. One need only observe extremely young children to see how soon boys imitate their fathers and girls their mothers. Soon after,

they start imitating media images of mothers and fathers, women and men. This imitative process makes it clear that they have assimilated not only gender differentiation but differences in power. The identification with the father and the devaluation of the mother is not a response to the mother's power but a reflection of her powerlessness.[36]

Thus for Gottlieb the identity of "young children" is determined far more by their perceptions of the "real power" relations between women and men both inside and outside the family than it is by any actual power that their mothers may have exercised over them. In short, girls and boys come to devalue women merely because a patriarchal society teaches them to do so. But one very obvious problem (among others) with the substitution of this behavioristic, learning-theory account for Dinnerstein's psychoanalytic account of the origins of individual identity is that it is simply implausible to assume that during the first two years of their lives "young children" are more likely to be aware of, and affected by, the way in which their mother stands in relationship to their father (if they even have one), or to men in the society at large, than they are by how *they* stand in relationship to their mothers. However power*less* their mother may be in relationship to men, she—as their "will's first, overwhelming adversary"[37]—will be experienced as power*ful* in relationship to them. Gottlieb shows that he is aware of this objection when he says that "it might be replied [to his account] that the emotional dynamic described by Dinnerstein takes place at such a young age that differences between male and female power cannot be recognized." Indeed. But he quickly counters this objection with the argument that it "only raises another difficulty with Dinnerstein's theory: her highly questionable attribution to infants of emotional states that would seem more appropriate to more fully developed humans."[38]

There are a number of problems with this rejoinder. First, Gottlieb's "alternative reading" of infantile experience (to which I have already referred) presumes just as much emotional and cognitive capacity on the part of the young child as the Dinnersteinian reading he contests. But I will not press this point, since Gottlieb specifically disclaims any commitment to the truth of this "thought experiment."[39] Instead I will refer the reader to observational studies of Margaret Mahler and her colleagues that lend substantial empirical support for the preoedipal fantasies and associated feeling-states assumed by Dinnerstein.[40] Of course the conclusions that Mahler and her associates draw about the inner life of young children are themselves theoretically informed interpretations of their observable behavior. Because Gottlieb would undoubtedly contest their object-relational theoretical starting point he would therefore also reject their conclusions in favor of an interpretation derived from his alternative (behavioristic) theoretical standpoint. Since theories are always under-determined by the facts, no direct appeal to the facts can arbitrate the theoretical dispute between Gottlieb and Dinnerstein.

But this dispute is nonetheless amenable to indirect empirical arbitra-tion. Rather than attempt to prove the truth of Dinnerstein's assumptions about the fantasies of infants and young children, we can simply treat these assumptions as a more or less useful starting point to an effort to explain what she wants to explain—namely the universality of misogyny. Judged by this pragmatic criterion, it is difficult to avoid the conclusion that her theoretical assumptions have enormous explanatory power. They enable her to explain a culturally universal devaluation of women as the conse-quence of an equally culturally universal female monopoly on mothering. Moreover, they encourage a practical-revolutionary "test" of this theory in the form of the commitment to coparenting.

No such parsimonious or politically attractive explanation, in contrast, can be derived from Gottlieb's theoretical assumptions. Those assump-tions lead him to argue, as we have seen, that omnipotent-mother fanta-sies are not the cause but rather the consequence of the "economic, political, and cultural devaluation of women." But it is precisely that universal de-valuation of women that this argument leaves *entirely unexplained.* It is true that Gottlieb points us in the (Marxist) direction of an explanation when he urges us to "study the connection between modes of production and fundamental categories of thought."[41] Presumably he means to hypothe-size that different modes of production give rise to (and are reproduced by) different modes of male domination. But this Marxist hypothesis, as I have shown at length in *Marxism and Domination,* cannot account for a *common* fear and loathing of the female that cuts across all hitherto exist-ing modes of material production.[42]

At this point Gottlieb would likely reiterate his claim that Dinnerstein does not account for important *variations* on an arguably universal theme.[43] This claim is correct. But it is all too easy to criticize Dinnerstein for not doing something she did not set out to do. The question is not whether Dinnerstein herself explains those variations but whether a plausible ex-planation for them can be *derived* from her theoretical assumptions. In *Marxism and Domination* I demonstrate that it can. From Dinnerstein's assumptions I derive the hypothesis that the intensity of misogyny across different societies will vary directly both with the intensity of the identi-fication between boys and their mothers, and with the radicalness of the enforced separation between them, and I show that this hypothesis is completely consistent with a broad range of ethnographic and cross-cultural studies.[44] It is of course always possible that these findings can be explained in some other equally consistent way, although I know of no such alternative explanation. At any rate, the fact that an hypothesis derived from Dinnerstein's assumptions survives the test of cross-cultural falsification suggests that—*pace* Gottlieb—her theory cannot simply be dismissed as empirically inadequate.[45]

Patricia Elliot also takes Dinnerstein to task for treating "patriarchal valuations" as a dependent rather than an independent variable.[46] For the most part she relies on the arguments of Gottlieb that I have already called into question. But to these arguments she adds a thought experiment of her own. She envisions a situation in which "patriarchal culture" persists but there is "exclusive mothering by men" and concludes that under those circumstances "it is hard to believe that the [devalued] fate of the female caretaker would befall the male should he be in her position." The fact that the "devaluation of femininity and the idealization of masculinity" would obviously survive the imagined change in child rearing is supposed to demonstrate that the determining power of "patriarchal norms" is far greater than the determining power of child rearing arrangements.[47]

But it seems to me that it demonstrates nothing of the sort. Depending on what Elliot means by "exclusive mothering by men," her thought experiment is either clearly rigged from the outset against Dinnerstein's theory or might in fact result in its confirmation. If exclusive mothering by men means that it has replaced exclusive female mothering as the statistically normal way of raising children, then the hypothetical she envisions is already *ruled out* by Dinnerstein's theory. According to that theory, "patriarchal norms" are the *result* of exclusive female mothering and thus they would not exist in its absence. The very terms of the thought experiment ostensibly designed to test the truth of Dinnerstein's theory presuppose that Dinnerstein must be wrong. Hardly a fair test of the truth of her theory.

If, on the other hand, "exclusive mothering by men" simply means that *some* men are the only primary caregivers for their children in the context of a society in which "exclusive female mothering" remains the statistical norm, then Elliot's hypothetical is not ruled out by Dinnerstein's theory and we *can* have a fair test of the hypothesis that the mode of child rearing is more determinative of misogynistic attitudes toward women than prevailing patriarchal norms. But then it is by no means as self-evident as Elliot believes that "the fate of the female caretaker would [not] befall the male." It is entirely possible, notwithstanding the persistence of patriarchal norms in American society today, that the several hundred thousand of exclusively father-raised young girls and boys[48] will turn out to hate men more than women and that the gender-based differences in their object relations would be exactly the reverse of what they have been hypothesized to be under exclusive female mothering. Similarly, it is also perfectly plausible to hypothesize that even in the absence of any large-scale change in patriarchal norms coparented children are far less likely than exclusively mother-raised children to demonize women and idealize men (as well as far less likely to demonize men and idealize women than exclusively father-raised children), and that the differences in their object relations would be significantly attenuated if not entirely eliminated.[49] Confirmation of either of these hypotheses would constitute a compelling case for the determining power of the mode of child rearing over the extrafamilial factors favored by Elliot. Of course these hypotheses might turn out to be wrong. But the problem is that Elliot's position (like Gottlieb's) discourages us from participating in the only real experiments that could possibly test them.[50]

(3) Whereas Gottlieb and Elliot replace what they take to be Dinnerstein's *psychological* determinism with a "political, cultural, and economic" determinism of their own, Jean Elsthain rejects Dinnerstein's psychological *determinism* in favor of "an account of language as that which makes human beings vitally and irrepressibly self-defining and self-creating." Because Dinnerstein "put[s] so much weight on the stage when we do not use language—because she insists "that the oral stage and preverbality set a powerful *causal* context for all that follows"—she "eviscerates the possibility that human beings, through language, can 'talk' their way into and out of alternative ways of being by changing their self-descriptions."[51] Thus she concludes that Dinnerstein's determinism prevents us from understanding how we can—and (supposedly) often do—"talk our way" into nonpatriarchal "ways of being."

Elsthain grants that there is a "partial truth" in Dinnerstein's picture of "a child lurk[ing] in each of us, threatening to erupt, disrupt, or fall apart" and that "human beings, at least some of the time, overdefine themselves as 'real men' or 'true women'" as a defense against this threat.[52] But she insists that "that is not all we are" and that "to reduce male activity to the defensive and destructive history-making of naughty boys and female activity to the play-acting of maternal menials or coy sex kittens . . . is to sink into [a] one-dimensionality"[53] that ignores the way in which the "minds [of language-users] can be put to purposes not ultimately or finally or 'really' reducible to infantile drives, desires, or wishes." Because Dinnerstein ignores these irreducibly adult purposes her "one-dimensional" patriarchal picture is "a serious distortion." It erroneously presumes a "social situation of unrelenting debasement or infantilisation" to which women "have [somehow] given their consent" that contradicts the fact that "we know of no human society based on such debasement which has enjoyed a continuing existence."[54]

Dinnerstein's claim, of course, is exactly the opposite: that "we know of no human society which has enjoyed a continuing existence" that has *not* been based, at least in part, on such debasement. For me this claim is all too clearly confirmed by the cultural universality of rape and many other ugly violations of female bodily integrity as well as by the omnipresence of the misogynistic myths that condone or even encourage those violations.[55] Thus my reading of the cultural and historical record leads me to conclude that Dinnerstein can justifiably plead guilty to Elsthain's charge of "eviscerating the possibility" that human beings can simply "talk themselves out" of their patriarchal "ways of being." The stubborn resistance of these ways of being to our changing self-descriptions suggests that we should instead take seriously a psychoanalytic account of language that assumes that (1) our self-descriptions are routinely at odds with—and thus lead us to misrecognize—our actual "ways of being"; and (2) our actual ways of being regularly serve to defend us against the very "infantile drives, desires, or wishes" that Elsthain believes our self-descriptions enable us to overcome. To put this more pithily: we need a theory whose "determinism" matches the tenacity of the (patriarchal) phenomenon of which it must give an account. Anything less is idealism.

Of course we also need a theory whose determinism is relative, in the sense that it does not rule out—and can in fact clarify—the possibility of overcoming male domination. It seems to me that Dinnerstein's psychoanalytic theory fits this bill. If it teaches us that we cannot merely "talk our way out" of our patriarchal ways of being, it also teaches us that a new, psychoanalytically informed "self-description" that matches rather than masks these ways of being can be the first step toward transforming them. But only the *first* step. We will only transform our ways of being if the new self-description leads to a confrontation with the "infantile drives, desires, and wishes" against which those ways of being defend. This confrontation can either take place intra-generationally, in therapy, or intergenerationally, in coparenting. Conventionally raised adults *can* learn in therapy to mourn the loss of the infantile omnipotence that is a central source of the rage against our mothers that poisons our relationships with women. Their coparented children *may* learn to mourn that loss as a matter of course and thus come to harbor far less hostility against *either* parent. Thus Dinnerstein is as committed to what she calls "our gift for self-creation"[56] as Elsthain. She simply recognizes that this process is a far more arduous one than Elsthain imagines.

I am not aware of any criticisms of Dinnerstein's admittedly incomplete account of the relationship between mother-dominated child rearing and the domination of nature. I will therefore now turn to criticisms of my effort in *Marxism and Domination* to complete that account.

My Critics

You will recall that I proceeded from Dinnerstein's assumptions that the mother is the child's first representative of the world and that the child's relationship with the mother therefore establishes the template for the adult's symbolization of nature. In short, my starting point was the claim that the mode of symbolization is engendered by the mode of child rearing.[57] Although neither Heydebrand nor Simon addresses Dinnerstein directly, they do challenge this Dinnersteinian point of departure in the course of their respective reviews of my book. Thus Heydebrand excoriates the "rampant psychological reductionism implicit in the concept of a mode of symbolization as based on patterns of child rearing," and Simon complains that "with Balbus, the positions of sociology and psychology have been reversed completely. . . . The world, external nature, becomes a reflection of the categorical structure of our minds."[58]

Simon's formulation of my position goes much too far. The concept of a mode of symbolization *does* entail the claim that the way in which nature *appears to us* is always mediated by the "categorical structure of our minds." How, after Kant, could anyone seriously claim otherwise? But the assumption that the mode of symbolization is determined by the mode of child rearing denies that there is *one* such unchanging categorical structure and asserts to the contrary that different categorical structures result from different *real* relationships with the mother. Thus my position, *pace* Simon, is *not* that "it is our consciousness, or rather, our unconscious, that determines social relations."[59] Rather it is that one particular "social relation"—namely the mode of child rearing—determines both our unconscious and our consciousness. This position is hardly a "complete reversal" of "the positions of sociology and psychology."

Heydebrand's "mode of symbolization . . . based on patterns of child rearing" is, in contrast, a fair characterization of my position. In what sense, then, is he entitled to describe this position as "rampant psychological reductionism"? Since he cannot mean that I reduce "social relations" to "psychology" he must mean—as far as I can make out—that I reduce *conscious* to *unconscious* symbolization. The target of his critique, then, appears to be my assumption that (an intersubjectively shared) mode of symbolizing nature is an outgrowth of the object relations of individuals. This is, of course, a perfectly contestable assumption. But to dismiss it rhetorically as "rampant reductionism" is to ignore at least two important things that can be said in its favor.

First—as I discovered some time after the publication of *Marxism and Domination*—there is not only psychoanalytic, but also cognitive developmental, support for my assumption. Piaget argues in *The Child's Conception of the World* that the child's feelings of "participation" and "communion" result from a "continual response of the [maternal] environment" and thus from a "complete continuity between its parents' activities and its own." Consistent maternal gratification, in other words, "ensures an absence of differentiation between the world and the self." This sense of differentiation—for Piaget, the disappearance of feelings of participation and communion—only develops with the child's "liberation from the bond that ties him . . . to his parents." The dissolution of this bond between mother and child, in turn, is set in motion by the frustrations that the former imposes on the latter. Thus Piaget's argument about the early childhood origins of our conception of the world is completely consistent with my claim that the symbolization of nature is determined by the mixture of maternal gratification and frustration experienced by the preoedipal child.[60]

Second, my assumption has (what Lakatos would call) considerable "heuristic power." By this I do not merely mean that the hypotheses I derive from it are corroborated by "the facts" but also that they lead us to "predict [a number of] novel, hitherto unexpected fact[s]."[61] Heydebrand and Simon unwittingly testify to this in the course of (what they take to be) their critique of my hypothesis that the instrumental mode of symbolizing nature was engendered by the peculiarly harsh child-rearing practices of the early modern West. That hypothesis, you will recall, was corroborated by a cross-cultural comparison that revealed that child-rearing practices were significantly more severe in modern instrumental than in traditional noninstrumental societies. Heydebrand refers to this comparison as "suggestive but [once again!] hopelessly reductionist" and Simon says that it provides "some anthropological and historical evidence to support [Balbus's] interpretation, but not nearly enough to overcome my initial skepticism." But in spite of their skepticism—and to their credit—each takes the hypothesis seriously enough to pursue its logical consequences. Both Heydebrand and Simon are sufficiently perceptive to infer that if my hypothesis is correct then there must have been a dramatic change in child-rearing practices on the eve of modernity in the West. This prediction, in turn, leads them both to look for an explanation. Thus Heydebrand asks, "Why was there a change in child-rearing practices which in turn gave rise to the rape of nature?" and Simon wonders, "What caused this . . . change in the basic mode of child rearing?" Not stopping there, Simon speculates that in order to answer this question either "some theory of internal contradiction [must] be developed" or it must be conceded that the mode of child rearing is "effected [sic] by other factors." And he wants to know whether they are the kind of "social and economic variables" that would take us "back to finding room at the base of the theory for sociology, perhaps even Marxism."[62]

All excellent questions, all eminently worth pursuing. But the point is that it would not have occurred to Heydebrand and Simon—or anyone else—to ask them unless they were wrestling with an hypothesis that had been derived from my assumption of the determining power of the mode of child rearing. Surely the fact that this assumption gives rise to such interesting questions says more about the heuristic power of my theory than the mere fact that I did not answer them in *Marxism and Domination*. If Lakatos is correct to claim that the mark of a "theoretically progressive" research program is its ability to "predict some novel, hitherto unexpected fact," then the "prediction" of Heydebrand and Simon would seem to attest to the theoretical progressivity of my research program.

I want to go further and show that my research program is not merely theoretically but also empirically progressive in that it not only predicts novel facts but has actually led to their *discovery*.[63] I will therefore conclude this essay with a brief summary of my effort since *Marxism and Domination* to corroborate the prediction of Heydebrand and Simon and to develop an internally consistent explanation for that prediction. What follows, in other words, are my answers to the questions they have been insightful enough to ask.

Conclusion

In *Emotional Rescue: The Theory and Practice of a Feminist Father* I attempt to verify the hypothesis that the modern Western objectification of nature was preceded by a dramatic increase in the severity of child-rearing practices over those practices that must have long been in place in the West prior to the triumph of objectification. Within the limits of the available evidence, I demonstrate that children of a variety of different classes in Western Europe and the American colonies were subjected from the sixteenth through the eighteenth centuries to a form of (what was then called) "family government" that was substantially more strict than the regime that children of those classes typically experienced during the Middle Ages. I argue that it is reasonable to conclude from the existing studies of child-rearing advice, the personal diaries of parents, and the memoirs of those who recounted their childhoods during the two periods in question that early modern practices were much harsher than medieval practices. To confirm this conclusion I also rely on Norbert Elias's simultaneously entertaining and persuasive demonstration that the early modern period was marked by a dramatic increase in the level of shame associated with the bodily processes of adults.[64] Thus I discover exactly that change in child-rearing practices that the theory of the determining power of the mode of child rearing would lead us—and did lead Heydebrand and Simon—to predict.

I then turn to the problem of explaining this (as well as any other) transformation in the mode of child rearing that I had postponed in *Marxism and Domination*. To make good on that omission, in *Emotional Rescue* I derive what I call a *gender-struggle theory* of transformations in child-rearing practices from the assumptions of both Dinnerstein and Nancy Chodorow. My theory holds that the mother-monopolized structure of child rearing necessarily engenders an opposition between the parenting interests of women and the parenting interests of men, with fathers (or father-substitutes) both preoedipally and oedipally predisposed toward repressive (or "underprotective") practices, and mothers (or mother substitutes) psychologically prepared for indulgent (or "overprotective) child-rearing practices. It follows from this assumption that child-rearing practices will reflect the balance of power between mothers and fathers and that a change in those practices will be the result of a change in the nature of that balance of power. This leads me to hypothesize that the marked early modern increase in the severity of child-rearing practices was the result of an equally sharp shift from maternal to paternal control over the mode of child rearing.

I then show that substantial support for this hypothesis is supplied by historians who argue that the transition from the late medieval to the early modern period was indeed punctuated by a pronounced increase in the father's power within the home. According to Lawrence Stone, "the powers of fathers over children and of husbands over wives . . . became greater than they had been in the middle ages."[65] Stone is echoed by a number of other scholars who argue that the early modern period was in fact the period par excellence of the patriarchal family in Western Europe.[66] Of course the corroboration of my hypothesis of an early modern shift from maternal to paternal control over the mode of child rearing leads us, in turn, to ask *why* that shift occurred. My answer is that a number of inter-related, extra-familial factors—the dissolution of the ties of extended kinship, the development of the domestic economy, statification, and pa-triarchal Protestantism—combined to produce a dramatic increase in the father's power within the home.

Notice that my explanation for changes in the mode of child rearing is based both on the assumption that the mode of child rearing necessarily engenders a conflict between the parenting interests of mothers and the parenting interests of fathers, *and* the assumption that the outcome of this conflict will be determined by a number of mutually reinforcing external factors. Thus it combines what Simon calls a "theory of internal contra-diction" with a specification of "other," including "social and economic variables" that "overdetermine" the effect of that contradiction. Whether "we are back to finding room at the base of [this] theory for sociology, perhaps even Marxism," is a matter of interpretation. On the one hand, there would have been no increase in the severity of child-rearing prac-tices without the dramatic increase in the power of the early modern fa-ther over child rearing for which the social, economic, political, and religious forces to which I have referred *were* responsible. On the other hand, none of these factors—or any combination thereof—can properly be said to have required or called forth the increase in the severity of child-rearing practices that was associated with that increase in paternal power. Child-rearing practices, I argue, did not become harsher because harsh practices were necessary for, or even a direct consequence of, the opera-tion of the nuclear family, the domestic economy, the centralized state, or evangelical Protestantism. Rather, they became harsher because the en-hanced paternal power produced by these social, economic, political, and religious forces unleashed a paternal parenting predisposition the exis-tence of which does not depend on those extrafamilial forces. The deter-mining role of these cultural and historical factors, in short, was decisively mediated by the transcultural, transhistorical force of *gender.*[67]

The same point can be made about the ultimate origins of the instru-mental mode of symbolization for which—to return for a final time to the thesis of *Marxism and Domination*—the harsh child-rearing practices of the early modern era were immediately responsible. To the extent that the nuclear family, the domestic economy, statification, and the Reformation helped make these child-rearing practices possible, they must be understood as important determinants of the modern industrial worldview. This point would appear to sustain the claim of a variety of different theoretical traditions—including Marxian, Weberian, and Durkheimian—concerning the contribution of these social, economic, political, and religious forces to a modernity that was uniquely Western in origin. But only in part. Neither the founders nor the followers of any of these theoretical traditions have grasped that the contribution of these culturally and historically specific factors to modernization was contingent on their contribution to the triumph of the paternal over the maternal interest in the rearing of children. None has recognized, in short, that modernity was made possible by a hitherto unprecedented *masculinization of the mode of child rearing*.

This claim, finally, clarifies the sense in which it is possible to speak of patriarchal production in Marx. In the second and third sections of this chapter I argued that Marx's category of production is patriarchal because it entails a commitment to the domination of nature that is an historically and culturally specific form of the domination of men over women. If the domination of nature was, in turn, the consequence of a gender struggle that replaced maternal with paternal control over the mode of child rearing, then we can add that "production" is patriarchal because it was the *conceptual child of the father-dominated family*. Thus, to move beyond Marx is—in more ways than one—to bid farewell to the "world of our fathers."[68]

3   The Butler Didn't Do It: Why "Gender Identity" Survives Its Deconstruction by Judith Butler

Introduction

The feminist object-relations theory on which I rely in *Marxism and Domination* and defend in the two preceding chapters is vulnerable to the objection that it ignores important differences in the quality of parenting *practice* under the prevailing, mother-dominated *structure* as well as the differences in that practice that might outlive the transformation of that structure in the direction of coparenting. Thus in *Emotional Rescue* I elaborate a partial synthesis of feminist mothering theory and contemporary psychoanalytic theories of narcissism that enables me to assess the relative contributions of structure and practice to the problem of male domination and to argue on behalf of what might be called *"good-enough" coparenting* as a necessary solution to that problem. This synthesis incorporates the argument of feminist object-relations theory that mother-raised boys must in some sense dis-identify from their mothers in order to become men. This claim, you will recall, is based on the assumption of an inevitable opposition between a boy's core gender identity and an earlier primary identification with the mother that is normally resolved in favor of the former and against the latter.

The assumption of core gender identity entails the claim that children will normally develop "a cognitive sense of gendered self, the sense that one is [either] male or female"[1] that corresponds to their anatomical sex. They will make use of genital and other physiological markers to determine whether they are girls like their mothers and unlike their fathers or brothers, or boys unlike their mothers and like their fathers or brothers. Although Robert Stoller—who is chiefly responsible for the development of the concept of core gender identity—claims that core gender identity is normally established during the second year of life and is firmly and irreversibly consolidated by the end of the third,[2] the precise periodization of this process may in fact be subject to cultural variations. But the outcome of the process is not. To make use of a theory that is based on the assumption of core gender identity is to assume that the overwhelming majority of the members of any conceivable society—even a society in which all children are coparented—will be *gendered*, in the elemental sense that they will be constrained by their embodiment to think of themselves as either male or female rather than both male and female, something in between, or something entirely different.

Notice that this assumption does *not* entail the claim that (what are sometimes called) gender role identities—shared expectations about masculine as compared to feminine attributes or actions—are culturally universal. To the contrary: feminist object-relations theory simultaneously relies on the assumption of core gender identity *and* hypothesizes that gender-based differences in the "role identities" of coparented children would be significantly attenuated if not entirely eliminated. It predicts that anatomically male and female coparented children would continue to think of themselves as either boys or girls, and then women or men, even as girls and women become more "oppositional," and boys and men become more "relational," than their conventionally raised counterparts.

This prediction is based on the assumption that the primary identification of coparented boys and girls would no longer be exclusively female, since both boys and girls would have a same-sex and an opposite-sex primary caregiver on whom they were dependent and with whom they were identified. The coparented boy could tell himself "I am male like the father-with-whom-I-am-one" just as the conventionally raised girl can tell herself "I am female like the mother-with-whom-I-am-one." Thus the boy would no longer have to disidentify from his caregiver—to repudiate his primary identification—in order to prove that he was a man. In fact he wouldn't have to *prove* his manhood at all, since the source of his manhood would already be inside him.

Thus feminist object-relations theory is as dependent on the assumption of a primary identification—of an "early, non-verbal, unconscious, almost somatic sense of oneness"[3]—with the first parent(s) as it is on the assumption of an anatomically based core gender identification. It argues that it is the conflict between these two identifications that creates the problem for/of the mother-raised boy and that it is the congruence between them that creates the solution of/for the coparented boy.

Butler's Critique

Both the assumption of core gender identity and the assumption of a primary (female) identification have been called into question by Judith Butler in her extraordinarily influential *Gender Trouble: Feminism and the Subversion of Identity*, published in 1990, and in *Bodies That Matter: On the Discursive Limits of "Sex,"* published three years later.[4] In *Gender Trouble* she counters Stoller's concept of core gender identity with the striking claim that "there is no gender identity behind the expressions of gender." Instead, "that identity is performatively constituted by the very 'expressions' that are said to be its results."[5] In other words, the performance of "masculine" and "feminine" roles is not the expression of some underlying, more essential sense of maleness and femaleness, but rather that which constitutes that sense of maleness or femaleness in the first place. By treating that sense as an essential cause rather than a contingent effect, the discourse of core gender identity disguises the constitution of that sense and thereby helps ensure its efficacy. Thus this discourse must itself be understood as one of the *"regulatory practices* of gender formation and division,"[6] that is, as one of the practices that produce both masculinity and femininity as well as the illusion that they are expressions of a male and female core gender identity.

Moreover, in producing these oppositions object-relations theories "offer story lines about gender acquisition which effect a narrative closure on gender experience and a false stabilization of the category of woman [and the category of man]."[7] Consider the "story" that begins with the assumption that a primary identification with the mother is the source of the girl's gender identity but an obstacle to the boy's gender identity, and that culminates in the conclusion that women are "relational" and men are "oppositional." Even if this story is told by feminists like Nancy Chodorow and Jessica Benjamin, who remind us that it holds true only so long as women "mother" and men do not, it remains "effectively essentialist" because the assumption of unified and opposing masculine and feminine identities "forecloses convergences" across genders as well as "all manner of dissonance" within them.[8] Thus the "stabilization of the category of woman [and man] effected by object-relations theory is not only false but exclusionary."[9]

Object-relations theory can effect this stabilization only because it is based on the unwarranted assumption of "an orderly temporal development of identifications in which the first identifications serve to unify the later ones."[10] For example, unless we assume that the girl's initial identification with the mother is primary in the sense that her subsequent identifications with her father or with her brother "are easily assimilated under the already firmly established gender identification with women . . . we would lose the unifying thread of the narrative."[11] If "the temporal prioritization of primary identifications" were "fully contested," then we would "have . . . the gender equivalent of an interplay of attributes without an abiding or unifying substance."[12]

But then we would also be beyond "the regulation of sexuality within the obligatory frame of reproductive heterosexuality."[13] It is precisely the "heterosexualization of desire" that "requires . . . the production of discrete, asymmetrical oppositions between 'feminine' and 'masculine,' where these are understood as expressive aspects of 'male' and 'female.'"[14] (Or, as Butler puts it more pithily in *Bodies That Matter*, "'It's a girl' anticipates the eventual arrival of the sanction, 'I now pronounce you man and wife.'"[15]) Since, as we have seen, Butler claims that object-relations theory produces exactly those oppositions (between "feminine" and "masculine") and exactly that understanding (of these oppositions as "expressive aspects of 'male' and 'female'"), it follows that object-relations theory must be considered one of the disciplinary practices that serve "the interests of the heterosexual construction and regulation of sexuality."[16] In short, object-relations theory necessarily normalizes heterosexuality and marginalizes homosexuality.

The Critique of Butler's Critique

I do not believe that *any* of Butler's claims can be sustained. Let me begin with the last, the claim that object-relations theory is inherently heterosexist. Butler's argument that a commitment to the categories of "women" and "men" necessarily culminates in a normalizing commitment to "feminine women" loving "masculine men" cannot in fact be squared with the object-relational understandings of the relationships among "core gender identity," "gender role identity," and "sexual identity."

Although it is true that for both Freud and Lacan all three identities are established in one fell oedipal swoop, so to speak, for Stoller and Chodorow (as we saw in Chapter 1[17]) core gender identity is established during rapprochement and therefore well before the oedipal stage. Moreover, the object-relational concept of gender identity leans on Freud's claim in *Group Psychology and the Analysis of the Ego* that "identification is known to psychoanalysis as the earliest example of an emotional tie with another person" rather than his subsequent assertion in the *Ego and the Id* that "the ego is a precipitate of abandoned object cathexes."[18] For object-relations theory, identification is not a substitute for object love but something prior to and separate from it. The theory is therefore vulnerable to the objection that this separation of identification and desire makes it difficult to *explain* sexual identity, and heterosexual identity in particular. But even if this objection is correct, there is a world of difference between an inability to explain heterosexuality and a normalizing presupposition of its existence.

That object-relations theory is not in fact wedded to the presupposition of normative heterosexuality can be seen from what it has to say, or rather *does not* have to say, about homosexuality. If a commitment to the concept of core gender identity entailed a commitment to the "heterosexualization of desire," we would expect that relational psychoanalysts would argue that homosexuals typically suffer from gender identity disorder. But they do not. A recent report concludes that "most homosexual men have not experienced boyhood Gender Identity Disorder, which is relatively rare."[19] The fact that an overwhelming majority of gay men think of themselves as men (and that, presumably, the overwhelming majority of gay women think of themselves as women) is not an anomaly for, but is rather entirely consistent with, the assumptions of object-relations theory.[20]

So too is the possibility of widespread bisexuality in a future society of coparented children. In fact we can derive this prediction from the assumption of a primary identification with primary parents as well as the assumption of core gender identity—as long as we are willing to add to the assumption of primary identification the additional assumption that the relationship that gives rise to that identification is also an erotic relationship. If, in other words, we assume that sexual desire is born in the eminently embodied interaction with the primary caregiver, we can hypothesize that when female and male infants are caressed by their fathers as well as their mothers they will grow up to be women and men whose core gender identities are intact but whose love-objects are as likely to be same-sex as opposite-sex. This hypothesis may turn out to be wrong, but the fact that it is in no way ruled out by the twin assumptions of primary identification and core gender identification means that object-relations theory can justifiably plead not guilty to the charge of enforcing "compulsory heterosexuality" and thereby marginalizing homosexuality.

I believe that it is also innocent of the charge of imposing unified "gender role identities" on women and men that foreclose gender "convergences" and "dissonances" and exclude the women and men who enact them. In *Emotional Rescue* I demonstrate (but here have only space to assert) that at least four different types of men and four different types of women are consistent with the object-relational assumption of core gender identity and primary [female] identification. Differences in the ways boys and girls are treated by both their mothers and their fathers, I show, produce important variations on the theme of oppositional men and relational women. The point is that a good deal of difference can go hand in hand with an object-relational concept of gender identity, and that far many more women and men can find themselves in the gender-generalizations of object-relations theory than Butler believes.

Of course at this point Butler is likely to object that it is only the unwarranted "assumption of an orderly temporal development in which the first identifications serve to unify the latter ones"[21] that enables me to continue to speak of four types of *women* and four types of *men*. Unless we assume, for example, that the subsequent identifications of physiologically male individuals are always assimilated to their prior core gender identification, there is no good reason to group the father-identified, physiologically male individual and the non-father-identified physiologically male individual under the same gender category. But this objection merely reiterates Butler's opening argument against core gender identity, and the force of that argument depends entirely on the plausibility of her alternative, "performative" account of gender.

That account, I want to argue, is simply not plausible. To understand why, consider the following passage:

Acts, gestures, and desire produce the effect of an internal core or substance, but produce this *on the surface* of the body through the play of signifying absences that suggest, but never reveal, the organizing principle of identity as a cause. Such acts, gestures, enactments, generally construed, are *performative* in the sense that the essence or the entity that they otherwise purport to express are *fabrications* manufactured and sustained through corporeal signs and other discursive means. That the gendered body is performative suggests that it has no ontological status apart from the various acts which constitute its reality. . . . [W]ords, acts and gestures, articulated and enacted desires create the illusion of an interior and organizing gender core.[22]

According to this account, then, core gender identity is a "fabrication" in the twofold sense that it is both manufactured and an illusion. The conviction that comes to almost all anatomically female and anatomically male children before the end of the third year of their life that they are either girls or boys, and not both or something else entirely, reveals no "truth" about who or what they really are but rather only the power of the "words, acts, and gestures"—the "corporeal signs and other discursive means—that compel that conviction. It is not clear whether Butler wants us to construe these "words, acts, and gestures" as those of the parent or those of the child, or both. But what is clear is that she treats these signs as arbitrary, "contingent acts that create the appearance of a naturalistic necessity."[23] For Butler, anatomy functions not as destiny but as alibi. The illusion that the signifiers of core gender identity represent (re-present) our bodies is precisely what enables these signifiers to construct them.

But if the signifiers of "core gender identity" are body builders that are entirely unconstrained or "unmotivated" by the bodies they build, then it would seem that "gender itself becomes a free-floating artifice, with the consequence that *man* . . . might just as easily signify a female body as a male one, and *woman* . . . a male body as easily as a female one."[24] Although Butler considers this position problematical, it is not clear how she can avoid it. She insists that gender is not "a set of free-floating attributes" but is rather "compelled by the regulatory practices of gender coherence."[25] But this formulation merely reproduces the problem of voluntarism at the level of culture: although individuals are constrained by the "regulatory practices of gender coherence," these regimes themselves seem to float freely from the bodies they construct. So why couldn't there exist a regime that radically separates gender from anatomical sex? Why not the cultural construction of three, four, or a hundred genders rather than two? Why not, indeed, unless "gender" is constrained by the very bodies it "constructs"?

To her credit, Butler addresses this problem in *Bodies That Matter*. She tries to solve it with the notion of construction as "constitutive constraint."[26] That notion is designed to transcend what she describes as the "tired" opposition between a "radical constructivism" that dissolves the materiality of the body entirely into discourse, and an "essentialism" for which the body is simply "prediscursive" and unconstructed.[27] The difficulty with radical constructivism is that it can be read (as I have read it above) as a linguistically deterministic denial "that there are, minimally, sexually differentiated parts, activities, hormonal and chromosomal differences that can be conceded without reference to 'construction.'"[28] To overcome this difficulty a concept of construction must be constructed that does not claim that discourse "originates, causes, or exhaustively composes that which it concedes."[29]

To do this we must "rethink . . . the meaning of construction" so that it is no longer understood as something "artificial and dispensable" that is opposed to something "natural and necessary."[30] A defensible "constructivism needs to take account of the domain of constraints without which we would not be able to think, to live, to make sense at all," without which "there [might] be no 'I,' no 'we.'"[31]

Although this kind of constructivism denies the determinism of discourse, it still insists on its formative power. It thereby maintains its distance from an essentialism that fails to grasp that "there is no reference to a pure body which is not at the same time a *further formation* of that body." Unlike essentialism, it understands that "the constative claim is always *to some degree* performative."[32]

It seems to me that this reformulation rescues Butler's performative account of gender from linguistic determinism at the exorbitant price of virtually eliminating the distinction between her account and the very account of core gender identity that she contests. Is not the claim of the theorists of core gender identity precisely that physiologically male and female children are constrained by their physiology to construct an elementary sense of maleness or femaleness, without which they "cannot make their way" in the world and that is inseparable from their sense of "I" or "we"? Doesn't this mean that there is now rather more "identity" than "difference" between Butler and Stoller?

Of course to keep her distance Butler might argue that Stoller and his followers continue to ignore the power of an always physiologically constrained but nonetheless "formative" gender discourse, the extent to which the discursive "reiteration of a . . . set of [gender] norms"[33] by the parents performatively constructs the gendered body of the child. But that is simply not the case. Stoller specifically argues that core gender identity is the result of an interaction between "biologic forces" on the one hand and the "sex assignment" made by, and the "attitudes" of, parents on the other.[34] Perhaps Butler would reply that Stoller grants rather too much to biology and rather too little to discourse. But then she would be making an empirical claim about a difference of degree rather than a principled argument about a difference in kind. She would be making a gender point that mattered. But she would no longer be making gender trouble.

4 Against the Idealism of the Affects

Introduction

Rationalists from Plato through Kant to Habermas rely on reason for principles of social obligation that can override our supposedly selfish appetites and thus secure the possibility of a genuinely just society. Realists from Hobbes through Nietzsche to Foucault counter that these principles are themselves merely weapons wielded in the war against others and that justice is merely the name we give to the outcome of that war. Thus the common assumption that the appetites are inherently *agonistic* underlies the obvious opposition between the rationalists and the realists. This assumption precludes that possibility of sensuous sociality that a venerable and still-valuable tradition calls *solidarity*.

Postmodernism, in contrast, does not simply rule out the possibility of solidarity. But the search for its source is short-circuited by the assumption that the need for solidarity (or, for that matter, for anything else) is merely an effect of the discourses that determine it. The origins of solidarity are obscured by postmodernism's dedication to the deconstruction of any concept of a "real" self that might serve as solidarity's source.

The great virtue of the four works under review in this chapter[1] is their search for exactly such a self. Yet in their preoccupation with the sources of solidarity in the self, they all ignore—or at least seriously underestimate—the selfly sources of what subverts it. Because our authors treat agonistic affects as external to the self that suffers from them, they are in no position to clarify the conditions under which their ideal of solidarity is more, or less, realizable. For this reason I think that it is fair to claim that all four works, their considerable merits notwithstanding, suffer from what might be called the *idealism of the affects*.

The Idealism of the Affects

Nel Noddings

The form of Nel Noddings's *Starting at Home* is admirably consistent with its content: her commitment to an ethic of care is matched by the care with which she constructs her concepts. Her assumption, as the title of her book implies, is that we can best learn how to create a more caring society by learning more about the origins of care in the domestic domain. Her argument, in a nutshell, is that "[l]earning to care about depends on learning to care for, and that in turn depends on oneself having been cared for." By *caring for*, Noddings means a receptive attention to the needs of intimate others that entails both a commitment not only to their "expressed" but also to their "inferred" (by the caregiver) needs *and* a sensitivity to the potential dangers of that distinction. It is motivated neither by self-interest nor ethical obligation but rather "arises more or less spontaneously out of affection or inclination" for the person who is being cared for. Thus, according to Noddings, a care ethic is neither deontological nor utilitarian, but it *is* consequentialist in its concern for "the effects on recipients of our care."[2]

Caring about involves the extension of this concern from those whom we know to those whom we don't: it "moves us from the face-to-face world into the wider public realm." According to Noddings, this move entails both change and continuity. Although we cannot care for strangers in the same direct way we care for intimates, we *can* experience a "fellow-feeling" for them that leads us to act on their behalf. In fact, what distinguishes genuine "caring about" from a cheap, overly abstract substitute is precisely a commitment to help "establish social conditions in which care [in the sense of "caring for"] can flourish." Thus "caring-about is empty if it does not culminate in caring relations."[3]

The need to *be cared for* is, according to Noddings, a culturally universal need. It grows out of what she calls, by way of obvious contrast to John Rawls's original position, the "original condition." Because the original condition—infancy—is one of "utter dependency,"[4] all human beings depend on others—mostly mothers—to fulfill their basic needs. Here Noddings follows Sarah Ruddick[5] in identifying these as the needs for "preservation, growth, and acceptability."[6] Thus a child who is "cared for" has a caregiver who ensures his or her physical safety, promotes the realization of his or her potential, and helps him or her learn to distinguish between necessary and superfluous social norms.

Noddings's claims, then, are (1) that children who have been cared for in this way will grow up to be adults who are "naturally" inclined toward attentively caring relations with intimate others, and (2) that adults who are involved in attentively caring relations with intimates will care enough about strangers to work to create the social conditions that maximize the possibility of caring relations (with intimates). Neither of these claims is adequately defended by Noddings. But it is on the first that I want to focus.[7] This claim sits rather uneasily with her own insistence that *women* are disproportionately likely to develop an ethic of care. That ethic, according to Noddings, "arises more naturally from the sort of experience provided for women than from that provided for men."[8] Here the causal claim is that socialization for, and the experience of, caregiving engenders the inclination to care for intimate others. One way to reconcile this claim with the (first) claim, which roots that inclination in having been cared for, is to argue that girls have been more adequately cared for than boys. But Noddings nowhere attempts to make this case, and it would of course be a difficult one to make. It would also be possible to argue that having been *cared for* is *necessary but not sufficient* for developing an ethic of care, and that only a combination of having been *cared for* and being a *caregiver* engenders that ethic. Indeed at one point Noddings points parenthetically to just this argument: "people who are directly responsible for the care of others (*if they themselves have been adequately cared for*) will likely develop . . . an *ethic of care*."[9] But the argument that being *cared for* is necessary but insufficient is inconsistent with her assumption that "the need to be cared for, the most basic expressed need, *triggers* a desire to care."[10]

Noddings's first claim is also vulnerable to the objection that she has an incomplete conception of what it means for a child to be cared for. As we have seen, she assumes that the "utterly dependent" infant has three great needs: the need for physical protection, the need for adequate "mirroring," and the need to fit in with (at least certain) social groups. Thus she ignores entirely the need of infants and children to *express and integrate their aggression*. Whether we understand aggression to be innate, or (as I would prefer to understand it) as the necessary consequence of the frustrations inevitably imposed by even the most solicitous primary care-givers, those caregivers cannot but become the targets of the rage of those for whom they care. Whether the structures and practices of caregiving encourage children to reconcile their (incipient) hate with their love for their caregivers surely helps determine whether they are well cared for, and thus (on Noddings's assumption) whether they will develop a desire to care for others.[11] Children who have been physically protected, sup-ported, and socialized to be acceptable but who have not learned to toler-ate emotional *ambivalence* will *not* in fact be inclined toward attentively caring relations with intimate others. We should instead expect that their unintegrated, split-off rage will transform their relationships with inti-mates into relationships of domination and subordination. Noddings is, of course, aware of such aggressive inclinations, but her account of the "original condition" gives her no way of *explaining* them. Faced with a particularly egregious example of human hostility she can only indignantly ask (but never attempt to answer): "What sort of self accumulates and exudes such hatred?"[12] Her moralistic outrage is no substitute for an analy-sis that would yield an answer to that crucial question.

Kelly Oliver

Neither do we find an answer to this question in Kelly Oliver's *Witness-ing: Beyond Recognition*. What we do find—unlike in Noddings's work—is a good deal of conceptual confusion. As her title and subtitle announce, Oliver's central concept of *witnessing* is constructed in opposition to what she takes to be Hegel's notion of *recognition*. She argues that "recogni-tion itself is part of the pathology of oppression and domination" be-cause, as conceptualized by Hegel (and his contemporary followers, e.g., Charles Taylor and Axel Honneth), it presupposes both a hierarchical relationship between the one who recognizes and the one who is recog-nized and the inability of the former to acknowledge the separateness or otherness of the latter. "In the Hegelian scenario the hope for recip-rocal recognition . . . is won through enslavement and domination . . . difference is the threatening otherness that alienates and motivates the murderous urges inherent in the struggle for recognition." While rec-ognition flattens difference into sameness, witnessing, in contrast, in-volves an authentic, ethically admirable openness to the other that enables us to learn something new and unexpected about her: "Address-ability and response-ability are what I identify with the process of wit-nessing." Witnessing, in turn (and not, *pace* Hegel, recognition), is the social source of subjectivity: "Having a sense of oneself as a subject . . . requires that the structure of witnessing as the possibility of address and response has been set up in dialogic relation with others. Dialogue with others makes dialogue with oneself possible."[13]

In my judgment Oliver's critique of recognition rests on a complete misreading of the chapter on "Lordship and Bondage" in *The Phenomenology of Mind*. This misreading has a long history, to which both Sartre in *Being and Nothingness* and Levinas in *Totality and Infinity* have made signal contributions. In effect, Oliver merely recycles Levinas's claim that Hegelian recognition is "not a relation with the other as such, but the reduction of the other to the same . . . [it] is a philosophy of power."[14] But this claim, as Robert Williams has persuasively demonstrated, entails a failure to distinguish between the "*concept* of recognition [and] a particular *determinate instance* of recognition."[15] Although Hegel's historically informed account begins (perhaps arbitrarily) with a struggle to the death that culminates in the master–slave relationship, he clearly considers that relationship to be a fatally flawed form of what he calls "the pure conception of recognition," or "recognition proper."[16] Recognition proper is described by Hegel as a process in which "each is to itself and to the other an immediate self-existing reality, which, at the same time, exists thus for itself only through this mediation. They recognize themselves as mutually recognizing one another."[17] This means, as Williams has emphasized, that for Hegel "genuine reciprocal recognition requires . . . letting the other go free. . . . The recognition that really counts is the recognition from the other that is *not* at the disposal of the self."[18] Thus, as Derrida once noted, "Levinas is very close to Hegel. . . . As soon as he speaks against Hegel, Levinas can only confirm [him]."[19] The same can be said for Oliver.

With one important exception. Although the master–slave relationship is only one possible outcome of the struggle for recognition, "conflict of some sort *is* [for Hegel] an essential structural feature of recognition."[20] Hence the term, the *struggle* for recognition: mutual recognition is only won through arduous efforts to overcome the tendencies that oppose it. Oliver's concept of witnessing, in contrast, explicitly disclaims the inevitability of those tendencies.[21] Thus she takes Julia Kristeva, Judith Butler, and other theorists of "abjection" to task for ontologizing what she argues is an historically specific, uniquely patriarchal conflict between mother and child, and for ignoring or underestimating in the process the maternal and infantile sources of the capacity to bear witness. In fact Oliver says some very interesting things about the affective sources of sociality.

Borrowing from psychologist J. J. Gibson and feminist theorist Theresa Brennan, she argues that "the possibility of subjectivity is founded on responsiveness to psychic and affective energy" and that "we are by virtue of our response to the biosocial energy that surrounds us."[22] She also relies on Merleau-Ponty to reconceptualize vision as something that connects rather than separates us. But there are also, as I have suggested, undeniably sensual sources of *separation*. Oliver wishes these away when she argues that theories of abjection (that assume an inevitable split between mother and child) "are based on a false notion of an antisocial mother–child dyad . . . that must be violently broken in order for the child to become social."[23] But we do not have to assume that the mother–child relationship is either "antisocial" or a purely "natural unity"[24] to recognize that even the most eminently social mother–child relationship culminates either in the child's psychological separation or in a number of destructive defenses against it. These defenses set the emotional stage for the adult's experience of the other as a mere extension of his self and thus for his inability either to recognize or witness the other. The price that Oliver pays for her denial of this psychological fact of life, then, is an inability to explain the domination she deplores.[25] Instead she repeatedly invokes "patriarchy" to account for the very psychological processes that might account for *it*.[26]

Cynthia Willett

Like Oliver, Cynthia Willett argues, in *The Soul of Justice*, that "our intimate relationships with our mothers provide the prototype for all subsequent social relationships."[27] Although her account of the mother–child relationship is much thicker than Oliver's, it ultimately suffers from the same idealization of that relationship that plagues her colleague's work. On the one hand, Willett draws on Luce Irigaray and Daniel Stern, among others, to demonstrate "how the highest dimensions of subjectivity [are] cultivated in social interactions, beginning with erotic sources that are not regressive or primitive, but quite sophisticated, in the adult–child relationship." In contrast to thinkers (including, supposedly, Nancy Chodorow) who conceptualize that relationship as the source of a "minimalist" form of sociality that is limited to "rudimentary concerns for security," Willett argues that "pro-social drives originally embedded in lyric, tactile, and rhythmic sources of meaning in infancy form the basis for mature forms of moral development and culture." She agrees with Stern that what he calls the "affect attunement" between infant and mother is the sensual source of all social reciprocity.[28] Affect attunement as Stern understands it entails a prediscursive capacity of the infant to respond to the mother's behavior "with some behavior that does not literally copy but instead 'corresponds'" to that behavior.[29] In her earlier *Maternal Ethics and Other Slave Moralities*, Willett points out that this Baudelairean concept of correspondence implies that the infant's face-to-face play with the mother is the origin of the adult's capacity to make metaphors.[30] Aristotle's description of this capacity in his *Poetics* as "the greatest thing by far"[31] lends weight to Willett's claim that "mature forms of moral development and culture" are indeed rooted in the child's earliest relationship with the mother.

Willett relies on the concept of prediscursive affect attunement to develop a compelling critique of other contemporary thinkers who have tried—against the tradition of liberal individualism—to seek out the sources of human sociality. Care ethics—including the (earlier) work of Nel Noddings—is found wanting due either to its failure to provide "a psychological theory that can explain what motivates the caring attachments that this ethic presupposes," or because it relies on a Chodorowian object-relations psychology that, once again, can only yield a "minimalist" conception of sociality. Predictably—and to my mind correctly—Habermasian discourse ethics is taken to task for (among other things) neglecting the nondiscursive sources of ethical intuitions. And Willett argues that Seyla Benhabib's effort to synthesize Habermasian discourse ethics and an ethic of care effectively subordinates the latter to the former, both because Benhabib fails to call into question the inevitable partiality of ostensibly impartial, universalizing reason and because she relies on a thin, "quasi-natural" notion of "nurturing and care."[32]

On the other hand, Willett's concept of the self sheds no more light on its dark side than does Oliver's. Although she describes (and decries) the crime of hubris—the arrogant assertion of superiority on the part of the powerful over those of lesser status—she never attempts to explain its origin. This is particularly puzzling in the light of her own insistence that "we . . . need to acknowledge the inevitable impact of [aggressive] drives on human behavior before we can build a society evolving from and sustained by free libidinal relationships," and that "any dream of human society that does not acknowledge games of power as core to our existence is naively romantic."[33] Despite this promising insistence, Willett fails to incorporate "aggressive drives" and "power games" into her account of the formation of the self and thus fails to elucidate the sense in which they are "core to our existence." This failure, I would argue, follows from her explicit endorsement of Oliver's repudiation of Hegel's concept of the struggle for recognition, and with it the inevitable moment of conflict that it entails.[34] Similarly, she shares Oliver's dismissal of "any theory of individuation that renders normative a separation from the mother or other libidinal attachments within . . . the domestic sphere."[35] This dismissal effectively purges the mother–child relationship of any hostility and thus precludes the possibility of a psychodynamic account of the "aggressive drives" and "power games" that Willett acknowledges. Where they come from and how they operate remain entirely unclear.

Sonia Kruks

Sonia Kruks characterizes her *Retrieving Experience: Subjectivity and Recognition in Feminist Politics* as an effort to retrieve the "rich heritage of existentialist [and phenomenological] thought" from the undeserved obscurity to which French poststructuralism consigned it and to employ this conceptual heritage to grasp "the possibilities and limits of forms of solidarity that are respectful of differences among women."[36] This effort, in my judgment, is a largely successful one. It does not, however, include an adequate account of the origins of the *obstacles* to those forms of feminine solidarity. Such an account, I will argue, would require that existentialist phenomenology give way to—or at least be supplemented by—psychoanalysis.

Kruks effectively debunks the by-now received interpretation of existentialism and phenomenology as an Enlightenment philosophy of the (Cartesian) subject. She shows that the critique by Foucault, Derrida, and Lyotard was based on a caricature of existential phenomenology that either distorted or neglected many of its founding texts. A fair reading of those texts reveals that neither Merleau-Ponty in *The Phenomenology of Perception*, Beauvoir in *The Second Sex*, nor (even) Sartre in *Being and Nothingness* ever embraced a philosophy of a disembodied subject fully present to itself, but that instead all shared "notions of a subject that is above all *situated*: embodied, sentient, ambiguous, unable ever to coincide with itself in Cartesian self-reflexivity [or] to act as a pure constituting consciousness."[37]

Kruks then mobilizes this concept of an "embodied and socially situated self" on behalf of a devastatingly effective (if not entirely original) critique of poststructuralist efforts to dissolve the body/self in discourse. Foucault, Judith Butler, Richard Rorty, and Joan Scott are all taken to task for simultaneously overestimating the determining power of discourse and ignoring or denying the power of prediscursive experience, "those modalities of experience that, in themselves, elude speech—and yet which we come to 'know' through forms of non-intellectual, embodied, cognition." Thus poststructuralists "cannot give sufficiently full accounts of experiences such as humiliation, fear, anger, empathy, or care, out of which acts of resistance are often born." They cannot, in particular, account for the possibility of feminist solidarity.[38]

The last part of *Retrieving Experience* is preoccupied with this possibility. Kruks genders Merleau-Ponty's concept of the "body-subject" in order to explore the "role of embodied experience as an affective basis for solidarity among women." Against those postmodernist feminists who claim that "essentialist" efforts to establish commonalities among women across class, race, and culture necessarily exclude and/or marginalize the differences among them, Kruks suggests that "certain stable biological attributes to the female body—such as the fact that, "*in general* women menstruate, have a vagina, clitoris, womb, [and] are capable of being impregnated"—might serve as the source of "a respectful but concerned *affective* relationship of recognition with others significantly different from oneself."[39] By affectively "respectful recognition" Kruks—borrowing from Sandra Bartky's insightful *Sympathy and Solidarity*,[40]—means a *feeling with* (*Mitgefuhl*) that "involves a doubled awareness: both an immediate affective response to another's pain and a simultaneous awareness that my response is *not* the same as the other's suffering."[41] Thus otherness is preserved even as it is transcended. Unlike Oliver and Willett, then, Kruks both appreciates Hegel's concept of mutual recognition and appropriates it for feminist purposes. What she adds to Hegel is precisely the proposition that "certain 'invariants' to female embodiment" might make it possible for otherwise very different women to "feel with," and thus to recognize, one another despite their differences.[42]

Kruks emphasizes that feminine feeling-with does not necessarily lead to a common *feminist* political response. She is aware, moreover, that feminine feeling-with is itself in no way guaranteed by shared feminine embodiment: " I have not been arguing that the commonalities of feminine embodiment *ensure* a bond of sentience." Indeed, she argues that "it is very easy to refuse the attempt to [feel with]," and she details numerous examples of women who have "condoned or even participated in . . . the physical suffering of other women." Thus she concludes that "a moral choice [to feel with], however tacit, is necessary."[43] Here, I think, is where idealism substitutes for analysis: the absence of sustained reflection on the obstacles to feminine solidarity culminates in the wish that women *should* create it. At one point Kruks does seem to suggest that "differences of race, religion, or other highly charged dimensions of otherness"[44] are the main impediments to feminine solidarity. But this suggestion ignores the possibility that shared embodiment is—or at least has been—as much a hindrance as a help to female solidarity.

This is the possibility pursued by Dorothy Dinnerstein in *The Mermaid and The Minotaur*.[45] As we have seen, Dinnerstein argues that hostility among women is, under "mother-dominated" child rearing, the inevitable consequence of rage against the mother that—given shared female embodiment—first girls and then women both turn against themselves and project onto other women. This argument both leans on and significantly modifies the psychoanalytic assumptions of Melanie Klein. It is to these assumptions, and Dinnerstein's modification of them, that I want briefly to turn in my concluding remarks. These remarks should serve to clarify the way in which a neo-Kleinian psychoanalytic approach can illuminate the obstacles not only to feminine solidarity but also, more generally, to human sociality itself—and thus help us to overcome the "affective idealism" common to all four authors discussed here.

Conclusion

Melanie Klein assumes that (1) the infant's earliest experience of the mother is radically split between a fantasy of a gratifying, all-good mother who becomes the object of its love and a fantasy of a frustrating, all-bad mother who becomes the object of its hate; (2) the child's realization (when he achieves "object permanence") that the bad mother he hates and the good mother he loves are in fact the same person engenders ("depressive") anxiety and guilt for (the fantasy of) having harmed her; (3) depressive anxiety and guilt give rise to urges to repair the mother that facilitate the integration of the child's love and hate for her; (4) these reparative urges are countered by the child's tendency to defend against depressive anxiety and guilt by either idealizing or demonizing—that is, continuing to split—the mother; and finally (5) that the capacity of the child to integrate his love and hate for the mother, and thus to relate realistically to her as a necessarily imperfect, genuinely separate other, depends on the relative strength of reparative as compared to defensive tendencies.[46] Thus the Kleinian message is that the ability of the adult to recognize the other depends on the (always precarious) ability of the child to integrate his love and hate for the mother.

Dinnerstein modifies this message by demonstrating the way in which the very structure of (what might be called) the maternal mode of child rearing militates against the integration of love and hate for the mother, and thus for the women who later come (unconsciously) to represent her. Wherever it is the case that a woman is the sole primary caregiver and a father (or father-figure) is therefore available as a blameless refuge from her power, it will also be the case that women will become the objects of both demonization and idealization. It follows from this diagnosis that a necessary (but not necessarily sufficient) condition for the integration of love and hate for the mother—and thus for women—is the (equal) sharing of primary care for children by at least one woman and one man.[47] Coparenting, as I have consistently argued over the past two decades, is an essential prescription for the elimination of patriarchy.

None of the authors whose works I have reviewed engages this Dinnersteinian argument, or even shows any awareness of it.[48] This is, I believe, a most unfortunate sign of the times. These times, I take it, include political opposition on the part of some feminists to any theoretical position that would *appear* to normalize or even mandate heterosexual parenting arrangements.[49] But political discomfort should not dissuade us from taking Dinnerstein's position seriously. As I demonstrate in Chapter 2, above, *none* of the criticisms addressed to Dinnerstein's argument over the past twenty-five years stands up to critical scrutiny. More than a decade after her death, it is high time to give Dinnerstein her due.

5 Remembering Melanie Klein

Introduction

It is hard to hope after the Holocaust. To remain *realistically* optimistic in the face of this most horrible of twentieth-century horrors demands a firm grasp of the potential for both good and evil in the human condition. It also requires the realization that the growth of goodness depends decisively on our willingness to face up to, and attempt to repair, the damage done in the name of our more malevolent motives. This increasingly widespread, welcome realization helps to explain the recent and remarkable renaissance of interest in the thought of Melanie Klein. Klein described more vividly than any psychoanalytic thinker before her (and perhaps after her as well) the infantile sources of love and hate, as well as the way in which the conflict between these most primitive passions continues to reverberate throughout our lives. She was also the first to insist that the always fragile triumph of love over hate requires that we recognize, and make reparations for, the harm done by our hate to the mother, and then to the others, whom we love. Thus it is not surprising that she has become one of the most important teachers of realistic optimists at the dawn of the twenty-first century.

Klein on Individual Development

Melanie Klein's great teacher was Sigmund Freud. Analyzed as a young woman by two original members of Freud's inner circle—first by Sándor

Ferenczi in Budapest and then by Karl Abraham in Berlin—she arrived in London in 1926 at the invitation of Ernest Jones, himself a faithful follower, and subsequently the official biographer, of Freud. Almost immediately she established herself as a leading figure within the British Psychoanalytical Society and—her Freudian patrimony notwithstanding— soon came to challenge the master's account of the childhood origins of the adult personality.[1] Freud had located the oedipal triangle as the crucible in which the self is shaped: the child—or at least the male child, who serves as the model child in what was later challenged as Freud's phallocentric account—loves the mother whom he wants to monopolize, hates the father for enforcing the prohibition on incest, and eventually resolves this oedipal conflict by internalizing the paternal prohibition in the form of a harsh superego. Thus for Freud it is the father who represents civilization against the erotic impulses of the child—what he called the "reality principle" against the "pleasure principle"—and it is the identification with the father on which the reproduction of civilization depends.

For Klein, in contrast, it is the *mother* who enforces both the pleasure principle *and* the reality principle. Even a mother who is deeply dedicated to satisfying the imperious oral and other needs of her infant necessarily frustrates those needs as well. Thus it is she who becomes (long before the father typically enters the scene) the target of both the infant's love and its rage. (Klein assumes that maternal gratification and frustration only reinforce innate libidinal and aggressive impulses, or what the later Freud called the life and death drives, but most contemporary analysts influenced by Klein have jettisoned this assumption.) In its earliest months the infant is, of course, unaware that the source of its dramatically different sensations of pleasure and pain is one and the same person. Lacking what cognitive developmental psychologists call "object permanence," the infant, Klein inferred from her pioneering analysis of young children, imagines both a "good breast" and a "bad breast" as separate sources of the antithetical experiences of blissful maternal presence and terrifying maternal absence. She also argues that the infant reacts to its otherwise self-destructive rage by projecting it onto the bad breast, against whose imagined aggression the infant protects itself with further imaginary attacks. Thus Klein calls this initial infantile emotional position the "paranoid-schizoid" position: schizoid because the infant's experience of reality is radically split between an all-good and an all-bad "object," paranoid because its rage against the latter is felt as coming from the outside rather than from within the infant itself.

When the infant acquires object permanence (Klein locates this as early as the third month of life but we now know that it typically doesn't emerge until the last third or even quarter of the first year), it enters into what she calls the "depressive position," the successful negotiation of which becomes for Klein and those who follow her the chief task on which the emotional development of the child depends. The realization that the mother of gratification and the mother of frustration—the target of both its worshipful love and its murderous rage—are in fact the same person engenders the terrifying anxiety of having destroyed the very mother to whom it is so ardently attached and on whom all its feelings of goodness and security depend. Great guilt also necessarily accompanies the child's awareness of its matricidal motives. "Depressive" anxiety and guilt, Klein argues, will induce the child to attempt (first in fantasy and then in reality) to repair the damage to the mother, whose positive responses to these reparative efforts will serve to reassure the child that the mother has, after all, survived his or her aggression, thus inaugurating a benign cycle of love given in return for love. Thus if all goes well depressive anxiety and guilt are self-limiting, and culminate in the child's recognition that the mother—as well as the self, which Klein assumes is the product of "introjections" of aspects of the mother—is neither all-good nor all-bad but nonetheless worthy of care.

But all may not, in fact, go well. The child may be tempted to defend against depressive anxiety and guilt in ways that permanently postpone the task of integrating its love and hate. Chief among these defenses are "idealization" on the one hand and what Klein calls "manic denial" on the other. Idealization wards off depressive anxiety and guilt through the fantasy of a mother who is too perfect ever to be the object of rage; typically the rage is split off and directed either against the self and/or others. The child who resorts to manic denial, as the name implies, defends against depressive anxiety and guilt by denying any dependence on, or love for, the mother and omnipotently transforming her into an object of contempt and control. Children who succumb to either of these defenses (as well as a number of others) will be plagued as adults by unstable, unrealistic object relations, alternately idealizing or demonizing the others they encounter and unable to develop or maintain mature relationships with them. Klein assumes that most children will eventually overcome defensive temptations and thus avoid this fate. But subsequent sources of stress—such as the loss of a parent, or other loved ones—will reawaken defensive temptations and threaten the integration of love and hate. Depressive integration is thus a deeply difficult, lifelong accomplishment.

From the Individual to the Group

In the four decades since Klein's death Kleinians have applied her account of the dynamics of individual development to the dynamics of groups, or even entire societies. Freud and Freudians assume that groups are bound by attachments to leaders that are rooted in feelings for the father.[2] Kleinian social theorists, in contrast, have explored the way in which the relationship between the individual and the group reproduces the relationship between the child and its mother.[3] They have argued that individuals unconsciously experience groups as simultaneously gratifying and frustrating mothers that inevitably evoke their gratitude and their rage. Thus the group that is loved is also necessarily the group that is hated. The development of the group demands that its members learn to respond reparatively to the anxiety and the guilt aroused by this ambivalence, that is, that they come to understand that their group is neither all-good nor all-bad but nonetheless worthy of care. But this happy outcome is always threatened by the temptation of individual members to defend against the group equivalent of depressive anxiety and guilt, either by denying their dependence on the group (the group analogue of manic denial) or by denying their rage against it (the group analogue of idealization). Manic denial leads to dropping out of the group but also entails an obsessive preoccupation with, and denigration of, the very group from which one has dropped out. Idealization creates a demonized out-group that unwittingly becomes a target for all the rage that cannot be expressed within the in-group. Thus the Kleinian message is at once hopeful and ominous. It reassures us that harmonious relations among groups *are* possible if group members cultivate their capacity to acknowledge and work through, rather than defend against, the ambivalence and guilt that inevitably accompany membership in their group. But it also warns us that the failure to cultivate this capacity can culminate in murderous relations between groups.

Sympathetic critics of Klein's account of individual development claim that her preoccupation with infantile *fantasy* greatly underestimates the impact of maternal *reality* on the child's capacity for depressive integration. Thus for example the English pediatrician and psychoanalyst D. W. Winnicott argued that what he called "good-enough" mothering—which includes "holding" the child in order to facilitate trust in its environment, "mirroring" the child's autonomous efforts in order to foster an initially grandiose sense of agency, and "optimally frustrating" the child in order eventually to reduce that sense of agency to more realistic dimensions—is a prerequisite for the child's ability to integrate his or her love and hate for the mother.[4] Feminist followers of Klein, including especially Dorothy Dinnerstein, have (as we have already seen) insisted that even good-enough mothering is not good enough. As long as the father is not equally involved in early child care, he (or a male substitute for him) will always be available as a blameless refuge from maternal power and thus as the object of a defensive identification that enables both boys and girls to evade the task of depressive integration, that is, to continue to harbor split-off hatred of the mother. Dinnerstein argues that all those who come to represent the mother, namely women in general, cannot but inherit this hatred. It follows from Dinnerstein's argument that misogyny—a fear and loathing of women that is shared by men and women alike—will persist until children of both sexes are more or less equally dependent on, and identified with, their mothers *and* their fathers. Combining Winnicott's and Dinnerstein's arguments, we can say that "good-enough coparenting" is at once the necessary condition for healthy emotional development and for the passing of patriarchal passions.

These arguments have implications for the Kleinian account of group development as well. The capacity of group members to integrate their love and hate for their group, it would seem, depends on the level of individual emotional development they have achieved; individuals who can tolerate or even embrace ambivalence in their intimate relationships are unlikely to idealize an in-group and demonize an out-group. It follows that the development of healthy groups is as dependent on good-enough forms of coparenting as is the development of healthy individuals. But if healthy individuals are necessary, they are not sufficient for healthy groups. Depressively integrated individuals will be reluctant to devote their emotional energies to groups if the groups themselves are not structured in ways that facilitate "owning" and working through the intense ambivalence that inevitably accompanies life in groups. Thus Klein has taught us something new and important about the emotional demands of democracy.

The Kleinian Legacy

Few twentieth-century thinkers have encouraged us to think as deeply about the human condition as Melanie Klein. Against the currently fashionable postmodernist claim that what appears to be *the* human condition at any given time is merely an historically specific, culturally contingent "social construction," Klein reminds us that there *are* universal problems—the relationships between love and hate, women and men, and individual and group—with which human beings will inevitably be confronted. But against those who would counsel resignation in the face of the enormity of those problems, she also insists that there are better and worse ways to deal with them, and gives us reason to hope that better ways *can* be found. For all these reasons she deserves a prominent and permanent place in the pantheon of twentieth-century thinkers.

Part II

Mourning and Modernity

6 Working through Benjamin: Walter Benjamin and the Work of (Counter) Cultural Mourning

Introduction

At unspeakable cost we have finally learned that the modernist murder of the past only feeds the fundamentalist fantasy of resurrecting it. To arrest this deadly dialectic—to counter the modern assault on memory without mobilizing the noxious weapons of nostalgia—is surely one of the central political tasks of our time. We are indebted to Walter Benjamin for embracing this task long before less prescient mortals were even aware of its necessity. As we shall see, Benjamin offers "anamnestic solidarity" with our "enslaved ancestors" as an antidote to a modernity that is hell-bent on either obliterating or idealizing the past.[1] The trick of the historian—and ultimately we are all historians—is to conjure up images that capture, or create, a "coincidence of past and present" struggles against oppression that redounds to the advantage of each. These "dialectical images" serve simultaneously to rescue the past from a "conformism that is [always] about to overpower it" and to enable the present to "blast" itself out of the catastrophic continuum called "progress."[2]

Benjamin's message, then, is that we can only redeem ourselves by redeeming the claims of the past. He was well aware that these claims "cannot be settled cheaply" and that they call for "courage, humor, cunning, and fortitude."[3] But settling these claims, I will argue, is even more difficult than Benjamin imagined. He barely recognized that making good on the damage done to past generations demands that the present generation confront the *guilt* aroused by the fact—or even the wish—of having escaped that damage.[4] Moreover, his appeal to an identification with past struggles against oppression that would reawaken current struggles against it entirely ignores the stake that the oppressed have in their own oppression. The failure to remember, and to work through this identification with oppression, we now know, is a certain recipe for its repetition.[5] In short, the ghost of domination haunts the Benjaminian project of overcoming it. Working through Benjamin will be my effort to exorcise that ghost.

Hope in the Past

"The devotion to happiness which has been denied is won only through a regretful sorrow."[6] Adorno penned these words in praise of Walter Benjamin's effort to transform this Proustian insight into a political project. Of course Benjamin's historical situation was very different from ours. His task was to revive a moribund working-class movement by awakening its identification with the heroic struggles of its proletarian predecessors. In the face of fascism he could only dream of a revolution that would redeem those failed struggles. Less than thirty years after his self-inflicted death, the members of the generation of 1968 took this dream for reality, convinced that our movement of personal and political transformation was as irreversible as it was profound. Unlike Benjamin's workers, then, we who (we thought) made this (nonproletarian) revolution and have since seen it succumb to what Herbert Marcuse, as early as 1972, correctly identified as a "counter-revolution,"[7] must redeem a loss that we ourselves have suffered. But we too are faced with the task of finding "hope in the past"[8] in order to reanimate a petrified present. Thus our project can learn both from the merits and the limits of the way in which Benjamin conceived his.

To grasp what Benjamin wants to rescue from the past we need to understand his account of what has been lost to the present. This account can be captured with the claim that modernity murders the twin capacities of *mimesis* and *anamnesis* and thus the rich relationship with reality that depends on them. Benjamin defines the "mimetic faculty" as the "capacity for producing similarities" and the "gift of seeing resemblances"[9] between humans and their world. The "capacity for producing" *and* the "gift of seeing": similarities or resemblances are neither wholly *created* nor wholly *found*. Rather, these "natural correspondences assume their decisive importance only in the light of the consideration that they stimulate and awaken the mimetic faculty that responds to them in human beings."[10] Benjamin locates the source of this capacity to *imagine what exists* in childhood play: "children's games are everywhere interlaced with mimetic modes of behavior, and their range is not limited at all to what one human being imitates from another. A child not only plays at being a grocer or a teacher, but also at being a windmill or a train."[11] Thus from the very beginning our relationship to reality is constituted by the capacity to *see one thing as another*, or what might be called a primordial metaphorical faculty.

Ontogeny recapitulates phylogeny (or so Benjamin claims). In ancient times this fanciful faculty was the capacity of the entire culture. It enabled an enchanted kinship between humans and their world, an "ecstatic contact with the cosmos ... scarcely known to later periods."[12] Scarcely known to later periods because the "advance" of civilization entails "the increasing decay of the mimetic faculty."[13] This decay culminates in the thoroughly "disenchanted" world of modernity in which a separate "subject" either constitutes or is confronted by an alien "object." This subject–object relationship precludes the imaginative awareness of "similarities" and secures what Benjamin, in his early critique of Kant, calls "an experience ... of the world ... of the lowest order."[14] This impoverished experience of the world as an alien object, moreover, cannot but engender the drive of the subject to overcome it: (capitalist) technology transforms the "wooing of the cosmos" into the "lust for profit" and in the process "turn[s] the bridal bed into a bloodbath."[15] This bloodbath will persist as long as mankind fails to understand that not the "mastery of nature" by man, but rather the "mastery of the relationship between nature and man ... is the purpose of technology."[16] If the "relationship between man and nature" is or ought to be mimetic, then the technology that masters this relationship would have to embody the very "mimetic faculty" that modernity maims.

Modernity is as hostile to memory as it is to metaphor. More precisely, modernity carries out an "unprecedented disassociation" between what Benjamin, following Proust, calls "voluntary" and "involuntary memory."[17] By voluntary memory Benjamin means memory "that is in the service of the intellect" and that therefore produces "information about the past [that] retains no trace of it."[18] *Mémoire involuntaire*, in contrast, presupposes a state of "mental relaxation" and "self-forgetfulness"[19] that opens us to the power of a present object "instantly" to recall an object in our past to which it "corresponds." As such, it can be considered the temporal counterpart of the "mimetic faculty": the work of involuntary memory reveals a world of "similarities" or "resemblances" between the present and the past through which the past is effectively brought back to life. Thus it is that Benjamin is able to describe *mémoire involuntaire* as a "rejuvenating force which is a match for the inexorable process of aging."[20] Anamnesis is as integral to *life* as mimesis.

Voluntary and involuntary memory are, in principle, by no means mutually exclusive. In fact Benjamin argues that the "rituals . . . ceremonies [and] festivals" of traditional societies "kept producing the amalgamation of these two elements of memory over and over again. They triggered recollection at certain times and remained handles of memory for a lifetime." This traditional amalgamation of voluntary and involuntary memory is precisely the condition for an authentic experience of reality: "where there is experience [*Erfahrung*] in the strict sense of the word, certain contents of the individual's past combine with material of the collective past."[21] *Erfahrung* enables the individual to place a contemporary event within a coherent personal narrative and to locate this personal narrative within the narrative of the collectivity to which he or she belongs. Memory (in the twofold sense) is thus the thread with which the authentically experienced individual weaves the present into the fabric of what has gone before and what is yet to come.[22]

But modernity cuts this thread and rends this fabric in pieces. As storytelling gives way to print and broadcast media the patient passing-on of experience from generation to generation and from "mouth to mouth" is supplanted by the dissemination of unassimilated information intended for private and instant consumption.[23] The sequestration of death—the fact that "in the course of modern times dying has been pushed further and further out of the perceptual world of the living"—likewise weakens the links in the "chain of tradition" by inhibiting our ability to remember the dead.[24] Involuntary memory is also undermined by the frequent "shocks" of modern urban life against which an ever more vigilant consciousness must defend by reducing the "forgetful" receptivity to impressions on which our openness to historical correspondences depends.[25] And memory is further eroded by commodities whose form forces us to forget their origins and whose function is to become obsolete as soon as they are no longer "new."[26]

For all these interrelated reasons Benjamin argues that modern experience is less and less a matter of *Erfahrung* and more and more a matter of *Erlebnis*. *Erlebnis* is Benjamin's word for discrete, immediate events that are merely lived through rather than experienced as integral elements of a coherent personal and collective past.[27] Put otherwise, *Erlebnis* describes the "atrophy of experience"[28] that inevitably accompanies the decline of involuntary memory in modernity. Unmediated by the work of involuntary memory, each fragmentary experience ultimately becomes like every other. Thus for Benjamin modernity "designates a temporal structure of experience [characterized by] the repetitive succession of identical instants"[29] or what he calls, in the "Theses on the Philosophy of History," "homogeneous, empty time."[30] What goes by the name of "progress" is, in fact, "the time of hell," the "new as ever-always-the-same."[31] To "blast open" this hellish "continuum of history" is precisely the task of our time.[32]

An explosion cannot be a restoration. The "historical materialist" knows that "cultural treasures" are merely the "spoils" of the age-old war waged by the oppressors against the oppressed: "[these treasures] owe their existence not only to the efforts of the great minds and talents who have created them, but also to the anonymous toil of their contemporaries. There is no document of civilization which is not at the same time a document of barbarism."[33] Thus we cannot draw on the "tainted" resources of the official past in order to rescue the present from *Erlebnis*. Recapturing *Erfahrung* requires instead that we "wrest tradition away from a conformism that is [always] about to overpower it"[34]— that is, it demands that we uncover the *emancipatory traditions of the oppressed* that have been buried by a history that until now has always been written by the oppressors.

Thus an "anamnestic solidarity" with the liberation struggles of the past is Benjamin's antidote to the modern domination he decries.[35] This solidarity requires, in the first instance, that we acknowledge the claim that the oppressed past has on our "weak messianic power," that is, on our power to give *new life* to the defeated struggles of those who "expected . . . our coming," by embracing these struggles as our own.[36] Only by redeeming the claims of the past can we redeem ourselves; only by giving the past a future do we give ourselves a present. The historian does this when "he grasps the constellation which his own era has formed with a definite earlier one."[37] In these constellations, or "dialectical images," the "Then and the Now come together . . . like a flash of lightning"[38] that jolts the present out of the continuum of empty homogenous time. *Erfahrung* is (fleetingly) recaptured in the form of an intense communion with an "oppressed past"—an enchanted experience that Benjamin calls *Jetztzeit*, or the "time of the now," that anticipates the future end to all oppression.[39]

Working through Benjamin

Let me sum up what I take to be Benjamin's many and important contributions to our contemporary project of reviving our radicalism. First, his relentless theoretical critique of the inauthenticity of modern experience anticipates the practical struggles of the Sixties to reanimate experience, and thus stands as a living reminder of the enduring significance of those struggles. Benjamin helps us remember that the Sixties are well worth remembering. Second, he reminds us of our *obligation* to remember them. He takes seriously the claims of the past on the present and insists that these claims must be redeemed through the cultivation of the capacity for collective remembrance.[40] Thus his message is that we owe it both to ourselves and to others to honor our utopian dreams by recalling our youthful efforts to take them for reality. Third, Benjamin understands that we have no time to waste: "every image of the past that is not recognized by the present as its own concerns threatens to disappear irretrievably."[41] To defer our memorial work to the future is to risk losing forever an image from our countercultural past that we might otherwise have been able to reclaim for the present. Fourth, Benjamin appreciates not only the great urgency but also the great *difficulty* of this labor of remembrance; he stands in solidarity with those of us who know just how difficult is the daily struggle to rescue the tradition of the Sixties from the various official versions that always threaten to overpower it. Fifth, and finally, he gives us reason to hope that the results will be worth the struggle, that our efforts to awaken the "then" of the Sixties will help give new life to the "now" of the new century. For all these reasons, Benjamin is our indispensable ally.

But from our present standpoint it is nonetheless necessary to locate four limits to his contribution to that struggle.

1) His own account of modernity suggests that its soil is far too depleted for the cultivation of the capacity for collective remembrance to which he is committed. If modernity murders both mimesis and anamnesis then there is in fact no modern ground in which remembrance can grow. Thus Benjamin is obliged to look elsewhere for its source. At one time he pointed to a "classless," prehistorical "collective unconscious" as the timeless template of the dialectical image.[42] For this Jungian lapse he was taken to task by Adorno, who justly accused him of ahistorical mythology.[43] At other times Benjamin looked not to the childhood of the species, but rather to the childhood of the individual for the origin of the dialectical image. As we have seen, he finds in the spontaneous fantasy of the child, who

"plays not only sales clerk or teacher but windmill and railway as well," evidence of the cognitive capacity to "perceive and enact" the nonsensuous similarities recalled by the dialectical image.[44] Thus "the child can do what the adult cannot . . . he [sic] can recognize the new."[45] And children are therefore considered by Benjamin to be "representatives of paradise."[46] But this ontogenetic account is no more convincing than the phylogenetic one he eventually abandoned. In fact Benjamin argues that this playful capacity to imagine reality is precisely what modern—for Benjamin, bourgeois—education tends to discipline out of existence.[47] There is nothing in Benjamin's account of modernity that would suggest why it should ever be otherwise.

Yet less than three decades after Benjamin's death the West witnessed a massive rebirth of both the *mimesis* and the *anamnesis* over whose absence he despaired. The world was reenchanted as all manner of magical "correspondences" between all manner of things were everywhere at once created and found. An entire generation "turned on" in search of the "profane illuminations" to which, Benjamin pronounced prophetically in his essay on surrealism, "hashish, opium or whatever else can serve as an introductory lesson."[48] With or without the aid of drugs, millions of young people intuitively "grasped the constellation that [their own era] formed" with the preindustrial and even the primitive past. For the members of this modern tribe *Jetztzeit*—the time of "the now"—became more real than the empty, homogeneous time of modernity, which they rejected when they decided they would no longer wear their watches. That this time— "the time of hell"—has long since reasserted itself with a vengeance in no way negates our experience of a fundamentally different kind.

Because we have had this experience our task of remembrance is, at least in one sense, easier than Benjamin's. He wanted the oppressed to find hope in a past which was not of their own making, to identify with failed struggles against suffering of which they themselves had no direct experience. In short, it was not *their own losses* that they were invited—or incited—to mourn. It is, in contrast, precisely our present task to mourn the losses of the Sixties that we ourselves have suffered. Because we suffered them we have memories of them—*loving* memories of them—that we can uncover without the aid of the dialectical images of the materialist historian. We need to rely on, and learn more about, our own resources of remembrance.

2) Benjamin's insistence on separating a "pure" tradition of the oppressed from the tainted "official past" that enshrines the traditions of the oppressor purges any feelings of *ambivalence* from the political mourning

process. The surgical operation of the dialectical image severs the movement of liberation from the domination against which it struggles and thus
precludes the awareness of the possibility that the former is "infected" by
its contact with the latter. But not even Benjamin's magic can conjure away
the elements of domination that inevitably surface within the very movements that are committed to its elimination. And the reproduction of
domination within the lost movement is an irreducible source of *anger*
against it, for whose expression any adequately *critical* political mourning process must make room. Even those of us who were most seduced by
the Sixties suffered many Movement excesses that justifiably gave rise to
our rage. The Movement that we loved was also the Movement that we
hated. Mourning the Movement will require that we wrestle with this
intense ambivalence.

3) It will also demand that we deal with the *guilt* inevitably aroused by
this ambivalence. It is already possible to argue that Benjamin ignored
the way in which the task of maintaining "anamnestic solidarity" would
inevitably be complicated by the (survivor) guilt resulting from the inability of the currently oppressed ever *really* to undo the damage done to
their oppressed ancestors.[49] Is there not likely to be far more guilt over
failed struggles for which we ourselves bear no small measure of responsibility? When we have helped to kill our own dreams is it not that much
harder to keep them alive? Thus the task of mourning the Movement must
include a confrontation with, and an overcoming of, the measures by which
we defend against our guilt for having contributed to its demise. Since
this was not Benjamin's problem he did not and could not contribute to
its solution.

4) Finally, the only possible outcome of a political mourning process
that has been emptied of any ambivalence (hence too of any guilt arising
from it) is a simultaneously unstable and idealized identification with what
has been lost. In fact with Benjamin it is misleading to speak of a mourning *process* at all. The identification established between the currently
oppressed and their enslaved ancestors is the result not of the slow, patient, and persistent labor of sorting out the loved and hated aspects of
their political traditions, but rather of the instantaneous "lightning flash"
of the dialectical image. But any identification that bypasses the painful
work of mourning is fated to be fleeting; as the dialectical image "flashes
by, never to be seen again"[50] the animating identification that it sparks is
likewise lost. "The rescue that is . . . effected, can only take place for that
which, in the next moment, is already irretrievably lost."[51] Hope (in the
past) is not kept alive. Thus it would seem that the fate of the current

struggles can be no different from the failed struggles of the past that they are supposed to redeem. The "repetitive succession of identical instants" of the "homogeneous, empty time" of modernity is mirrored by the repetitive failure of the enchanted efforts to transcend it.

Perhaps this is because Benjamin's oppressed are never really in a position to learn from the mistakes of their predecessors. To learn from those mistakes they would have to be acknowledged. But they are never acknowledged because the identification that the oppressed establish with their predecessors is not the result of, but rather precludes, a critical evaluation of their practices. Benjamin's "anamnestic solidarity," we might say, is purchased at the price of the idealization of his "enslaved ancestors." His idealization of the oppressed, moreover, goes hand-in-hand with his demonization of the oppressor: the oppressed are supposed to remember the sufferings of their "enslaved ancestors" so they will not "forget [their] hatred"[52] for their current oppressors. That an identification with past suffering culminates in hate rather than love is surely a sign of what Gillian Rose calls Benjamin's "aberrated mourning."[53]

Because's Benjamin's account of political mourning excludes the possibility of a lasting, selective, and loving identification with lost liberation struggles, I believe that we must look elsewhere for a concept of identification that can inform our project of saving the Sixties.

I hope that my critique of Benjamin has clarified the criteria that would have to be satisfied by a more adequate theory of political mourning. This theory would have to (1) locate the incentive for mourning in the strength of our love for what we have lost; (2) make room for our hatred as well as our love for the lost "object"; (3) identify the mechanisms for defending against the guilt aroused by this ambivalence and thus clarify the emotional obstacles to successful mourning; and (4) specify the kind of identification with the lost object in which successful mourning culminates. I will argue in the next chapter that a theory of political mourning derived from the psychoanalytic theory of mourning of Melanie Klein can satisfy these criteria.

7 Mourning the Movement

Introduction

We are all still haunted by the ghost of the Sixties. For thirty long years we have not ceased either to lament or celebrate the death of this singular decade. The remarkable longevity of this death of the Sixties story unwittingly testifies to the survival of its subject. For many of us who cut our political teeth on the civil rights, antiwar and student movements, the Sixties live on as a longing for a golden age that has been lost to a permanently pallid present. But nostalgia for the Sixties is only the most obvious sign of their ghostly presence. Other progressives are still so spooked by them that they cannot refrain from periodically presiding over their burial.[1] The intensity of these efforts to exorcise the Sixties, I would suggest, only serves to confirm the survival of their spirit.

I argue in this chapter that this recurrent pattern of nostalgia for and denigration of the Sixties on the Left is both a sign of and a defense against a profound political-cultural loss from which we have yet to recover. Both the longing for (an idealized version of) what has been lost and the (seemingly) sober message that nothing valuable was ever really lost ward off the sorrow—and the guilt—that would inevitably accompany a fully embodied awareness of the magnitude of our loss. Both serve, in other words, to defend against the deeply difficult but absolutely indispensable task of mourning (what we used to call) the Movement. This task is indispensable, I maintain, because the consequence of evading it is precisely the profound political pessimism from which we presently suffer. We have lived through a transition from a time when—as so many have remarked—everything seemed possible to a time that seems bereft of any political possibilities at all. I would not want to underestimate the current political-economic reasons for this loss of our radical political imagination. But I also want to insist that our inability to mourn a Movement in which the imagination was actually—if only briefly—in power is at least as responsible as those objective factors for the current impotence of our imagination.

My argument, in short, is that the atrophy of our imagination is a symptom of our *political depression.*[2] Political depression is every bit as much the result of unmourned intersubjective losses as individual depression is the result of unmourned personal losses. In either case hope is crushed under the accumulated weight of unexpressed grief. Thus the renewal of political hope—the resuscitation of our currently moribund political imagination—requires that we summon up the strength for our simultaneously emotional and political task of giving in to our grief.

In the next section of this chapter I call on the psychoanalytic theory of Melanie Klein to help us appreciate both the necessity and the difficulty of mourning *individual* losses. The third and final section summarizes the effort of Kleinians and others influenced by her work to extend her model of mourning to political-cultural or intersubjectively shared losses, and concludes with an application of this model of *group mourning* to the specific problem of mourning the Movement.

Melanie Klein and the Psychoanalysis of Individual Mourning

It was in fact not Klein but Freud who first supplied the warrant for a psychoanalytic theory of political mourning. "Mourning," he announces in "Mourning and Melancholia," "is regularly the reaction to the loss of a loved person, *or to the loss of some abstraction which has taken the place of one,* such as one's country, an ideal, and so on."[3] An "abstraction . . . takes the place" of "a loved person" in the sense that the libido originally "invested" in this person is displaced onto that abstraction. Because our ideals serve as substitutes for the people we love, the loss of the former can give rise to reactions of grief that are comparable to the feelings that follow the loss of the latter. Thus the implicit message of Freud's famous definition is that the mourning of cultural or political losses may be as necessary to our emotional well-being as the mourning of the individual losses on which the rest of his essay is explicitly and exclusively focused.

But Freud's model of individual mourning does not satisfy, and in fact is inconsistent with what I take to be the criteria for an adequate theory of political mourning. His concept of the "loved person" as the "cathected object" of the libido of the bereaved prevents him from grasping both the depth and the tenacity of the ties between ourselves and those whom we have lost. Since successful mourning is defined by Freud as a "detachment of libido" from what has been lost, anything that interferes with eventual "de-cathexis" is considered to be a sign of melancholia rather than of normal mourning. His text works (although not without some internal inconsistency) to confine ambivalence toward, guilt over, and identification with the lost object to the category of the pathological.[4] Thus it cannot serve as the foundation for the theory of political mourning that it authorizes.

But Klein's text can. All the features of mourning that are marginalized in Freud's "Mourning and Melancholia" become central to Melanie Klein's concept of mourning, as set out in her "Mourning and Its Relation to Manic-Depressive States."[5] Unlike Freud, Klein plumbs the emotional depths of the relationship between the mourner and the love (s)he has lost. Freud was aware, of course, that every person repeats his relationship with his parents in the course of his ostensibly adult relationships. But it was left to Klein to grasp the meaning of this repetition for mourning. Beneath the loss of the adult other, she argues, there always lurks the threatened loss of the (internal) mother: "the poignancy of the actual loss of a loved person is . . . greatly increased by the mourner's unconscious phantasies of having lost his *internal* 'good' objects as well."[6] This is why, according to Klein, mourning is typically both so painful and prolonged: "early mourning is revived whenever grief is experienced in later life."[7]

By "early mourning," Klein means the "anxieties, guilt, and feelings of loss and grief derived from the depressive position"[8]—that is, the turbulent emotional atmosphere surrounding the very young child's separation from the mother. She argues that the adult mourner will choke in this atmosphere if the child never learned how to breathe in it. Learning to breathe in the depressive position, moreover, is no easy matter for the young child. Because the mother is the source of both the satisfaction and the frustration of the imperious needs of the infant, Klein argues—as we have already seen—that the infant necessarily phantasies both a "good mother" (actually she says "breast") who is the source of all its pleasure and a "bad mother" who is the source of all its pain. The "good mother" thus becomes the object of the infant's love and the "bad mother" becomes the target for its rage. Successfully negotiating the depressive position requires that the infant "work through" and eventually overcome this split between its love for the all-good mother and its hate for the all-bad mother. But this integration of the good and bad mother is invariably threatened by the profound anxiety and guilt that accompanies the child's dawning awareness that he or she has destroyed—in fantasy, but for the very young child there is of course no difference between fantasy and reality—the very mother whom the child loves and on whom he or she so deeply depends. The anxiety and guilt will ordinarily awaken the child's impulse to make reparations to the mother, which—if made and accepted—will eventually enable him to discover that she has survived his rage. Thus, if all goes well, depressive anxiety and guilt are self-limiting, and do not prevent depressive integration'. But all may not go well, because the child is always vulnerable to the temptation to defend against his anxiety and guilt, either by denying that he depends on his mother ("manic denial") or by denying that he hates her ("idealization"). These defenses interrupt the integration of love and hate on which the emotional development of the child depends.

Winnicott adds that defensive temptations will be irresistible if the actual mother is not "good enough," that is, if the mother does not encourage her child's reparative impulses and thus enable him to alleviate his own anxiety and guilt. A mother who is generally able both to encourage her child's flights from the nest and to welcome him back to the nest when he falters will engender more love, and less hate, than a mother who normally either suppresses his separation or prematurely pushes him away. And the more favorable the ratio of love to hate, the stronger the reparative inclinations of the child are likely to be. But even the most supportive mother will—indeed should—frustrate the demands of her child, and will therefore become the object of his rage. The way in which she responds to her child's rage, in turn, also affects the intensity of his depressive anxiety and guilt. An actual mother who calmly withstands her child's rage is far more likely to foster an internal representation of a caring mother who has survived his destructiveness than a mother who either retaliates or falls to pieces in the face of that rage. The reality of good-enough mothering is thus the most important single contribution to the creation of an internal representation of a good-enough mother on which the successful negotiation of the depressive position depends.[9]

According to Klein, the successful negotiation of the depressive position is, in turn, the key to successful mourning as an adult: "If in an individual the depressive position has been achieved and fully established, then the reaction to loss is grief, or sadness. Where there is some degree of

failure at the depressive position the result of loss is depression."[10] Since
the separation from the loved one reproduces the separation from the
mother, the bereaved cannot but hate the "object" for having "abandoned"
him and cannot but feel guilty for hating the object he also loves. This
guilt is only compounded by the phantasy that the hatred that (s)he sometimes felt for the loved one while (s)he was alive was somehow responsible for his or her death.[11] If the bereaved adult never learned as a child
how to respond reparatively to depressive guilt—if she has no confidence
that love can triumph over hate—then she will succumb to the temptation
to defend against it, either by denying her love or by denying her hate.
The former entails a (manic) "denial of the meaningfulness of the loss"
and the latter entails a "persistent [idealized] attachment to the lost
object."[12] Either form of denial will transform mourning into melancholia.
Conversely, this pathological outcome can only be avoided if the mourner
has the emotional wherewithal simultaneously to acknowledge both his
hatred and his love for the lost object. Making room for his rage will engage the reparative impulses of the "depressively integrated" mourner and
will eventually enable him to experience "in full force . . . the pining for
the lost object."[13] This intensely painful pining, in turn, is essential for
the completion of the mourning process: "[When] grief is experienced to
the full and despair is at its height, the love for the object wells up and the
mourner feels more strongly that life . . . will go on after all, *and that the
lost love object can be preserved* within."[14]

Thus for Klein the successful work of mourning culminates in a certain
kind of *identification* with the lost object. We can infer from her insistence
on the mourner's need to recognize and work through his ambivalence
toward the lost object that this identification must be *selective* in the sense
that only positive attributes of the object are taken in by, and become part
of the self, while others are left behind. What is implicit in Klein is made
explicit by subsequent theorists of mourning who have been influenced
by her account, including Volkan:

> A successful resolution of the grief process depends on a . . . healing iden-
> tification with valued aspects of the deceased person. The uncomplicated
> mourner is able to discriminate realistically among the traits of the de-
> ceased and identify those he values positively. . . . In contrast the depressed
> mourner experiences a *disruptive* identification with ambivalently related
> representations of the deceased that eventuates in a continuing internal
> struggle—a struggle between cherishing the self and wanting to do away
> with it.[15]

and Smith:

> Identifications for purposes of growth are not imperative, emergency, "in toto" internalizations. The various aspects of the objects can be experienced and specific ones can be relinquished or coordinated as enduring aspects of the self. The difference is between relatively enforced and relatively optional identifications. The latter tend to be with the loved and admired traits of the object.[16]

Klein claims that the selective identification of the bereaved with his lost object often results in his enhanced "productive activity":

> At this stage in mourning, suffering can become productive. [It can] stimulate sublimations, or even bring out quite new gifts in some people, who may take to painting, writing, or other productive activities. . . . Others become more productive in a different way—more capable of appreciating people and things, more tolerant in their relations with others—they become wiser.[17]

Thus we can say that for Klein (successful) mourning is a process in which *grief transforms loss into growth*. But she also insists that this must happen twice if it is to happen even once. As we have seen, the loss of the adult other necessarily threatens the loss of the (adult) child's (internal) mother. Any current loss will confront even the most securely "depressively integrated" adult with the task of "reinstating . . . his loved *internal* objects [which] are felt to have gone under."[18] According to Klein, "the successful work of mourning" requires the "rebuilding of this inner world."[19] Thus the selective identification of the bereaved with his currently lost other, on which his development depends, is contingent on the reconstruction of his identification with his long-lost mother. Klein's ultimate message, then, is that grief can only transform current loss into growth by "*recovering* what . . . has already [been] attained in childhood."[20] Only by rescuing his past does the mourner give himself a future.

Conclusion: Mourning the Movement Mother

If we assume, with Freud, that *ideals take the place of the loved one*, and with Klein, that *the loved one is ultimately the mother*, then it follows that the account of individual mourning I have outlined can also serve as the skeleton for my account of mourning the Movement. In order to flesh out this account, however, I need to say something more specific about the way in which countercultural "ideals [took] the place of the loved one," that is, about the precise sense in which *the Movement was a mother* to its youthful members.

As we saw in Chapter 5, contemporary Kleinians have extended Klein's analysis of the relationship between the child and his mother to the relationship between the individual and his group.[21] To reiterate: the assumption is that groups are unconsciously experienced as simultaneously gratifying and frustrating mothers that inevitably evoke both the gratitude and the rage of their members. Thus the group that is loved is also necessarily the group that is hated. The development of the group demands that its members learn to respond reparatively to the anxiety and the guilt aroused by this ambivalence, that is, that they come to understand that their group is neither all-good nor all-bad but nonetheless worthy of care. But this happy outcome is always threatened by the temptation to defend against the group equivalent of depressive anxiety and guilt, either by denying one's dependence on the group (the group analogue of manic denial) or by denying one's rage against it (the group analogue of idealization). Manic denial leads to dropping out of the group but includes an obsessive preoccupation with, and denigration of, the very group from which one has dropped out. Idealization creates a demonized out-group that unwittingly becomes the target for the all the rage that cannot be expressed within the in-group. Thus the Kleinian message is that the development of the group (as well as the development of its individual members) depends on the capacity of its members to acknowledge and work through, rather than defend against, the ambivalence and guilt that inevitably accompany membership in the group. Group development is possible but precarious.

It seems to me that this general account does much to illuminate the specific psychodynamics of the Sixties. In the light of that account it makes sense to say, to begin with, that the Movement was a particularly gratifying mother. Its pervasive presence protected us from the dangers of an often hostile outside world and gave us a feeling of belonging to something much larger than ourselves. Through our common identification with our Movement mother, we who would have otherwise encountered each other as strangers immediately became "brothers" and "sisters" with whom food, dope, or shelter could be shared. That the language of kinship was regularly employed to express the ties that bound people to one another itself testifies to the maternal origins of the sense of, and need for, *community* that ran so deep during the Sixties. The words of one activist help us recall just how deeply we desired it: "You've got to build

community above all else . . . I never had it until I [joined the Movement]
and I haven't been able to live without it since."[22] *I haven't been able to live
without it since.* For this movement activist, as well as many others, to be
separated from the beloved community was to be separated from the source
of life itself. But within the matrix of the Movement we were safe from
the stultifying "seriality" of "*la vie quotidienne dans le monde moderne.*"[23] Thus
the Movement was, in Sartre's sense, a gigantic "group-in-fusion" in which
"each [member] saw in the Other the same project as his own [and]
impersonality, isolation, [and] atomization were washed away."[24]

The Movement on which we so deeply depended, moreover, was also
the Movement that encouraged us to "do our thing." Like Winnicott's
good-enough mother, it mirrored us even as it held us: it applauded the
widest—often the wildest—possible use of our imagination and thereby
bolstered our confidence in our capacity to act creatively in and on the
world. Just as the child mirrored by its mother "not only plays at being a
grocer or a teacher, but also as being a windmill or a train,"[25] so the youthful members of the Movement mobilized (what Walter Benjamin would
call) their "mimetic faculties" simultaneously to find and create all kinds
of connections among all manner of ostensibly separate material things.
This qualitatively different sense of space, moreover, was accompanied by
a radically transformed sense of time. For those of us who inhabited this
radically reenchanted world, Benjamin's *Jetztzeit*—the magical time of the
now—became more real than the "homogeneous, empty time"[26] of modernity that we rejected when we threw away our watches. In short, we were
no longer merely "marking time" but actually (or so we thought) *making
history.* This perhaps unparalleled sense of collective agency gave clear and
compelling purpose to our daily lives. Small wonder that for so many of
us the Sixties survive as the memory of an Eden from which we were long
ago exiled.

But we have many painful memories of that period as well. The Movement was no exception to the general rule that even the most gratifying
group inevitably frustrates the needs of its individual members. Our patience for participatory democracy was tested, and in many cases worn
thin, by the seemingly endless Movement meetings that devoured so much
of our time (and for which the women among us were expected to keep
the food and coffee coming). Long-standing personal and professional
dreams were deferred, and in some cases permanently sacrificed, to the
demands of political activism. The Movement's message that "if you can't
be with the one you love [you should] love the one you're with" took a
terrible toll on the personal lives of so many of its members. In short, the

protection and the mirroring of the Movement was often purchased at the high price of its intolerance for many of the values to which many of us were still at least ambivalently committed.

That the Movement was a *counter*cultural movement compounded the personal pain that it provoked. To be a member of the Movement we had to cut many of our ties to the straight society to which it was opposed. Since membership in the Movement was in large part generationally defined, moreover, cutting our ties to that society very often meant cutting ourselves off from our *parents*. Thus many of the children of the Movement lost the support of the culture and the families that had given birth to them. But I do not remember a single Movement meeting at which these terrible losses were discussed. It was if lamenting those losses would have been a sign of disloyalty to our newly adopted, jealous Movement mother.

I believe that the inability to grieve these losses had grievous consequences. *The very things that we lost became targets for the rage that could not be expressed against the Movement that was, in part, responsible for our losing them.* The defense against our ambivalence took the form of an idealization of our adopted Movement Mother and a demonization of the cultural and biological parents against which we protested. We transformed cops into "pigs" and rewrote "America" with a *k* as a sign of our struggle against a "fascism" from which we believed we were entirely free. Our warning that no one over 30 should be trusted was an implicit proclamation that we were completely trustworthy. Why should we who were so good have to lament the loss of "they" who were so bad?

Of course "they" all too often acted like the "bad mothers" we took them to be. The actual hostility of both the state and our parents confirmed our paranoid projections and further fueled our rage against the system. This only led, of course, to still more repression. And so on. Eventually the loving countercultural community was lost to this vicious cycle of schizoid opposition between the Movement and the system. "Burned out" or afraid of being "rubbed out," we left in droves the Movement that we loved. We have been politically depressed ever since.

At the outset of this chapter I suggested that this depression will not lift until we are finally able to mourn the Movement. Now it should be clear what mourning the Movement would mean. It would mean doing *now* what we were unable to do *then*: acknowledging and working through our intense ambivalence toward our countercultural Movement mother. It would require that we own the anger against it that we did not have the strength to express when we first felt it and that we split off with such fateful consequences. It would also require that we confront our buried

guilt both for hating the Movement we loved and then for leaving it because we spoiled it with our split-off hate. Facing our anger and our guilt
should engage our reparative impulses and remind us just how much we
still love what we have lost. Then "grief could be experienced to the full
[and] the lost loved object [could] be preserved within"—that is, then
mourning the Movement might culminate in a *selective identification* with
those (loving) aspects of the Sixties that are truly worth saving. If Klein
is correct, this selective identification with the Sixties should "stimulate
[the] productive activity" of our political imagination and even encourage us once again to "take our dreams for reality." Thus, through a "regretful sorrow," might we win back our "devotion to happiness which has
been denied."[27]

This sorrow, finally, will have to find both public and private expression. From Klein we have learned that our real adult losses awaken early
childhood losses and that our capacity to mourn the former will in important part be determined by our capacity to mourn the latter. If we have
not learned to tolerate our ambivalence for our internal objects we will
not be in an emotional position to tolerate our ambivalence for the Sixties. Thus the individual struggles of so many Sixty-Eighters both inside
and outside therapy to mourn their internal mothers (and fathers) are a
necessary complement to the shared mourning of the Movement on which,
I have argued, their development equally depends.

It was precisely a commitment to the Movement that motivated many
of us to begin long ago the individual grief-work that has since become
necessary for the successful mourning of that very Movement. Those of
us who were committed to the principle that we should live our lives as if
the good society already existed were soon forced to face the fact that the
only way in which we could live up to this principle was to do compensatory emotional work on our selves. We recognized that a "prefigurative
politics"[28] required a personal transformation: there could be no successful struggle against the domination in our society without a successful
struggle against the domination within *us*. I believe that many of us are
now far more emotionally prepared for prefigurative politics than we were
thirty years ago: we have caught up psychologically with our political
commitment to combat domination. But ironically the very political task
for which we are now emotionally prepared seems virtually unimaginable.

This loss of political imagination, I have argued in this chapter, is the
result of a collective failure to mourn a Movement that gave birth to a
profound and pervasive sense of social solidarity and collective agency.
All the individual grief-work in the world will not help us to work through

the terrible loss of that sense of solidarity and collective agency we have suffered and for which we are, in part, responsible. Social losses—intersubjectively shared losses—can only be properly mourned in a properly social setting.[29] Thus ongoing individual grief-work is a necessary complement to, but no substitute for, the collective grief-work that we have yet to accomplish. Mourning the Movement and reclaiming our childhood are two equally essential, reciprocally related routes to that "hope in the past"[30] that would reanimate our petrified present. Personal and political grief-work are, in short, two sides of the same emancipatory coin. The same coin, but two different sides. The personal both *is* and *is not* the political. This is, it seems to me, one of the hard-won, enduring insights that must be saved from the Sixties.

8   The Psychodynamics of Racial Reparations

Introduction

The once nearly moribund movement for reparations for African Americans has recently gained new life. A number of American city councils as well as *The Philadelphia Inquirer* have called for the creation of a national reparations commission, a team of prominent African-American lawyers, including Harvard professor of law Charles Ogletree, has announced plans to seek legal damages from both the federal government and companies that profited from slavery, a number of companies have issued formal apologies for having done so, and the Declaration of the United Nations World Conference Against Racism held in Durban in September 2001 describes slavery as a "crime against humanity" whose consequences states have a moral obligation to "halt and reverse."[1] In short, we are witness to a resurgence in the rhetoric of racial restitution.

To this point the scholarly literature on reparations has understandably focused on the issue of whether blacks *ought* to receive them. This very general normative question has been divided into a number of rather more specific ones. What is the injustice that reparations are designed to remedy— slavery, Jim Crow, or their persistently lethal legacy as well? If the object of reparations is slavery and/or Jim Crow, is it fair to ask whites who were born long after the end of these evils, and thus could not have been responsible for them, to contribute to the compensation of those who continue to suffer from their sequelae? Correspondingly, who should be the beneficiaries of reparations—just the descendants of slaves or all African Americans? How long should the benefits last, just for the members of this generation of African Americans or for the members of future generations as well? Who should pay for them—the federal government, businesses that profited from slavery, or both? How much should blacks benefit, and how should the benefit be determined, for example, by calculating the current monetary value of slave labor, the value of denied opportunities under slavery and legal segregation, or by some other method? All of these normative questions have been thoroughly and vigorously debated.[2]

Yet there is a sense in which this debate—like all exclusively normative debates—is beside the political point. Arguments about what should be are rarely a match for the needs that negate them. Thus white Americans are unlikely to be moved by principled arguments in favor of reparations if they have a deep psychological stake in resisting them. In this chapter I argue that this is indeed the case. I draw on the psychoanalytic theory of Melanie Klein to make and clarify the claim that the movement for reparations for African Americans encounters powerful unconscious resistance on the part of many of the white Americans who would—in some sense—be responsible for making them.

My Kleinian account of the roots of this resistance, however, will culminate in the conclusion that whites would reap enormous emotional benefits from working it through. Thus I do not argue here that blacks deserve reparations but rather that reparations are in the emotional interest of whites.[3] The perhaps unexpected consequence of my effort to supplement standard normative arguments in favor of reparations with a psychoanalytic account of the reasons for the resistance to them is a transformation in the nature of the normative case itself. That case would no longer be based on the assumptions that the benefits of reparations are predominantly *material* and that *blacks* would be their exclusive beneficiaries, but on the assumptions that reparations would also yield *emotional* benefits of which *whites* would be the recipients.

In the next section of this chapter I summarize the Kleinian account of the role of reparations in the psychological development of the individual. The mark of the emotionally mature person, Klein argues, is precisely her capacity to repair the (real or fantasied) damage resulting from her (real or fantasied) aggression against the (m)other. Learning to respond reparatively to, rather than to defend against, the "depressive" anxiety and guilt that inevitably accompany the awareness that we have harmed those whom we love is a *work of mourning* whose importance is matched only by its difficulty.

In the third section I explore the implications of this account for the future of American race relations. A genuinely reparative response to African Americans on the part of whites, I argue, would require a painfully successful confrontation with the anxiety and guilt necessarily accompanying the acknowledgment of the harm that they have done—or fantasized doing—to blacks.[4] Because this confrontation is so deeply difficult, there is a powerful temptation on the part of whites to defend against that anxiety and guilt by denying responsibility for the suffering of blacks. Thus current calls for reparations are a challenge for whites to overcome the very resistance that they evoke.

This argument—the application of the Kleinian concept of reparations to the question of racial reparations—presupposes that white Americans in some sense love the very black Americans they have harmed.[5] It is precisely this perhaps counterintuitive point that I intend to pursue. I argue that white love as well as hate for blacks can reasonably be inferred from the persistence of parallel idealizing and demonizing white racial fantasies. For every negative stereotype of blacks that is fueled by aggression there is, I suggest, a corresponding positive stereotype that is charged with libido. Blacks, in short, are the containers of both the hate and the love that whites have projected into them.[6] It follows—or so I will argue—that demands for reparations unconsciously remind whites that they have harmed those whom they also love and that these demands inevitably evoke the very anxiety and guilt that a successful program of reparations would have to overcome.

I then explore what it would mean for whites to "overcome." I suggest that an authentically reparative process would culminate in a decline in idealizing and demonizing white racial fantasies and the emergence of more realistic representations of and relationships with blacks. Because the ultimate source of the projected love and hate that infuses idealizing and demonizing fantasies is split-off parts of the self, I also argue that this process of overcoming idealization and demonization would necessarily include a fundamental transformation in—and thus a hitherto absent integration of—the fractured psyches of racist whites. These whites would, I propose, in some ways become more like what they take blacks to be.

In the fourth and final section I derive practical recommendations for reparations from this theoretical account. I argue that the prospects are bleak for any program of reparations that is not sensitive to the powerful emotional dynamics I describe. More specifically, any demands for restitution that do not address both the profound resistance of, and potential benefits to, whites will either fail to garner sufficient support or will be supported for the wrong reasons. Thus an overriding preoccupation with financial reparations is misplaced. The call for reparations must be understood as "as much a call for mourning as it is for [financial] restitution."[7]

The Role of Reparations in Individual Development

Klein argues that the psychological well-being of the individual depends decisively on the development of his or her reparative capacities. More specifically, making reparations is the only way in which the child can resolve the profoundly painful conflicts endemic to what Klein calls the "depressive position." The comprehension of the conflicts that comprise this centrally formative emotional position, in turn, requires an appreciation of the emotional position that is said to precede it, namely the "paranoid-schizoid position."

Because even the most solicitous mother necessarily frustrates the infant she seeks to gratify, she—or in the first instance the "part-object" with which the infant is in most continuous contact, namely her breast—necessarily becomes an object of both intensely positive and intensely negative feelings. On the one hand, the infant's oral gratification will give rise to a fantasy or internal representation of an all-giving, all-good breast—and eventually of a perfect mother—that is the savory source of that gratification. The blissfully pleasurable sensations that are later experienced at the site of organs other than the mouth—such as the anus and the genitals—will likewise contribute to the infant's love for the "good mother" who attends to them. On the other hand, the intense pain that the infant feels when the breast is withheld, the sphincters are constrained, or the genitals declared off-bounds perforce promotes a fantasy of an "all-bad" mother that becomes the target for a rage whose intensity more than matches the pain she is felt to inflict.

Klein assumes that the libido and aggression evoked by the gratifying and frustrating features of the "external object" are magnified by internal sources of love and hate—which Klein considers to be the ontogenetic corollaries of the life and death instincts—and thus she insists that the intensity of love and hate for the object is never directly proportional to the actual ratio of gratification and frustration that the mother supplies. Even if we jettison (as I believe we should) Klein's assumption that the infant's love and hate are innate, there remains a good Kleinian reason for the disproportion between the intensity of that love and hate and the actual treatment it receives at the hands of its mother. Since the infant experiences its own feelings of love and hate as coming from the mother's breast—because it projects its inner libidinal and aggressive states onto what (it does not yet recognize is) the outer world—the breast is endowed with far more goodness and badness than it actually possesses: " [an] inner world is . . . built up in the child's unconscious mind, corresponding to his actual experiences . . . and yet altered by his own phantasies and impulses."[8] Thus the breast of even the most loving mother will become the fantasied target of vicious (counter) attacks designed to protect the infant from its (fantasied) attacks. Eventually the infant will make full use of all the physical means at its disposal: its fantasies will include oral, anal, and genital attacks on the "bad breast": "the instinctual aims of the sadistic impulses (to bite, soil with excrement, cut up, burn, etc.) become . . . the weapons in fantasy of an object relationship aimed at the annihilation of the object."[9] The rage that motivates these counterattacks, moreover, will in turn be projected onto the bad breast, leading to yet further fears of annihilation: "The projection into the object of the split-off parts of the self, because motivated by a wish to control the object, gives rise to the fear that it may take its revenge by itself controlling the parts projected into it."[10] In short, the infant at this point is trapped in a vicious circle of projected hate and fear. Hence Klein's initial description of this position as the "paranoid position."

But the term on which she eventually settled was the "paranoid-schizoid position." In its earliest months the infant has no way of knowing that the mother of gratification and the mother of frustration are in fact one and the same person. Lacking what cognitive developmental psychologists call "object permanence"—in this case the capacity to recognize that one and the same "object" can be the source of such radically different stimuli as intense pleasure and intense pain—the infant does not realize that the target of its worshipful love and the target of its murderous rage are one and the same person. Thus the infant's initial reality is "schizoid," that is, radically split between the fantasy of a benevolent, all-good breast and the fantasy of a malevolent, all-bad breast. This splitting of reality—or rather this split experience of reality, since it is the result of the infant's cognitive immaturity and not its agency—is both the source of the infant's security and of all the emotional dangers to which it may eventually succumb. On the one hand, the fact that his or her fantasy or internal representation of an all-good breast is unsullied by any contact from the all-bad breast means that there is a libidinal source for that trust in a loving reality on which his or her subsequent capacity to give and receive love will depend. Introjection of an all-good breast, in short, is essential for good object relations. On the other hand, as we shall see, once the infant develops the cognitive capacity to confront the depressive position it will be tempted to revert to the paranoid-schizoid position and to make use of its sadistic weapons for purely defensive, and ultimately self-destructive purposes. Thus the paranoid-schizoid position is both the foundation for, and the chief obstacle to, the further emotional development of the child.

For Klein there can be no splitting of the object "without a corresponding splitting taking place within the ego."[11] This follows from her assumption that the ego is formed through the introjection of the object. That is, she assumes that the sense of self is the product of fantasied experiences and associated internal representations of the (m)other. Thus the experience and internal representation of an all-good breast/mother will give rise to the experience and internal representation of an all-good self, and the experience and internal representation of an all-bad breast/mother will engender the experience and internal representation of an all-bad self. To put this another way, because the infant does not initially distinguish clearly between self and (m)other, when that distinction begins to develop the all-good and all-bad feeling-states and fantasies that preceded the development of that distinction are easily transferred from (m)other to self and from self to (m)other.[12] In short, in the paranoid-schizoid position the self is as split as the (m)other.

When the child develops the cognitive capacity to recognize that the good and bad mothers are in fact one and the same—Klein dates this development to the third or fourth month but we now know that object permanence typically does not develop until the last third or even quarter of the first year of life[13]—he is faced with the terrifying consequences of his murderous rage. Not yet able to distinguish between fantasy and reality, the "omnipotent" child fears that it has destroyed the very being to whom it is so ardently attached and who is the source of all its worldly comfort and security. This profound "depressive" anxiety, Klein argues, is normally associated with an equally pronounced sense of guilt. Depressive guilt, according to Klein, entails genuine concern or "pity" for the mother and "remorse" for having harmed her.[14] Thus for Klein—in stark contrast to Freud—"there is no guilt without love."[15]

Depressive guilt, in turn, is the trigger for "an over-riding urge to preserve, repair, or revive the loved object," which urge Klein variously calls the "drive" or the "tendency to make reparation."[16] On the fate of this drive or tendency the entire subsequent emotional development of the child/ adult will depend. If the child's reparative efforts are matched by the mother's reassuring responses (and, Klein adds, if the child's paranoid-schizoid tendencies are not too strong), then a benign cycle of love given in return for love will be established and the child will be able to overcome his or her fears of having irretrievably destroyed the mother. The relief that results from the recognition that the real mother has survived his assaults, moreover, will help him to bear the pain—to mourn—the loss of the perfect fantasy mother that also necessarily accompanies the recognition of her imperfect reality. Thus successful negotiation of the depressive position[17] culminates in the child's recognition that the mother is neither all-good nor all-bad but nonetheless worthy of care. This integration of love and hate for the mother simultaneously entails the integration of love and hate for the self; the overcoming of the split within the self goes hand in hand with the transcendence of the split within the object: "[I]t is not only an object about whom guilt is experienced but also parts of the self which the subject is driven to repair or restore."[18] Thus the depressively integrated individual is prepared for relationships with self and others that are based on a realistic appreciation of the inevitability of ambivalence within those relationships.

But depressive integration is by no means an easy or inevitable accomplishment. The very depressive anxiety and guilt that encourage reparations are also likely to trigger defenses against the need to make them. Chief among these defenses are idealization and what Klein calls "manic denial." Idealization wards off depressive anxiety and guilt with the fantasy of a mother who is too perfect ever to have been the object of the infant's rage.[19] Thus the task of overcoming the split between the good mother and the bad mother is postponed through the effective denial of the existence of the latter. In manic denial, in contrast, the child defends against depressive anxiety and guilt not by idealizing but by denigrating the mother; she denies her need for and love of the mother and treats her instead as an object of contempt and omnipotent control.[20] In this case an exclusively demonizing fantasy short-circuits the process of mending the split between the good and bad mother.

Although Klein (prematurely) dates the onset of the depressive position to the second quarter or third of the infant's first year, she also argues that the child continues to wrestle with the depressive position for at least the next three years.[21] According to Petot's painstaking, comprehensive reconstruction of Klein's corpus, "four years . . . are allotted . . .

for the successful working though of the depressive position."[22] This means
that the depressive position is "worked through"—or not—in the course
of all the orthodox Freudian stages of libidinal development. In fact Klein
reconceptualizes the conflicts resulting from the parental repression of
oral, anal, and genital impulses as the source of depressive anxiety and
guilt, and the characteristic ways of defending against those conflicts as
stage-specific defenses against that anxiety and guilt. Thus she identifies
both idealizing and demonizing defenses against the depressive anxiety
and guilt accompanying oral, anal, and genital conflicts. The overcoming
of these conflicts and the defenses against them, in turn, is understood to
be the result of reparative urges and practices that are themselves colored
by the particular libidinal stage at which they appear.[23]

Although Klein has often been taken to task for privileging the "constitutional" over the "environmental" origins of the emotional conflicts
of early childhood,[24] she does not in fact ignore the role of the real mother
either in facilitating or hindering the resolution of these conflicts. Indeed,
she insists that "a good relation to its mother and to the external world
helps the baby to overcome its early paranoid anxieties" and thus successfully to work through the depressive position.[25] Thus "frustrations which
can be avoided should not be inflicted on the child." Consistent with this
claim, she advises mothers to nurse their infants on demand and wean them
gradually, to toilet train them gently and with an appreciation for the
"pleasure [the child] takes in his excretory functions and his excreta," and
to "not interfere with the child's masturbation" and demonstrate instead
a "really friendly acceptance of sexuality in her child." Frequent cutaneous contact is likewise recommended.[26]

These recommendations imply that Klein is aware of what might be
called the precarious parental preconditions for depressive integration.
Nevertheless she claims that most children will eventually negotiate the
depressive position with success (even though the losses they cannot but
suffer as adults will oblige them continually to renegotiate it).[27] But there
are good reasons to believe that she drastically underestimates the barriers to depressive integration. In fact, in the next section of this chapter
I will argue that the core fantasies of white racism are manifestations of
pervasive splitting at the oral, anal, and genital stages of libidinal development, and thus that the overcoming of white racism would require a
great depressive leap forward in the emotional maturity of those Caucasians who have succumbed to it. Making reparations for racism, in short,
would both require and encourage a long overdue confrontation with white
racist fantasies and the psychological splits that fuel them.

The Psychodynamics of Racism and Reparations

Racism

In previous work I have argued that both the structure and practices of Western child rearing militate against depressive integration at the oral, anal, and genital stages of individual development. The culturally universal fact that a woman—either the biological mother or a female mother-substitute—is uniquely responsible for both the gratification and frustration of the earliest needs of the child, and the culturally specific fact that the ratio of gratification to frustration in the West since the seventeenth century is tipped far more toward frustration than elsewhere, combine to encourage the development of individual defenses against depressive anxiety and guilt that reinforce the splitting-up and off of oral, anal, genital, and other bodily needs.[28] In this chapter I will not rehearse that argument but rather assume that defensive splitting on the part of individuals is pervasive, and will argue instead that culturally shared demonizing and idealizing white racial fantasies both feed off and reinforce those individual defenses. My claim, in other words, is that white racism is fueled by the primitive passions of the paranoid-schizoid position *and* that it discourages people from transcending that position.[29] Racism is, in short—and among other things—a cultural defense against the poignant pain of depressive anxiety and guilt. Like all defenses, however, racism leaves individuals vulnerable to a different form of the very anxiety and guilt against which it defends. Calls for racial reparations inadvertently exploit that vulnerability and thus reproduce on the level of the group the individual distress that racism defers. That, at any rate, is the argument I will make in this section.

To make it I begin with a brief summary of what I take to be four pairs of demonizing and idealizing fantasies about blacks that are central to white racism in America.

Blacks as "lazy and shiftless" vs. blacks as "laid back and cool"

The stereotype of the lazy, shiftless black has long had a prominent place in the rhetoric of American racism. Ever since Emancipation those who have commanded the labor-power of African Americans have bemoaned their supposed unwillingness to work.[30] This picture of the black who *doesn't want to work* persists in the face of the reality of indispensable contributions of black labor to the construction of this country, not to mention the huge lines of the unemployed that typically form on the rare occasions when decent jobs open up in underclass communities. Equally resistant to the intrusion of reality is the image of the undisciplined, unproductive black who depends on the state (and thus on the taxes paid by independent, productive white workers) instead of his or her own efforts in order to survive. Thus welfare programs have consistently been stereotyped as programs for blacks notwithstanding frequent reiteration of the statistics that show that the majority of welfare recipients have always been white. For the white racist the image of the teenage black welfare mother who consumes huge quantities of junk food but produces nothing but babies provides irrefutable proof that blacks lack the initiative and independence that whites possess.[31] In short, *dependence* is one of the central meanings of "black" in the lexicon of American racism.[32]

At the same time it is definitely "cooler" in this culture to be black than white. Whites, and white youth in particular, who want to be "cool" typically affect the mannerisms—the dress, speech, and body movements— of blacks. The association of "cool" with "black" runs so deep in our culture that many years ago George Carlin could evoke prolonged peals of laughter from his (mainly young white) audience merely by imagining a situation in which black teenagers tried to imitate white teenagers rather than the reverse. The preposterousness of Carlin's hypothetical equation of cool and white served strikingly to confirm the naturalness of the cultural equation of cool and black.

"Cool" has many connotations, but a central one is surely the capacity to remain calm and composed in the face of the insistent pressures to which more anxious people would surely succumb. Keeping one's cool, moreover, is intimately related to being able to "cool it," that is, to slow down and take it easy. And closely connected to these two meanings of cool is the cool of "playing it cool," which is, according to *Webster's New Collegiate Dictionary*, to act in a "casual and nonchalant manner [and] not really involve [one]self"—in short, to go with the flow. To "go with the flow" in turn is to surrender to, and to affirm one's dependence on (rather than attempt to master) the inevitable uncertainties of everyday life. Notice that one cannot be cool and productive at one and the same time. The person who "takes it easy," "plays it cool," or "goes with the flow" cannot be a disciplined worker. (It is no surprise, then, that disenchantment with industrial discipline—with the straight world of work—characteristically takes the form of the commitment to be and act cool.) In short, "cool" idealizes what "undisciplined" demonizes. Thus it should come as no surprise that blacks are praised for being cool even as they are pilloried for being lazy.

This suggests that conflicting feelings about dependence are the common source of the demonizing and idealizing fantasies I have described. From Klein we learn that these conflicting feelings first arise at the oral stage of libidinal development, the stage at which the infant meets the world with its mouth. The oral frustrations that are mandated by the mother and that reach their peak at weaning give rise to rage against her that is turned against the self in the form of a militantly independent negation of neediness. Through what Klein calls "projective identification"—the process by which unwanted parts of the self are projected into the other and control over these parts is achieved through control of the other— the bad, needy, oral part of the self will typically and subsequently be projected into a variety of others who, because they now contain a hated part of the child's self, will be unconsciously experienced as greedy persecutors sucking at the maternal breast. Thus by means of a double idealization, first of the mother and then of the self, the child wards off depressive anxiety and guilt but is thrown back—or rather throws himself back— into the paranoid-schizoid position.[33] Needless to say, his fear and loathing of the oral neediness of others will coincide with his own repudiated and thus necessarily unsatisfied need for unlimited gratification from them.

If blacks are hated for "their" dependence, this can only be, from a Kleinian psychoanalytic point of view, because they become the containers of the split-off, unwanted, and feared dependent part of the white racist self. And if they are also loved for essentially the same qualities, this only proves the psychoanalytic rule that split-off (and therefore necessarily unsatisfied) infantile needs insistently press for their satisfaction and take the perverse form of the desire for (what Kristeva calls) the *abject*.[34] In this case they find their satisfaction in the fantasy of the "laid back" black who "goes with the flow"and is too "cool" to be concerned.

Blacks are "dirty and smelly" vs. "blacks are beautiful"

Ever since whites first encountered blacks in Africa they have complained that blacks are a dirty and foul-smelling people.[35] Cutaneous contact with blacks long figured prominently among the dangers against which segregation was designed to defend. But ardent segregationists are by no means the only whites who are averse to black skin and the odor that it is said to emit. Studies have shown that 3- and 4-year-old American preschool children in mixed-race preschool settings frequently describe both black children and black dolls as "dirty," "stinky," and "smelly," and often worry that the "dirt" will rub off on them.[36] In fact prolonged and in-depth observation of nursery school and kindergarten children led Marjorie McDonald to conclude that early "skin color anxiety" is in fact a "normal and necessary internal response to confrontation with skin color differences," and to warn that this anxiety will engender overt racial prejudice if it is not adequately resolved.[37] Pervasive adult aversion to black skin suggests that it often is not. The infamous *Time* cover photo that blackened the skin of O. J. Simpson was only one of the most recent and blatant examples of this aversion. A perhaps less obvious—but more telling—example is the fact that black skin still repels white votes: only three African Americans have been elected to the United States Senate since Reconstruction, and only two of them (Carol Mosley-Braun and Barak Obama) were obviously black. In short, there is ample evidence of white fear and loathing of dark skin.

On the other hand dark skin is also an object of white admiration and envy. Every year millions of Anglos head for the beaches—or the tanning parlors—in order to perfect their tans. That even the fear of cancer does nothing to dissuade them is an indication of just how deeply committed they are to darkening their pale faces. Until relatively recently this covert effort to make themselves *look more like blacks* was typically unaccompanied by overt admissions that they actually liked the way blacks looked. But at least since the 1960s, when increasingly large numbers of blacks came to insist they were, indeed, beautiful, increasingly large numbers of whites have been inclined to agree. Is it too much to suggest that whites are now as likely to look to a young Muhammed Ali, Sugar Ray Leonard, Michael Jordan or (for the younger generation) Tyrese as they are to (a young) Paul Newman, Robert Redford, or Brad Pitt for examples of what it means to be a good-looking man, and to consider Halle Berry, Naomi Campbell, and Tyra Banks clearly as comely as any of their white female counterparts? Madison Avenue apparently thinks not, at least if we judge from the frequency with which black flesh is used to peddle their products. Thus we can say that whites have come to profess with their purchases what they have always already known, namely that black *is* beautiful.

A Kleinian approach suggests that both the demonization and the idealization of dark skin are defenses against depressive anxiety and guilt arising at the anal stage. According to Klein, rage against the mother for delaying the pleasure of unrestrained defecation gives rise to the anxiety and guilt of having destroyed the very being whom one loves, which anxiety gives rise to reparative urges which at this point typically take the form of gifts of "good" excrement designed to please the mother.[38] But if these gifts are not appreciated, and/or the mother's prohibition on contact with his excrement has convinced him that it is bad, the child is likely to defend against anal depressive anxiety and guilt by redirecting his rage against his own anus and what comes out of it. Thus the price he pays at this point for an idealized, shit-free mother is the experience of the *self* as shitty or dirty, which experience will be followed by a projection of his dirty self into others and, in all likelihood, the development of a compulsive cleanliness as the sequelae to his own need to defend against dirt.[39]

Thus distaste for dirt is a sublimated form of disgust with shit. If blacks are stigmatized as dirty and smelly, this can only be—when seen from a psychoanalytic point of view—because they serve as the targets of the anal projections of whites. First Lawrence Kubie[40] and then Joel Kovel at much greater length a few years later in his provocative *White Racism: A Psychohistory*, argued that the fortuitous resemblance of the color of shit to the dark pigmentation of African-American skin conspires to select blacks as the "natural" containers for those projections. Thus whites are driven to separate themselves from blacks in order to cleanse themselves of their own filth. "Cleanliness is next to Godliness" becomes the watchword of the American who purifies himself at the expense of blacks, who become the object of his anal-compulsive efforts to control them.

Historians like Sander Gilman and Noel Ignatiev have implicitly called this analysis into question by pointing out that oppressed groups such as the Jews and the Irish have been stigmatized as "black" even though the color of their members' skin is not measurably darker than that of their oppressors.[41] In other words, "black" becomes a kind of floating signifier of badness that can be applied to anyone of any race. Yet Kovel could counter that he has provided an *explanation* for the arguably culturally universal or at least near-universal association between black and badness that his critics merely take for granted. The linguistic fact that "black" is metaphorically associated with evil or danger in so many cultures, he contends, testifies to the persistence of unresolved anal conflicts in those cultures. Black becomes bad, in short, because shit is considered bad, and white becomes "good" because it symbolizes the absence of shit.[42]

Idealization of black skin also has an anal explanation. Infants initially delight in the smell and taste of their bodies as well as their bodily products. Defecation in particular is an eminently pleasurable experience. And its product, we have seen, is the proud young child's first gift to the mother. Thus shit is initially experienced as good. But the joyful relationship to our excrement is soon sacrificed to the demands of continence and the shame of failing to achieve it. However, this relationship, like all repressed relationships, is not entirely lost but rather resurfaces, I am proposing, in the form of the love of the dark skin that unconsciously reminds us of the lost pleasures of "letting go." Thus it is possible that blacks represent for whites the forbidden *loss of control* that they crave. This interpretation fits with the fact that whites typically imagine blacks as more "soulful" and emotionally expressive than whites. The association between dark skin and a liberating letting-go is also strengthened, it seems to me, by the connection between whites getting a tan and whites being on vacation. Is it entirely accidental that whites are most inclined to darken their skin when they are relaxing their quotidian commitment to control?

Blacks as "sexual monsters" vs. blacks as "sexual marvels"

Whites have long been obsessed with what they imagine is the boundless sexuality of blacks; for whites blacks are, as Fanon remarked, the very "incarnation of genital potency beyond all moralities and prohibitions."[43] On the one hand, ever since whites first encountered black men they have stigmatized them as sexual beasts eager to prey on white women and thus to "mongrelize" the white race. As many historians have argued, in the white slaveholder's imagination the threat of slave revolts evoked the imminent danger that white women would be the victim of mass rapes carried out by liberated blacks.[44] His Southern Belle, Lillian Smith has suggested, was at least as rape conscious as he.[45] And, long after the demise of slavery, black men in the South and in parts of the North as well were all too vulnerable to savage reprisals carried out by white men ostensibly designed to protect the purity of *their* women. That lynching— often accompanied by castration—was the penalty imposed under slavery and Jim Crow for such "crimes" as having merely *looked at them* indicates the intensity of white fear of rampant black male sexuality.[46] This fear persists today, I would suggest, in the form of white susceptibility to sensationalistic news reports and Willy Horton–type campaign ads that convey the impression that white women are disproportionately in sexual danger from black men (even though statistics show that the overwhelming majority of the victims of rape carried out by black men are *black* women).

Black women also figure prominently, if less centrally, in the hostile white racial imaginary. Corresponding to the stereotype of the black male rapist is the stereotype of the black whore. Ever since slavery, black women have been stigmatized by whites as amoral sluts, the consequence of whose promiscuity is too many children from too many men. Thus in the white racist imaginary they are eminently deserving both of the street insults they often absorb from white men for "flaunting" their sexuality, and the animosity they often encounter from white women for tempting their men in the process.

On the other hand, there are many indications of white idealization of black sexuality. The mass media regularly portray black men as "sex machines" whose superior sexual skills and stamina enable them to get it on "all night long," and black women are stereotyped as uninhibited, naturally sensuous lovers who are eager to give pleasure to, and take pleasure from, their partners. The image of the black male stud has long had a particular prominent place in the white racial imaginary, and one only has to think of "John *Shaft*" to realize that this sexual deification of the black man is intimately related to the idealization of his proverbially prodigious penis. This collective "penis envy," moreover, is only the most obvious example of white fascination with the sexual potency of black men. In *Black Like Me*, John Griffin reports that southern white men who took him for the black he pretended to be regularly requested that he share with them his sexual secrets. Under the assumption that blacks "don't have the inhibitions we have" and that they "make more of an art . . . of your sex than we do," Griffin's fellow travelers were eager to learn all about "the different kinds of sex" in which blacks were assumed to excel.[47] Nor are white women immune to this voyeuristic relationship to the world of African-American sexuality. Calvin Hernton's research revealed that "Negro women working in white homes are awed by the obsessive questioning by white women regarding the sexual behavior of Negroes." Underlying this compulsive curiosity, Hernton speculates, is a sense that when her sensual maid returns to her sensual man they will partake of pleasures of which she has little or no knowledge. Thus what Hernton concludes of white men might also be said of white women: "sexually . . . he wants to *be* a Negro. He wants to enjoy the unbounded sexual vigor he imagines Negroes enjoy."[48]

Underlying the demonization and idealization of black sexuality by both white men and women is—as John Dollard was among the first to point out[49]—their illicit, publicly disavowed *desire* for black bodies. This was most obvious in the slave South, where slavemasters had unrestricted sexual access to the female slaves on whom they frequently forced themselves. Thus even as they railed against the potential mongrelization of their race by black men it was precisely *white men* who were responsible for that result. The fantasy of rapacious black male sexuality, in other words, was a projection onto black men of the *reality* of the slaveholders' rapacious desire for black women. This projection fulfilled a number of crucial emotional functions. First (like the corresponding fantasy of the "lascivious" female slave to whose charms he could not be blamed for succumbing), it assuaged his guilt for both his sexual crimes and his neglect of the children that resulted from them. Second, it punished his black male competitors for the sexual services of the slave women he wanted. Finally, it helped to allay his suspicion that his chaste Southern Belle might actually be as attracted to black men as he was to black women.

There were good reasons for this suspicion. Sexually deprived not only by a husband who idealized her purity and spent his passion in the slave quarters rather than the master bedroom, but also by the black Mammy who suckled her infants, it was scarcely surprising that her erotic energy would be absorbed by fantasies of taking her pleasure where her husband took his. Indeed, if we accept the psychoanalytic assumption that the strength of a taboo is directly proportional to the intensity of the desire that it prohibits, and if we take into consideration the fact that "the actual danger of the southern women being violated by the Negro has always been . . . much less . . . than the chance that she would be struck by lightning,"[50] it is difficult to avoid the conclusion—reached by Cash, Kovel, and Hernton, among others—that the intensity of the Southern white woman's fear of rape by black men betrayed an intense lust for them. If so, then the Southern white woman was as emotionally complicit in the murder and mutilation of the black men who were deemed to have defiled her honor as the Southern white man who carried out those dreadful deeds: both made the black man pay the price for their crimes against him.

This perverse sexual story did not end with slavery or even with Jim Crow. Even today "black people exist [for whites] to provide the means for expressing forbidden desire."[51] John Griffin reports that one of the Southern white racist men he met confided that "all the white men he knew craved colored girls."[52] Similarly, Malcolm X describes in vivid detail his efforts around the same time to procure black prostitutes for white men who had come to Harlem for the pleasures that they apparently could not find downtown.[53] And Calvin Hernton recounts tales of being taken for a pimp by whites who had come to Harlem for the same purpose.[54] There is no use belaboring the obvious: white men still have a "thing" for black women. Equally obvious, and for those who doubt it Hernton, Kovel, Young-Bruehl, and Fanon provide the evidence, is that white women still have a "thing" for black men.[55]

Why this should be the case is perhaps less obvious. The oedipal stage provides a crucial clue. At the genital stage the challenge of depressive integration is complicated by the father's triangulation of the child's relationship with the mother. Klein's account of the oedipal triangle draws on, but significantly modifies, the classical account of her mentor. She follows Freud in arguing that the boy loves—that is, at this stage, wishes sexual intercourse with—his mother and hates his father for prohibiting the consummation of that love,[56] and that the girl harbors similarly hostile, rivalrous feelings against the mother for monopolizing the father, whose penis she prizes. But Klein emphasizes far more than Freud both the boy's prior grudge against the "bad mother" (which grudge is reinforced by maternal prohibitions on masturbation) and how at this stage it assumes the fantastic form of specifically sadistic genital attack against her, as well as his preexisting love for the father that results from the transfer of his loving feelings for the good breast to the father's good penis. Thus for Klein, in contrast to Freud, the resolution of the boy's Oedipus complex—for her, the successful negotiation of the depressive position at the genital stage—requires fantastic efforts on the part of the boy to repair the damage (thought to be) done to both the mother and the father.

But these efforts may fail. If fear of the genitally dangerous bad mother, and fear of his own bad penis (his offending organ) combine to undermine the boy's confidence in his genitally based restorative powers, he is likely to defend against depressive anxiety and guilt by idealizing his mother and demonizing his father. Idealization makes it possible for the boy to maintain his infantile connection to the good mother by splitting off the genitally aggressive bad mother and projecting her into other women. Thus the boy's split between the good, asexual mother and bad sexual mother sets the emotional stage for the man's schizoid search for a madonna to take care of his inner baby boy, and a whore to satisfy his split-off, aggressive, and illicit sexual cravings. This idealization of the mother will typically be reinforced by the boy's identification with a "bad father" whom he will continue to experience as a persecutor who must be placated. His castration anxiety will persist in the form of his fantasy of possessing a dangerous, bad penis which, via the ubiquitous mechanism of projective identification, will characteristically be found in others who become the containers for his unacceptable oedipal urges. Thus the depressively unintegrated genital boy becomes the man who defends against his dangerous, incestuous sexual desires by attempting to contain the rapacious sexuality of other men.

As Dollard, Hernton, and Kovel have all pointed out, it is not difficult to fit the white male within this oedipal framework. The boy's split between the good, asexual mother and the bad sexual mother becomes the split between the supposedly sexually subdued white woman and the sexually voracious, seductive black woman. Thus white men live out their incestuous desires for their mothers in the form of dangerous liaisons, fantasized or otherwise, with their dark mother-substitutes.[57] In breaking the racial taboo they unconsciously break the oedipal taboo. At the same time, black men become the "bad fathers" against whom white men rage for enforcing this taboo and who, via the mechanism of projective identification, become the containers of their aggressively incestuous desires. Thus the white man unconsciously castrates his father when he heaps humiliations onto the black man. In short, he transforms the dangerously potent black man into a harmlessly impotent black "boy."

In certain respects the girl's oedipal situation is similar to the boy's. She too is faced with the task of integrating her sexual love and hate for both her father and her mother, and she too is able to rely both on her genitally based libido and her preoedipal love for both parents to carry out this task. But if her oedipal jealousy of her mother and/or her preoedipal grudge against her is too strong, or her confidence in her own restorative capacities—above all the capacity to bear children—is too weak, she will be tempted to defend against oedipal depressive anxiety and guilt by demonizing the mother and idealizing her father. As we saw in Chapter 1, according to Dorothy Dinnerstein's neo-Kleinian, feminist account of the "traditional emotional equilibrium that is known as heterosexual 'adjustment,'" the girl typically "transfer[s] to the father . . . much of the weight of [her] positive feelings [toward the mother], while leaving the negative ones mainly attached to their original object." By transforming the split between the good mother and the bad [genital] mother into the split between the bad mother and the good father, the girl "gains a less equivocal focus for her feelings of pure love, and feels freer to experience her grievances against her mother without fear of being cut off altogether from . . . a magic, animally loved, parental being." But the price she eventually pays for falling in love with her father is a "worshipful, dependent stance toward men" to whom she will sacrifice her agency—including her sexual agency—in order to repudiate her mother's.[58]

Dinnerstein's point is that the girl's repudiation of her mother's agency underlies the (heterosexual) woman's wish to be dominated sexually by a man and accounts for what Jessica Benjamin has described as "the pervasiveness of submission fantasies in [the] erotic life [of women]."[59] But it is unlikely that a woman's submission fantasies can be satisfied in the context of a monogamous relationship with a "safe" man who has chosen her as a mother instead of a whore. Thus she will be tempted to take her conventionally proscribed pleasure in the arms of a much more obviously dangerous, misogynistic man. In short, while the "good father" becomes the boy she wants to bring home to meet daddy and the man she will eventually marry, the "bad father" becomes her back door man.

In the racialization of this sexual split, the "back door man" becomes the black man and the boy-next-door becomes the white man. The combination of her idealization of her white boy-next-door and his idealization of her conspires to channel her lust to her "black-door man," who—perhaps because of a preexisting anally and/or orally based equation of black and bad—becomes a perfect container of her bad-father fantasies. Thus by sleeping with a black man the white woman succeeds in sleeping with her father. Like the white man, she crosses the oedipal line by crossing the color line. And, like her white male counterpart, she resents the "parent" who prevents her from crossing it. Beneath her obvious jealousy of her more sexually seductive black female competitor for her black man there lurks her oedipal jealousy of the mother who monopolized her father.

Blacks as "animals" vs. blacks as "athletes"

Blacks not only symbolize sex in particular but also "the biological" in general.[60] Thus they are both loved and hated for what whites take to be their proximity to nature. Every time they are condemned as "animals"— whether for their conditions of life or for their violent resistance to those conditions—the enmity of whites for the "natural" African American is all too evident. Caucasians contemptuously classify blacks as apes, monkeys, jungle bunnies, baboons, bucks, and coons in order to underscore their unbridgeable distance from whites and their kinship with the denizens of the animal world. In short, in the white racial imaginary whites are to blacks as culture is to nature, as mind is to body; just as civilization depends on the mental mastery of the body, so too it depends on white control over blacks.

Yet it is equally evident that blacks are admired—even adored—for their formidable physical feats. White fans are quick to glorify the black "natural athlete" with whose combination of agility, grace, power, and panache their supposedly more stolid white counterparts can scarcely compete. Two of the greatest black athletes of the second half of the twentieth century, Muhammed Ali and Michael Jordan, have succeeded in securing semidivine status in the minds of many Americans. In fact, if a visitor from another planet witnessed the profusion of what can only be called "Mikonography" on American television during the 1990s he or she or it could only have concluded that Michael *was* God. How else to explain the millions of whites who wanted to "be like Mike"?

But not just Mike and not just athletes. Gifted (in the eyes of whites) with a natural rhythm unknown to clumsier Caucasians, black musicians like James Brown, Janet Jackson, and Prince are also loved for what they can do with their bodies, captivating legions of white kids who try their best to mimic their moves.[61] Many years ago Norman Podhoretz confessed in *Commentary* that he envied blacks for their "superior grace and beauty" and that he was "capable of aching with all [his] being when [he] watch[es] a Negro couple on the dance floor, or a Negro playing . . . basketball. They are on the kind of terms with their own bodies that I should like to be on with mine, and for that precious quality they seemed blessed."[62] So too, I suspect, do many whites feel blessed who have learned to move their bodies like their idealized image of blacks.

By now the source of the splitting of the lived black body into the hated and loved black body should be clear. Idealizing defenses against depressive anxiety and guilt at the oral, anal, and genital stages characteristically culminate in a generalized need to deny (the pleasures of) the body in the name of the demands of a *dis*embodied mind. The child maintains his connection with an idealized mother at the cost of demonizing the bodily needs that she has suppressed; these dangerous bodily needs are controlled by projecting them into others who are consequently experienced as mindless animals that must constantly be contained by a civilized self (whose persistent envy of their proximity to nature, however, reveals an unconscious craving for the very body he or she consciously condemns).

The hated black body, then, is the white body that has been orally, anally, genitally, and otherwise repressed (thus the *racial* body fantasy condenses and completes the three previous fantasies), and that is projected into blacks who, either because they really *are* generally more comfortable with their bodies or because of the unconscious association of the (inside of the) body with darkness,[63] or both, become the apparently natural containers of these projections. Blacks, in short, become animals because whites hate their own bodies. Yet the repressed body returns in the form of the adoration of the miraculous physical moves of the African American (many of whom *can* dance but some of whom cannot). Thus does white nostalgia for the lost body of childhood become white idealization of black embodiment.[64]

Reparations

It should be clear that the racial fantasy structure I have reviewed prevents whites from realistically perceiving and relating to blacks, from recognizing that blacks are neither all-bad nor all-good but rather—like all people—a complex combination of the two. Thus whites who inhabit this racial fantasy world are defended against the racial analogue of depressive anxiety and guilt—that is, from the sorrow and remorse that would otherwise accompany the realization that they have harmed the blacks they love. Experiencing their hateful feelings (and actions) against blacks as necessary and natural responses to their badness, and strictly segregating bad blacks from good blacks, they are in no cognitive-emotional position to recognize that the blacks they hate and the blacks they love are in fact *the same people*. They are instead in the cognitive-emotional position of the character Pino in Spike Lee's wonderful movie, *Do the Right Thing*. The virulently racist Pino rages relentlessly against the "niggers," "animals," and "moulies" whom he is obliged to serve. At the same time he idealizes Magic Johnson, Eddie Murphy, and Prince. Challenged by Mookie to reconcile his hatred of the "niggers" and his love for his black superstar heroes, Pino responds: "Magic, Eddie, Prince . . . they're not niggers. They're not really black . . . they're different." In other words, Pino keeps his bad blacks and his good blacks so far apart in his mind that he it never occurs to him that Magic, Eddie, and Prince might have grown up in a ghetto similar to the hated one in which he works, and that the youthful ghetto residents he detests might have qualities similar to those of a Magic, Eddie, or Prince. Thus he is able to purchase his guilt-free rage at the exorbitant price of his arrested cognitive and emotional development. In this sense Spike Lee's picture of Pino accurately captures the psychological structure of all those whites who inhabit the racial fantasy world I have described.

It is precisely this psychological structure, I want to argue, that is threatened by calls for racial reparations. The fantastic segregation of good blacks from bad blacks is necessarily called into question by the claim that slavery, segregation, and their aftermath have harmed *all black people* and that *all black people* therefore deserve compensation. In effect, the advocates of reparations insist that individual blacks whom whites would otherwise demonize are "good-enough" to receive restitution and that individual blacks whom they might otherwise idealize have also suffered. This makes it more difficult—but not impossible—for the white racist to reaffirm an unbridgeable gap between the blacks he demonizes and the blacks he idealizes and thus more difficult—but not impossible—to continue to deny that his hate (along with any actions accompanying it) has harmed people who are worthy of his concern. Thus the call for racial reparations is likely to evoke the depressive anxiety and guilt of whites who would otherwise remain comfortably enclosed within the walls of their racial fantasy fortress.

This is, perhaps, precisely why such calls are vehemently resisted by so many of the whites who hear them. Recent polls reveal that although a large majority of African Americans favor a program of reparations for racism, most whites are adamantly opposed. According to a CNN/USA/ Gallup Poll conducted in February 2002, just over two-thirds of blacks believe that corporations that profited from slavery should apologize to African Americans, but less than a third of whites favor such an apology; three-quarters of black respondents support scholarships funded by those companies for the descendants of slaves, while almost two-thirds of whites oppose such scholarships; and more than half of blacks favor, while nine out of ten whites reject, cash payments to the descendants of slaves.[65] The shrill, sometimes even hysterical tone ("over my dead body!") of the anti-reparations rhetoric in the surprisingly numerous on-line discussion groups devoted to reparations, moreover, suggests that white opposition to reparations is as deep as it is wide.[66] The intensity of this opposition suggests that it is motivated by the need to defend against the racial analogue of depressive anxiety and guilt; in other words, white resistance to reparations is an expression of the collective version of manic denial. Just as the child manically defends against the anxiety and guilt accompanying his awareness that he has harmed his mother by denying his dependence on and love for her, so too whites ward off the sorrow and remorse that threaten to accompany the realization that they have harmed people who are worthy of their concern *by denying that they are worthy of their concern* and refusing to take responsibility for their fate. Thus the risk of the rhetoric of reparations is that it can trigger defenses against guilt that reinforce rather than reduce white racism. This pernicious emotional dynamic is exactly what Malcolm X had in mind in his *Autobiography* when he asked his followers, "Do you know *why* the White Man really hates you?" and then answered by insisting that it was because "every time he sees your face he sees a mirror of his crime–and his guilty conscience can't bear to face it."[67]

Yet later in that work Malcolm asked the questions: "Is white America really sorry for her crimes against the black people? Does white America have the capacity to repent—and to atone?"[68] and left their answers open. They still are. Although, as I have emphasized, there are formidable emotional obstacles, there are also enormous emotional advantages to a proper program of racial reparations. In fact white people have much more to gain from such a program than they have to lose. They already lose a great deal from racism: whites split blacks because they themselves are split. I have argued that the aggression that fuels racially demonizing fantasies is the hatred of those parts of the white self that have been repressed and split off, and that the libido that fuels racially idealizing fantasies is the loving return of those repressed parts. More specifically, I have suggested that the white racial fantasy structure is rooted in unsatisfied and therefore insatiable infantile (and adult) needs: the need to be taken care of, the need to let go, the need for a robust sexual life, and the need to embrace an animal existence. An authentically reparative process that challenged the white racial fantasy structure would therefore necessarily challenge the unconscious emotional structure of unsatisfied and split-off needs that sustains it.[69] In short, in repairing racism whites would be able to repair themselves. A properly reparative process would—in the wonderful words of James Baldwin in *The Fire Next Time*—"release [the white man] from his confusion and place him . . . in fruitful communion with the depths of his own being."[70] Thus whites would have nothing to lose but their psychological chains, and they would have an emotional world to win.

Conclusion: Recommendations for Reparations

South African psychiatrist Noel Chabani Manganyi argued some years ago that "on the collective level, the difficulties of working through the fantasy . . . structure supporting racism raises many practical problems which society prefers to ignore."[71] It is time to stop ignoring these problems. The argument of this chapter has been that reparations for racism would be an opportunity to "work through the [racial] fantasy structure," and that a "properly reparative process" would be obliged explicitly and directly to confront the difficulties—both the risks and the rewards—of working it through. Consequently any discussion of financial restitution should take place within an emotional context that encourages whites to confront their guilt for the (fantasized and/or real) harm done to blacks and to respond reparatively to that guilt. In the absence of this emotionally reparative process financial reparations are either unlikely to engender sufficiently strong white support or likely to engender support that mobilizes persecutory anxiety rather than genuinely "depressive" feelings. In this case restitution would be designed to placate blacks who would still be demonized in the white racial imaginary. Exclusively financial reparations would thus be the collective racial analogue to the "mock reparation" that Kleinians contrast to an effort to repair the mother that is motivated by genuine concern for her well-being.[72] Mock racial reparations are, in effect, what some blacks worry about when they express skepticism about a one-time financial compensation that would get whites off the emotional and political hook.[73]

In order to encourage whites to confront their guilt, an effective reparative program would have to include a relentless rehearsal of the history of harm done to blacks since their arrival on this continent. To counteract tendencies to maintain strict segregation between so-called good blacks and bad blacks, this history should recount the sufferings of even the most advantaged or idealized blacks as well as the positive contributions of even the most demonized among them. Thus any effective reparative program would entail a direct challenge to the conceptual-emotional segregation that is central to the white racial imaginary.

That program would, therefore, also have to be sensitive to the danger that the upsurge of anxiety and guilt inevitably accompanying the challenge to this conceptual-emotional segregation might engender a defensive rather than reparative response, for example, the denial of any need and concern for blacks rather than sorrow and remorse for their suffering. To counter this risk of racial manic denial the reparative educational program should emphasize the profound *dependence* of white Americans on black Americans—the fact that this country only is what it is because of black artistic, intellectual, stylistic, and athletic contributions—and thus the sense in which American culture *is already* an African-American culture. Whites who might otherwise be inclined manically to imagine an America without blacks should be regularly reminded of what Ralph Ellison pointed out three decades ago: namely, that an America without blacks would be entirely unrecognizable and thus would not be a country with which *they* could identify.[74] In short, whites must be persuaded that when they take responsibility for the future of blacks they take responsibility for their own future as well.

Their own future, I have argued, will also be dramatically improved if they are able to embrace the parts of themselves that have been split off and projected into blacks. Is it too much to expect that a "properly reparative process" would be informed by an appreciation on the part of its organizers of the terrible emotional price that whites pay to maintain the racial fantasy structure, and thus of the enormous emotional rewards that they might reap from participating in a reparative process that functioned to undermine it? That whites might be encouraged by psychologically sensitive political, religious, and cultural leaders to believe that by responding reparatively to the sufferings of blacks they might alleviate their own, and so become more willing to be cared for, less uptight and controlling, more sexually satisfied, and more in touch with their own bodies?

This raises a final point. To participate in a properly reparative process, whites would have to be confident that their reparative efforts (both to alleviate the suffering of blacks and their own) *would in fact make a difference.* After more than three decades of malign neglect, however, even well-intentioned whites are likely to lack confidence in their reparative powers and to succumb to the pessimistic prognosis that our racial problems are just too intractable to tackle.[75] Racially reparative leaders can help create a climate that can counter this pessimism. But the response of ordinary blacks to the reparative efforts of whites is likely to be even more important in this regard. Just as the mother who lovingly responds to her child's earliest reparative efforts reassures him or her that she has, indeed, survived his or her assaults, so positive responses from blacks to the initial reparative work of whites could bolster considerably the confidence of whites in their reparative powers. On this point I think there is reason for optimism. My sense is that sincere and sustained expressions of contrition on the part of whites would be met with an enormous outpouring of appreciation on the part of blacks,[76] and that this could trigger a benign cycle of love given in return for love—of racial healing—that just might culminate in an America that breathed reality into the old Movement dream of the beloved community.

9 The Infancy of Modernity: Cyberspace, Time-Space Compression, and the Grandiose Self

Immaturity and infantilism are the most effective categories for defining modern man.
—WITOLD GOMBROWICZ

Introduction

Worldwide Internet use has recently been estimated at more than 500 million people. If this figure is correct, roughly one out of every twelve people living on the earth today is currently online. (More than half of these people live in the United States, Canada, and Europe.)[1] If the current rate of growth in Internet use continues, by 2006 roughly a billion people in the world will be wired.

People who are wired depend on their personal computers for an extraordinarily wide variety of tasks: communicating with friends, conducting business, shopping, doing research, writing papers, listening to music, reading the news, making travel reservations, participating in discussion groups, constructing fantasy worlds, making art, and making love (or at least having sex). In short, an increasingly large slice of life in the West is lived "on the screen."[2] Correspondingly, people are spending more and more time online. According to a recent survey, America's teenagers now average between almost 13 and almost 16 hours online per week in ten of the largest cities in the United States.[3] Although European Internet use still lags considerably behind American use, the total monthly time online increased 94 percent in the UK, 225 percent in France, and 226 percent in Germany between June 2000 and February 2001.[4] Ethnographic research in the United States has revealed that so-called "heavy users" may actually spend between 70 and

80 hours a week in cyberspace.[5] In short, Internet use is fast becoming as intensive as it is extensive.

This chapter tries to explain why. The explanation I offer is not intended to supplant but rather to supplement those that already exist.[6] I assume that existing explanations require supplementation because none of them, at least as far as I am aware, has taken the full measure of the *seductions* of computer-mediated communication (CMC). More specifically, none has explored what might be called the psychodynamics of cyberspace. This is what I propose to do in this chapter. My argument is that computer-mediated communication dramatically accelerates the compression of time and space endemic to modernity and that this accelerated time-space compression promotes the proliferation and intensification of fantasies of infantile omnipotence off which modernity feeds and to which it contributes.

In the next section of this chapter I review psychoanalytic and cognitive developmental claims that the infant initially lacks any sense of spatial or temporal limits and thus omnipotently experiences the world as an extension of its actions. In the third section I argue that the child's inescapably painful confrontation with the reality of spatial and temporal limits, that is, with the resistance of the world to her will, engenders the temptation to defend against the loss of infantile omnipotence with fantasies of omnipotent control over the world (Kohut's narcissism of the "grandiose self"). Next I maintain that modernity both feeds off and reinforces the narcissism of the grandiose self by celebrating human progress as the increasing emancipation from natural limits, and that this fantastic commitment to overcoming natural limits includes an obsession with maximum possible speed and with the ever-accelerating time-space compression that is its consequence. The (current) culmination of modern time-space compression, I argue in my concluding section, is the virtually instantaneous and geographically unlimited communication of cyberspace. Cyberspace re-creates the infantile condition of a world without spatial and temporal limits and thus powerfully promotes and reinforces the grandiose fantasies of omnipotence that mark the *infancy of modernity*.

I hasten to add that this is not the whole story. As is always the case, there are countervailing tendencies. The very Internet that encourages omnipotence also supplies a space for those who seek the support required to contest it. Omnipotence knows no loss, but there are plenty of people online who are sharing their losses and helping each other to mourn them. But that part of the story is for another essay. This one is about how CMC militates against mourning.

Infantile Omnipotence

The infant of psychoanalysis enters the world as a stranger to time and space. It knows neither a separation between self and world nor any chronology of events in the world independent of its actions. Thus everything that happens in the world is immediately associated with whatever it wants. The fact that the breast appears whenever the infant is hungry engenders the illusion that the breast "is part of the infant . . . and under the baby's magical control."[7] Other magical ministrations by the mother are likewise felt to be mandated by a self that is somehow felt to include her: "as Freud pointed out, the fact that human infants receive such nearly perfect care seduces them into fantasies . . . of a world that automatically obeys, even anticipates, their wishes."[8] Thus the reality of the infant's complete *dependence* on a (good-enough) mother paradoxically gives rise to the fantasy that she—and therefore the world—is under his complete control. It is not for nothing, then, that Freud refers to the infant as "his majesty the baby."[9]

The research of Jean Piaget independently confirms this psychoanalytic account of that royal realm. Piaget demonstrates that in its earliest months the infant has no concept of space because it has no way of knowing that objects exist independently of its actions on them. Lacking object permanence, the infant is unable to recognize the distinction between the position and state of an object and is thus unable to recognize that objects are spatially situated.[10] Similarly, the infant's inability to conceive of a world of independent objects prevents him or her from perceiving an order of succession among them or the intervals between them: "as the child . . . perceives the order of phenomena only when he himself has been the cause, he remains incapable of conceiving the chronology of his universe independently of his own action."[11] Thus the infant distinguishes neither between here and there nor between now and then.

Since the concept of causality develops correlatively with those of time and space, it follows that the infant is unable to conceive of causal relationships among externally existing events. Neither, strictly speaking, does it conceive of action as "emanating from a self," since the infant at this stage does not distinguish between self and world.[12] Rather "it is to the dynamism of his own activity that the child attributes all causal efficacy . . . primitive causality may therefore be conceived as a sort of feeling of . . . efficacy linked with acts as such, always with the reservation that . . . one cannot say that he conceives of [the center of these acts] as either external or internal to himself."[13] Precisely because the infant "confuses his self with the universe . . . when the infant sees his limbs move at his own will, he must feel that he is commanding the world . . . and when [he] takes delight in movements situated in the outside world . . . he must feel an immediate bond between these movements and his delight in them."[14] In short, "during the first months of life the child does not dissociate the external world from its own activity. Perceptual images, not yet consolidated into objects or coordinated in a coherent space, seem to him to be governed by his desires and efforts, though these are not attributed to a self which is separate from the universe."[15]

Piaget describes a process of cognitive development through which this "egocentrism without an ego" or "narcissism without a subject"[16] is eventually surpassed in favor of a firm awareness of the distinction between the subjectivity of our desires and the objectivity of the world that "prevents us from believing in the automatic realization of our desires."[17] Psychoanalysis also assumes, of course, that the overcoming of infantile omnipotence and the ability to distinguish between fantasy and reality, subject and object, is a major marker of the distinction between the child and the adult.[18] But unlike cognitive developmental psychology, psychoanalysis insists on the profoundly painful nature of this process and thus on our tendency unconsciously and tenaciously to defend against its outcome. It teaches us, in other words, that we do not easily or happily give up the illusion of "the automatic realization of our desires" that was constitutive of our earliest relationship to reality.

The Grandiose Self

The end of infantile omnipotence and the beginnings of a more mature relationship to reality depend on the mother's "disillusionment" of the very infant she has "illusioned";[19] the frustration of her imperious child is the necessary condition for the development of any sense of separation between them. The distinction between self and world, or here and there, is born in the breach between desire and its satisfaction, and with it the distinction between now and then as well. Thus the development of both spatial and temporal distinctions is inseparable from the deeply difficult "discovery that circumstance is incompletely controllable, and that there exist centers of subjectivity, of desire and will, opposed to or indifferent to one's own"[20]—and from the feelings of *loss* and *rage* that inevitably accompanying that discovery. These feelings of loss and rage are compounded and complicated by the child's fear that his rage against the mother for the humiliations suffered at her hands has irreparably damaged her, as well as by the guilt that follows from that fantastic fear. In short, the loss of the illusion of omnipotence is, as Dinnerstein has felicitously phrased it, "an original and basic human grief."[21]

It is however a grief that too often we refuse to bear. Psychoanalysis teaches us both that we need to mourn the loss of infantile omnipotence and that there are multiple means to defend against it. To anticipate the analysis to come, I will ignore the many different defense mechanisms on which a more nuanced discussion would be obliged to dwell in favor of an exclusive focus on what Heinz Kohut calls the narcissism of the "grandiose self." The grandiose self, as the name implies, defends against the feelings of sorrow and guilt that would otherwise accompany the painful frustrations imposed by the mother by denying his dependence on and love for her and unconsciously experiencing her as an object, entirely under his control, whose only purpose is to reflect back to him his grandiosity. In other words, the (m)other is contemptuously fantasized as unworthy of concern and guilt and omnipotently fantasized as a mere extension of the self on whose constant mirroring the supposedly fiercely "independent" self is actually entirely dependent.

Children who succumb to this narcissistic defense mechanism become chronological adults who, in the words of Otto Kernberg, "present an unusual degree of self-reference in their interactions with other people, a great need to be . . . admired by others, and a curious apparent contradiction between a very inflated concept of themselves and an inordinate need for tribute from others."[22] Their excessive expectations of perfect recognition, however, can never be satisfied, if only because the people with whom they surround themselves are, after all, separate people with their own concerns in spite of their slave status in the psychic economy of the narcissist.[23] Thus the grandiose narcissist is vulnerable to repeated narcissistic injuries, to which he will angrily respond by immediately dropping those who never fail to fail him. But his rage against these dismissed others never gives rise to guilt because their failure to gratify him is experienced as proof that they are, after all, unworthy of his concern.[24]

Feelings of *depletion* are the inevitable result of receiving far less recognition than the narcissist requires. Thus Kernberg informs us that his narcissistic patients "describe a painful and disturbing subjective experience which they frequently refer to as feeling empty." This feeling of emptiness is sometimes accompanied by "chronic restlessness and boredom," sometimes by a "deadening sense of unreality or a blurring of any subjective experience." Thus an emotional deadness belies the narcissist's often frenetic facade. But strictly speaking, narcissists are not depressed: "they are especially deficient in genuine feelings of sadness and mournful longing; their incapacity for experiencing depressive reactions is a basic feature of their personalities."[25] Because narcissists are unable to mourn, they are particularly vulnerable to a variety of addictions—drugs, alcohol, sex, or food—which provide temporary relief from their feelings of emptiness and enable them to "'refuel' the pathological grandiose self and assure its omnipotence and protection against a . . . hostile environment in which gratification and admiration are not forthcoming."[26]

Because the sense of space and time are, as we have seen, born with the loss of infantile omnipotence, the narcissistic defense against this loss per-force entails the denial of spatial and temporal separation. Unconsciously experiencing the other as but extension of the self—treating the other as a "projective entity" rather than "entity in its own right"[27]—the narcissist emotionally denies the very spatial separation between self and world that he rationally recognizes. This denial of spatial difference, moreover, neces-sarily denies temporal difference as well: "because of his serious limitations in grasping the depth and uniqueness of human beings . . . [the narcissist] misses what is new in any relationship . . . and learns from experience that the 'exciting new' is [but] one more edition of the 'disappointing old.'"[28] His assiduous effort to ensure that there is no delay between his demand for and his receipt of recognition—to guarantee a completely continuous, predictable supply of the same social strokes—betrays an inability to toler-ate the inevitable contingencies of a temporally finite life. Thus the narcissist's assault on temporality typically takes the form of an inordinate fear of his own mortality. As Franco Ferrarotti has noted, "the unfolding of time involves the body and its processes of evolution and ultimately of de-composition. Time elects the body as its privileged vehicle, shows itself in its jointings, its heartbeats, its trembling, and its wrinkles."[29] We should not be surprised to learn, then, of the "exaggerated, artificial, and sometimes grotesque pseudo youthfulness of aging narcissistic personalities" and of their particularly deep difficulties in dealing with the ineluctable loss of their youth and decay of their bodies.[30]

Modernity as Grandiosity

My argument is that modernity is the cultural analogue of the grandi-ose self: the modern relationship between humans and (nonhuman) na-ture perfectly parallels the relationship between the narcissist and his exploited (m)others.[31] Just as the narcissist denies his dependence on the other and omnipotently experiences her as a mere extension of his self, so too modernity denies its dependence on nature and symbolizes it as a "disenchanted" object that only exists for the sake of the human subject. Just as the narcissist's denial of dependence on those whom he exploits is belied by his inordinate need for their repeated affirmations, so too modernity's omnipotent illusion of complete independence from and domination over nature masks a desperate, never-ending struggle to win recognition from it: as arch-modernist Marx would have it, "through and because of his production, nature appears as *his* work and his reality ... he contemplates himself in a world that he has created."[32] But the effort to wrest cultural meaning from a thoroughly humanized, subjugated world is bound to be as futile as the effort of the narcissist to stake his sense of self on the esteem of his denigrated others: contemporary claims concerning the "end of nature" notwithstanding, nature continues to assert its independence in the face of human efforts to tame it. Because nature has its own rhythms and requirements it will always fail to reflect back to humans just what they have made of it. Thus if we look only for ourselves in nature we will never really find ourselves. Cultural emptiness—modern meaninglessness—follows as surely from the grandiosity of modernity as individual emptiness follows from the narcissism of the grandiose self. And, just as the depleted grandiose self typically turns to a variety of addictions or compulsive disorders to evade its empty feelings and reinflate its punctured grandiosity, so a modernity that is empty of meaning over-relies on the consumption of *stuff* to prop up its ever-shaky shared sense of self. This desperate dependence on material products whose use-value is merely an alibi for their sign-value[33]—for the successful (e.g., rich, sexy, powerful) identities they signify—is merely the other side of a modern cultural coin whose face is the omnipotent effort to remake the material world in the image of human beings. Compulsive production and compulsive consumption are, in short, the reciprocally related elements of the self-defeating cultural cycle that make up the madness of modernity.

This self-defeating cycle can also be described in temporal terms. Modernity's commitment to the domination of nature—to collapse the space between the human and the nonhuman by symbolizing the latter as a mere extension of the former—can also be grasped as the commitment to "colonize the future."[34] In order to rob the world of its freedom from human control the "dangerously unpredictable elements of the future"[35] must be eliminated; in a culture dedicated to "planning the future . . . the different resolves itself into the already known."[36] Ferrarotti continues: "structural and sociopsychological changes do not take place. There is only transition from the same to the same."[37] Nowotny agrees: "we are about to abolish the *category* of the future and replace it with that *of the extended present.*"[38] Thus a stultifying stasis underlies the superficial dynamism— the melting of all that is solid into air—for which modernity is either celebrated or condemned. As Norman O. Brown argued long ago and Zygmunt Bauman has recently reiterated, a culture dedicated to the defeat of death—for that is what the goal of taming time amounts to—can only live in death's shadow.[39]

The elimination of the future in favor of an extended present is fostered by technologies that "have successfully reduced the distance that is needed to accommodate their own products."[40] The development of these technologies, in turn, has been driven by the determination to accelerate the cycle of compulsive production and compulsive consumption. Although the acceleration of this cycle can be viewed (as David Harvey has viewed it) as nothing other than the predictable consequence of the commitment of capitalists to maximize profits by shortening the "turnover time of capital,"[41] the progressive expansion of production and consumption that is both cause and consequence of shorter turnover time, I have argued, is itself fueled by the omnipotent fantasies of a grandiose modernity. Thus the much-vaunted time-space compression of (capitalist) modernity can be understood as the temporal consequence of its cultural omnipotence. So too therefore can the "cult of speed as a good in itself"[42] with which time-space compression is inextricably intertwined. Speed is, in the words of Paul Virilio, "the hope of the West" because it feeds the illusion that our wish is the world's command.

But speed kills. The early twentieth-century dream of the Futurists that "time and space died yesterday [and] we already live in the absolute, because we have created eternal, omnipresent speed"[43] has become our early twenty-first-century nightmare. A relentlessly accelerating pace of life, "a generalized . . . anxiety-producing and frantic . . . hurry,"[44] leaves us increasingly stressed and, arguably, increasingly vulnerable to diseases that are (at least in part) the consequence of our increasingly stress-compromised immune systems. The faster we do things, moreover, the *less* time we seem to have: "not enough time to do all the things I have to do" is perhaps our most commonly shared modern (or postmodern) lament. Thus are we defeated by the very time we are in such a hurry to defeat.

The Omnipotence of Cyberspace

My claim in this concluding section is that computer-mediated communication is the contemporary culmination of the time-space compression endemic to modernity. Anyone who is connected to the Net can communicate—or at least exchange information—virtually instantaneously with anyone else who is connected to it no matter what the physical distance between them. Thus "space is collapsed on the Internet because the physical location of [computers] is irrelevant to our connection to them."[45] This collapse of space is experienced as the sense of (virtual) co-presence we misleadingly call cyber*space*. Similarly, the "instant connection [the Net] provide[s] to distant realms and buried resources"[46] persuades us that we have transcended time in favor of the "extended present" envisioned by Nowotny. In short, on the Net everyone is *here* and it is always *now*.

Thus CMC creates an experience of spacelessness and timelessness that replicates the condition of infancy that both psychoanalysis and cognitive developmental psychology have described (or inferred). We should not be surprised to discover, then, that CMC also encourages the illusions of omnipotence that arise from that condition and to which, we have seen, adults are likely to succumb in their defense against its loss. More specifically, I argue that CMC facilitates the three fundamental fantasies of the narcissism of the grandiose self: the fantasy of total control, the fantasy of perfect recognition, and the fantasy of immortality.

Total Control

Once the world has been transformed into information it can be retrieved at will. The digitalized world is a world that is "available on call":[47] as CMC critics Arthur Kroker and Michael Weinstein have lamented, "here is the world of information completely at the beck and call of the possessive individual . . . here everyone is a god who, if they are not omniscient all at once, can at least entertain whatever information they wish to have at any time they wish to have it."[48] Not surprisingly, Bill Gates extols exactly what Kroker and Weinstein deplore. In 1987, Gates wrote that "in twenty years . . . the dream of having the world data base at your fingertips will have become a reality." That reality, moreover, is increasingly something that we will be able to *create*: "you'll even be able to call up a video show and place yourself in it."[49] Virtual reality prophet Howard Rheingold, much less of a technological huckster than Gates, warns us that "*we have to de-*

cide fairly soon what it is we humans ought to become, because we are on the brink of having the power of creating any experience we desire."[50] For Simon Cooper, Rheingold's virtual reality is merely a fantasy that "articulates the desire for mastery through which the subject is the absolute point of reference for, and creator of, its own experiences."[51] Never one to confuse fantasy and reality, Gates effusively translates: "It may be, you never know, that the universe exists only for me! If it were true, I have to admit I would enjoy that!"[52]

Thus both its critics and its celebrants agree that CMC seduces us because "we are enamored of the possibility of controlling all human knowledge."[53] Ethnographers of the Internet confirm that this omnipotent fantasy in fact informs the feelings of the heavy users they studied. All but one of Annette Markham's ten subjects acknowledged that the opportunity to exercise a form of control that was otherwise lacking in their life was *the* principal source of their attraction to online communication: "all the participants see control as a considerable benefit of, if not the very reason for, being online."[54] Most of them spend long hours in MUDs (multi-user domains)—virtual worlds or fantasy spaces that they may have helped to construct and over which they consequently have much more control than the offline world: "MUD players are MUD authors, the creators as well as consumers of media content."[55] Participants in these online worlds enact identities that may or may not correspond to their actual, offline identities. Because these identities are exclusively text-based—because all of the embodied dimensions of communication that normally render it ambiguous and open to interpretation are screened out—MUDers are able to exert much more control over the way that they present themselves to others than they can offline.[56] Markham's ethnography reveals that this possibility of complete control over self-presentation is one of the great seductions of CMC. Thus two of her informants claim that they "are more confident online" because they can "edit [their] thoughts before [they] let them loose" and "correct everything [they] say and therefore are."[57] The implicit message is that by controlling the self they can control the other. This message is made explicit by another of Markham's subjects: "I can dominate and control others' minds through my words." Thus for many heavy users the "sense of self becomes defined in terms of those things over which one can exert perfect control."[58]

There is reason to believe that even less-frequent users fall prey to illusions of omnipotence. How else can we make sense of the high-speed Internet ad on the next page, which shows a woman exploding in rage—*screaming like a baby*—because her Internet connection is too slow? What is it that engenders this rage if not the temporary loss of omnipotence, the painful reminder of the resistance of the world to the wishes of someone who *wants everything now*? How many of us have not felt at least something of this impotent rage in response to the sluggishness of our server or—even worse—the crash of our computer? How many of us cannot recognize in our own reactions the truth of John Carroll's claim that

> there is a singular feeling of impotence when the computer will not respond, when the user has made an error he cannot correct, or he fails to understand a function that has suddenly become indispensable, or the program has developed a flaw, or—horror of horrors—has caught a virus. . . . It is as if the power has been switched off, a parallel to the Homeric description

of the dying warrior being unstrung at the knees. A panic sets in, often leading to a stupid flailing around hitting keys or a tantrum searching for non-
existent files. It is as if an intimacy has without any warning been severed
and the unsuspecting lover is left to freeze.[59]

What better evidence, in short, that computer-mediated communication enables "imperial . . . fantasies of conquest and control"[60] than by the
severe separation anxiety that accompanies its disruption?

Perfect Recognition

Internet ethnographies reveal that heavy users crave recognition from the
very world they wish to control. Just as the performances of the grandiose narcissist are designed to extract maximum emotional supplies from
his admiring audience, so the heavy user diligently designs his self-
presentation so that others will reflect back to him exactly what he wants
them to see. "By removing the number of senses involved in our direct
relationship with others and the dimensions of responsibility and account-
ability that this might entail, we are able to relate to worlds of representation which are high in predictability for the individual user."[61] Thus the
medium enables the user to minimize the risks of nonrecognition. No
wonder that Markham's subjects report that they feel better understood
and more appreciated online than off. Or that some of them express a
preference for VR—virtual reality—over what they refer to as "RL"—real
life—for precisely that reason, and confess that they find it difficult to be
away even briefly from their computers. Heavy users, in short, are people
who are addicted to communication with others who exist to confirm their
existence. And so one of Markham's subjects tells her that his chat-room
partners only become real to him "when they reach out to me" and "when
I can see a part of myself in them."[62] When he can't—when they stub-
bornly insist on their separate selves—they can always be dropped. As
Borgmann has argued, "those who become present via a communication
link have a diminished presence, since we can always make them vanish if
their presence becomes burdensome."[63]

When their presence does become "burdensome," heavy users can find
other online ways to salve their narcissistic wounds. They can always leave
their MUDs and chat rooms, click on a search engine, and access the world
database that awaits their call. They can download vast quantities of the
information whose consumption is supposed to empower them. Until, that

is, they are overwhelmed by it. Then they can go shopping—without ever
having to log off their computer.

Immortality

I have already referred to the peculiarly *disembodied* character of
computer-mediated communication, the fact that "the computer network
simply brackets the physical presence of the participants, by either omit-
ting or simulating corporeal immediacy."[64] Relationships are formed, developed, and maintained among people who have no direct, reliable way
of knowing how their virtual interlocutors look, move, feel, or smell—
in short, among those who cannot sense the physical presence of the
other. In fact the disappearance of the body is clearly one of the major
sources of the seductiveness of cyberspace. Turkell's and Markham's ethnographies reveal that many heavy users experience their body as a
burden that they gladly leave behind when they enter the online world.
Thus Markham reports, for example "a two hour conversation with a
person [whom she calls Sherie] who said she would rather live life
through language because she could be herself through words better than
she could be herself through her body."[65] Sherie's description of the "face-
to-face" meetings she disdains as mere "flesh meets" eerily recalls the
characters in William Gibson's cyberpunk novel *Neuromancer*, for whom
"the body was [mere] meat" and who were desperate to escape "the
prison of [the] flesh."[66]
   Precisely for this reason cyberspace has been described as "Platonism
as a working product,"[67] and compared to the Christian conception of
heaven: "as with heaven, cyberspace is a place where we are promised
the joys of freedom, power, connection, and even love—a realm where
the failings of the body will supposedly melt away [and] the soul will
be free to express itself fully."[68] But for Plato bodily attraction is a necessary stage in the development of an Eros that culminates in the attraction of the mind; and in Christianity (at least pre-Reformation), the
incarnation of God in Christ is understood to symbolize God's presence
within *every* human body (and, arguably, within the material world as a
whole). Thus premodern conceptions of disembodiment do not in fact
adequately capture the hostility to the body to which cyberspace is host.
Rather it is the distinctively modern, Cartesian conception of the body
as inessential—indeed an impediment—to the mind of which the grandiose, virtual fantasies of radical disembodiment are a contemporary
counterpart.

Thus it seems to me that virtual reality utopians like Jaron Lanier are mistaken when they claim that the desire of cybernauts to be disburdened of the body is "universally human" . . . a "natural result of the human condition, and the frustrations associated with that."[69] The argument of this chapter has been that we should rather think of it as a manic mistrust of mortality that is specific to modernity. The message of modernity is that if we rise above our bodies we will not have to worry that they will decay. The war against the flesh, Norman O. Brown has taught us, is the war against death, and nowhere has this war been waged as relentlessly as in the modern West. But the relentless modern war against death, Brown warns us, cannot but mortify our life. It is in this sense that what Kroker and Weinstein call the "will to virtuality" can be understood as the most recent form of the death drive of the West.[70]

10 Toward Green Recovery

Introduction

In Chapter 9, I argued that compulsive production and compulsive consumption are two seamy sides of the same modern psycho-cultural coin. The fantastic declaration of independence from nature that fuels modern production engenders an emotional emptiness for which an equally fantastic overdependence on objects of consumption is the remedy that only renews the dis-ease. Otherwise put, the repressed (or rather split-off) need for nature resurfaces in the form of a desperate search for *stuff* that both defends us against, and (like all defenses) reproduces, the depression that results from the repression of that natural need. Thus is an omnipotent modernity compelled to repeat the damage it does to both the planet and its people.

In the next section of this concluding chapter I reformulate the diagnosis of this damage in specifically Kleinian terms in order to clarify how it might be repaired. I argue that modern underdependence on nature and overdependence on objects can be usefully understood as cultural defenses against depressive anxiety and guilt, and thus that a working-through of—that is, a reparative response to—that anxiety and guilt is the key to a more mature, depressively integrated relationship to our world and our products. This argument makes it possible for me in the third section of the chapter to penetrate the depth-psychological affinity between contemporary deep ecological challenges to compulsive production and contemporary twelve-

step struggles to recover from compulsive consumption, and thus to identify both as *reparative* responses to the damage that modern omnipotence
does both to nature and the self. Just as deep ecology decries an anthropo-
centric or arrogantly humanistic commitment to control nature in the name
of a biocentric relationship with a nature that is understood to have value
independent of the human uses to which it can be put, so recovery programs
demand that the addict relinquish his illusory effort to control his feelings
with whatever happens to be his drug of choice in favor of an explicitly acknowledged dependence on a "higher power," however he might understand
it. Thus both deep ecology and twelve-step recovery contest omnipotence
and affirm the necessarily *limited* nature of human power in the world. And,
just as deep ecology's insistence on the independent value of (nonhuman)
nature engenders a commitment to repair whatever damage is done to nature in the course of our inevitable alterations of it, so too the twelve-step
"surrender" to a higher power and concomitant renunciation of (what was
originally called) "alcoholic grandiosity" is the prerequisite to a process in
which the addict makes reparations to all those—including himself—whom
his hubris has harmed. In short, for both deep ecology and recovery it is
precisely the awareness of the limits to human power that enables its responsible exercise.

In the fourth and final section of this chapter I argue that there is not
only a depth-psychological, but also an organic connection between deep
ecology and recovery: the realization of the goals of each ultimately depends on the realization of the goals of the other. Thus there is both an
emotional and a strategic link between these two movements that supports the possibility of a unification of, or at least an alliance between them.
But at this point in time it is probably the case that most of the members
of the two movements are entirely unaware of the close connections between them. The absence of this awareness is, of course, a major roadblock to the rapprochement between recovery and deep ecology. The
political point of this chapter, then, is to promote that awareness and thus
help remove this roadblock. Green recovery is our goal.

Manic-Depressive Modernity

My Kleinian psychoanalysis of modernity starts from the assumption
that (nonhuman) nature is always a source of both gratification and frustration and that "she" is therefore always unconsciously experienced as
both a good and a bad mother.[1] On the one hand, nature is loved for the

goodness she grants. Just as the infant's life depends entirely on the mother who feeds it, so too nature is the ultimate ground of all the nourishment we need. Just as the mother is a predictably comfortable presence with whom the infant can merge, so too nature is the source of our sense that we are part of something larger and more stable than ourselves. And nature not only "holds" us but "mirrors" us as well: by watching the way it reacts to the way in which we work it, we gain a sense of our competence that parallels the emerging agency of the child whose autonomous efforts are recognized by his or her mother.[2] In all these ways—and more—nature nurtures us and is therefore loved by us.

But nature is also hated for harming us. Often it is a dreaded threat to the very human survival of which it is the source. Just as the child disdains his discovery that his mother has a separate, independent existence, so we decry the seemingly willful unpredictability of nature—its storms, its floods, its droughts—as an unpalatable indifference to, or even assault upon, our welfare. And even if we are lucky enough to evade these attacks we cannot avoid the fact that the very nature that secures our existence also appears to begrudge it. If it is true that nature is the ultimate source of our survival, it is also true that nature is never so bountiful as to prevent us from having to *work* in order to survive. Labor, Hegel tells us, "is desire restrained and checked, evanescence delayed and postponed."[3] Because nature makes us work, then, it obliges us to postpone gratification. In this sense even the most giving nature is a source of frustration and of the aggression to which frustration inevitably gives rise. Like the paranoid-schizoid child, moreover, we tend to project that aggression onto nature, which then becomes an even more monstrous mother than it would otherwise be. Thus the nature we love is also the nature we hate.

Of course we harm nature whether we want to or not. When humans work, nature winces. This suffering would be a source of considerable anxiety and guilt even if human work were not infused with the aggression that inevitably issues from the frustration that it imposes. But because work *is* infused with aggression, our anxiety and guilt are compounded by the unconscious fact that the harm we do is harm that we *wish* to do. No wonder that we are so disturbed by that natural damage.

A culturally reparative response to that damage, I want to argue, is every bit as much the mark of cultural development as the reparative response of the child to his mother is a sign of his development as an individual. Just as the child who successfully negotiates the depressive position painfully comes to the conclusion that his mother is neither all-good nor all-bad, but rather "good-enough" and therefore worthy of care, so culturally depressive integration would entail the symbolization of a nature that is good-enough to merit our ministrations.[4] Moreover, just as the depressively integrated child is able to relate to the (m)other not as a "projective entity" but rather as an "entity in [her] own right" with whom it is possible to establish a nonnarcissistic "object relation," so a depressively integrated culture would be able to achieve a "state of being in relation to [nonhuman nature] as something outside and separate."[5] And this experience of the nonhuman world as something separate with which we are nevertheless connected, in turn, is as essential for healthy cultural development as the child's "transitional" relationship to the mother is necessary for his individual development: "we are human only in contact, and conviviality, with what is not human."[6]

But this experience does not come easily. In fact it presupposes a work of cultural mourning that parallels the mourning of the child who is en route to depressive integration. Just as that child must grieve the loss of the all-good fantasy mother for whom she pines as well as surrender to her sorrow for having harmed (the one she now recognizes as) the real mother, so the culture must relinquish its fantasy of a perfectly nurturing nature as well as confront its sadness and guilt for having harmed the real, imperfect one. To abandon cultural omnipotence is to accept the inevitable recalcitrance of the world and thus to recognize that we must work on it—must alter it—in order to get what we want from it. Since there is no way to alter nature without doing some kind of damage to it, overcoming omnipotence *perforce* requires a confrontation with the anxiety and guilt that accompanies that damage. As Walter Truett Anderson has observed,

> there is guilt involved . . . in accepting the truth that we are all products of countless . . . acts of violence to the planet and its life. . . . The psychological conflict involved in human intervention in nature is at least as stressful as . . . the one. . . . the psychoanalysts deal with, between the instinctual and the symbolic sides of the human psyche.[7]

Precisely because this conflict is so stressful the temptation to evade it is so strong.[8] The difficult work of cultural mourning is threatened by mechanisms of defense that parallel those of the child whose depressive anxiety and guilt are simply too great to grieve. Like that child, modernity is in fact unable to carry out the difficult work of depressive integration. Rather, it defends us against the anxiety and guilt that would accompany an awareness that we hate the (mother)nature that we love by manically denying our need for nature and transforming it into the denigrated object of our omnipotent control. This fantastic transformation of nature into an all-bad, dangerous mother sets the psychological stage for its material transformation into a *real* threat to our existence. Having projected its own aggression into nature, modernity aggressively defends against this (its own) aggression by treating nature as an enemy that must be conquered, even destroyed. And the destruction of nature, in turn, leaves us terrified that "everything we breathe, eat, and drink is going to kill us," which only adds more fuel to our omnipotent fantasy "to be rid of it."[9]

Thus the progressive "abolition of nature" on which "reflexive modernists" insist, and that some postmodernists celebrate,[10] makes it increasingly difficult for us to "imagine that we are part of something larger than ourselves." McKibben continues: "We have deprived nature of its independence, and that is fatal to its meaning. Nature's independence *is* its meaning; without it there is nothing but us."[11] And if, to repeat Abram's claim, "we are human in only contact and conviviality with what is *not* human," then "when there is nothing but us" it is difficult indeed to feel fully human. If, in other words, the meaning of human life can only be established in relation to the meaning of nature, then to deprive nature of meaning deprives our lives of meaning as well. Thus the price of modernity's manic defense against natural depressive anxiety and guilt is the chronic feeling of meaninglessness that prevails in its midst. As Kernberg argues, "in narcissistic personalities, where the normal relations between an integrated self and integrated internal objects are replaced by a pathological grandiose self and a deterioration of internal objects, the experience of emptiness is most intense and almost constant."[12] What goes for a narcissistic personality goes for a narcissistic culture as well: the failure to introject a good-enough world precludes the formation of a good-enough self. Hence the modern "epoch of nihilism" of which Nietzsche despaired but to which his celebration of the "will to power" arguably contributed.[13]

Yet nihilism does not negate, but rather only intensifies, the need for the good mother in the form of an intense "hunger for objects" that, according to Melanie Klein, is "so characteristic of mania."[14] The message of consumerism, as John Carroll has argued, is "if you feel bad, eat!"— although what the consumer wants, above all, "is to be eaten up, absorbed by a larger universe than that of her lonely self."[15] In Kleinian terms, when it is unable to introject a good-enough world, the empty self defends itself against depletion through an omnipotent merger with objects that represent the "good mother" murdered by manic denial. Thus the split between the good and bad (mother) nature is transformed into the split between all-bad nature and all-good objects. The desperate drive for (re)union with the perfect mother explains why people will "shop till they drop" and accounts as well for the elation—the "commodity euphoria"[16]—they experience when that union is consummated. If compulsive consumers were to speak to their products, here is what they would say: "You are perfect, but I am part of you."[17]

But of course this perfection is not meant to last. Consumers are like lovers who disdainfully drop their overidealized partners as soon as they discover their inevitable imperfections; as soon as one product goes out of style it is quickly rejected and replaced by another. Thus the temporary elation at re-finding the perfect mother inevitably gives way to the depletion that results from losing her over and over again. Compulsive consumption, in other words, is a recipe for perpetual *dis*satisfaction, and it therefore functions to reproduce the very emotional emptiness against which it is supposed to defend. Yet the compulsive consumer knows no other way to fill himself up. If and when he gets sick of this self-defeating cycle, he will omnipotently declare his independence from the very objects he continues to crave. But this impossible struggle to defeat the object only serves to defeat the self: his repeated failures to give up the food, clothes, cars, and other objects on which he overly depends eventually make him face the humiliating fact that the (apparent) power of the object is far greater than his own. Thus does the guilt that results from damage done to nature culminate in shame that does damage to the self.

Repairing Modernity

Deep Ecology

The term "deep ecology" was coined in 1973 by the Norwegian philosopher Arne Naess in order to distinguish forms of environmentalism that were shallow in their failure to challenge anthropocentrism from the radical critique of anthropocentrism that he endorsed.[18] Over the course of the past three decades deep ecology has moved, in the words of one of its supporters, "from a proposal in a philosophical journal ... to a position that is now a bench mark in defining varieties of environmental philosophies."[19] It is an environmental philosophy, moreover, that can justly claim widespread political influence: "It has provided inspiration for resistance against nuclear weapons, nuclear power, military bases, new dams, and logging operations, and is closely related to activist groups such as Greenpeace, Earth First, Friends of the Earth, and Green political parties."[20] One of its leading critics, Tim Luke, writing in 1997 agrees: "Deep ecology . . . has inspired many new social movements' defense of the quality of their everyday life from the state and transnational commerce during the past decade and a half."[21] But there is something misleading in Luke's formulation: it is the quality not just of human but of *all* life that deep ecology defends. It is motivated, I will argue, by a commitment to repair the damage that we have done—and will inevitably continue to do—to the planet as a whole. If the influence of deep ecology on the new social movements is as great as Luke contends, then it is fair to conclude that this reparative sensibility is also widely shared among their many participants.

In the essay in which he introduced the term, Naess contests anthropocentrism—the restriction to humans of *the equal right to live and blossom*—in the name of the deep *dependence* of humans on nonhuman nature as well as their equally profound *ignorance* of the way in which they affect it. Against the denial of our dependence on (non)human nature he insists on what he calls an "intrinsic relation" between our being and all the other beings with whom we share the planet. He defines an "intrinsic relation" as one in which "the relation belongs to the definitions or basic constitutions of *A* and *B*, so that without the relation, *A* and *B* are no longer the same things." In short, the human being is only what it is by virtue of the total relational field—the biosphere—in which he or she participates. If the field does not "blossom," then neither will the human being. Thus "the attempt to ignore our dependence and to establish a master–slave role [in our relationship to nature] has contributed to the alienation of man from himself."[22]

The relational field on which we depend, moreover, is infinitely *complex*: "Organisms, ways of life, and interactions in the biosphere in general, exhibit complexity of such an astoundingly high level as to color the outlook of ecologists." More specifically, such complexity "makes for a keen, steady perception of the profound *human ignorance* of biospherical relationships and therefore of the effects of disturbances." Thinking that we can control these relationships is a recipe for disaster, both natural and human. What is needed, instead and "most importantly," is "more sensitivity towards . . . our state of ignorance." *Knowing that we do not know* is the sine qua non of "ecologically responsible policies."[23] "The notion of our ignorance about consequences," Naess insists, "implies a norm about limitation and careful control of our intervention."[24] Thus deep ecology is dedicated to "cultivating the virtues of modesty and humility."[25]

Naess contests modernity's denial of dependence on, and pretension to omnipotent control over, nature in the name of an image of nature that is by no means the idealization that some of his critics contend. In Chapter 2 we saw Tim Luke argue that the deep ecological conception of nature "appears to be a projection of an idealized humanity onto the natural world."[26] Yet Naess repeatedly points out that nonhuman nature has many features that are, from a human point of view, anything but ideal. "The process of identification," he tells us in *Ecology, Community, and Lifestyle,* "leads us to see much cruelty in nature. . . . Nature is not brutal, but from a human point of view, we do see brutality—as we see yellow in the sun; as we see these fantastically blue mountains outside this window." As an example of such cruelty or brutality he offers the example of a "desperately hungry wolf attacking an elk, wounding it mortally but . . . incapable of killing it," and tells us that it is "impossible not to identify with and somehow feel the pains of both" the elk that dies "after protracted, severe pains" and the wolf who "dies slowly of hunger." This sorrow, in turn, inevitably triggers the "search for means to interfere with natural processes on behalf of any being in a state of panic and desperation, protracted pain, severe suppression, or abject slavery. But this attitude implies that we deplore much that actually goes on in nature [and] that seems essential to life on Earth." Thus he concludes that the natural "process of identification" between humans and the other suffering beings on whom they depend precludes "any unconditional *Verherrlichung* [glorification] of life, and therefore of nature in general."[27]

Far from replacing the demonization with the idealization of nature, then, Naess insists that nature is neither all-good nor all-bad: it is, in that sense, "beyond good and evil." As such, nature is the inevitable source of *both* our joy and our sorrow. Or at least it is for people who are strong enough to feel both of these emotions: "With maturity, human beings will experience joy when other life forms experience joy and sorrow when other life forms experience sorrow."[28] Thus for Naess mourning is as central as celebration to a mature relationship with nature. To both mourn and celebrate with nature, moreover, is to *accept* it as a site of both great pleasure and great pain: "There is a kind of deep yes to nature which is central to my philosophy . . . there is a deep unconditionality, but at the same time a kind of regret, sorrow, or displeasure."[29] Without doing any violence to Naess's position we can translate it into the following specifically Kleinian terms: nature is neither all-good nor all-bad and therefore eminently worthy of care. The ecological analogue of depressive integration is the unconditional "yes" to which Naess yields.

It is precisely this simultaneously emotional and cognitive position, I would suggest, that supports the first and most controversial plank in the well-known platform of deep ecology proposed by Naess and his colleague George Sessions in 1984: "The well-being and flourishing of human and nonhuman Life on Earth have value in themselves (synonyms: intrinsic value, inherent value). These values are independent of the usefulness of the nonhuman world for human purposes."[30] The publication of the deep-ecological platform has given rise to a by-now voluminous literature purporting either to prove or disprove (what has been taken to be) this philosophical proposition.[31] This intellectual debate is, to my mind, largely beside the point. No one who has not reached the ecological equivalent of the depressive position will be persuaded by philosophical arguments in favor of the anti-anthropocentric "obligation" to respect and relate to nonhuman nature as an end in itself, and no one who *has* reached that position will be convinced by abstract, pro-anthropocentric arguments purporting to demonstrate that there is in fact no such obligation. The point is that one either feels or does not feel the need to respond to nature with the kind of unconditional "yes" with which Naess and other deep ecologists respond.[32] This, I think, is what Naess has in mind when he tells us that "we need not say today man's relation to the nonhuman world is *immoral.* It is enough to say that it lacks generosity, fortitude, and love."[33]

"Generosity" and "love" are exactly what are lacking in some of the more caustic critics of deep ecology. Their vitriolic, even rabid rejection of deep ecology is a sure sign that its anti-anthropocentrism is at least as threatening emotionally as it is intellectually. As Andrew McLaughlin notes, over the past two decades deep ecology has been accused of being "self-righteous," "arrogant," "antirational," "mystical," "rubbish," and "an ideological toxic dump."[34] Walter Truett Anderson condemns it as a "flight into irresponsible passivity" that

> generates a smug pseudo innocence, in which people displace onto others all responsibility for intervention while striving to convey the impression that they, personally, have no more impact upon the world than a butterfly and are profoundly in tune with nature. [This flight] can be found among environmentalists . . . who yearn to recapture the ecological wisdom of primitive societies and search for non-anthropocentric modes of relationship to nature. The aspiring "deep ecology" movement is a good example of this, and of the sort of cant it generates.[35]

That Anderson's "deep ecology" is a caricature becomes clear when we let deep ecology speak for itself. Just two pages after the list of the "basic principles" (platform) of deep ecology published in Devall and Sessions's *Deep Ecology*, Naess and Sessions emphasize, in their "Comments on the Basic Principles," that "the slogan of 'noninterference' does not imply that humans should not modify some ecosystems as do other species. Humans have modified the earth and will probably continue to do so. At issue is the nature and extent of such interference."[36] And in Naess's 1973 article inaugurating deep ecology he made it clear that "modifying" nature necessarily includes "some killing, exploitation, and suppression" of the nonhuman beings who inhabit it.[37] The inevitability of harm to nonhuman beings is in fact *already* implicit in the third plank of the deep-ecological platform: "Humans have no right to reduce [the] richness and diversity of [nonhuman life forms] except to satisfy *vital* needs."[38] It follows from this principle that deep ecology *does* allow for the destructive interference with nonhuman life when that interference really *is* essential to the satisfaction of those needs. Thus deep ecology can justifiably plead innocent to Anderson's charge of "pseudo-innocence."

Of course it follows from Naess's principle of "identification" that even the necessary harm that humans impose on nonhuman nature would be a source of great regret.[39] If mature human beings suffer from the suffering of the beings with whom they identify, then any harm done to those beings in the course of the satisfaction of vital human needs will inevitably be a source of human (as well as nonhuman) pain. Thus mature human beings will be motivated either to find alternative, nondestructive ways to satisfy their vital needs, or to reevaluate those needs if in fact benign ways of satisfying them cannot be found. To put this another way, deep ecology is dedicated to a dialogue in which individuals attempt to reconcile their needs with what they take to be the needs of nature. It encourages not "irresponsible passivity" but rather an active search for technologies that, in Naess's words, "satisfy maximally both the requirements of reduced interference with nature and satisfaction of human vital needs." Naess is aware that conflicts between these two goals are inevitable and that the best we can hope for is a kind of "equilibrium" between them.[40] But he also insists that the onus is on us to justify any "disequilibrium" that favors our needs over the needs of nature.[41]

The current disequilibrium between them is exactly what the fifth plank in the platform of deep ecology decries: "present interference with the nonhuman world is excessive and . . . rapidly worsening." It is followed, therefore, by a sixth plank that calls for policies that are designed to repair and reverse the terrible damage that has already been done, policies that "affect basic economic, technological, and ideological structures." The seventh plank makes explicit the kind of ideological change that Naess and Sessions have in mind: "The ideological change is mainly that of appreciating *life quality* (dwelling in situations of inherent value) rather than adhering to an increasingly higher standard of living. There will be a profound awareness of the difference between big and great."[42] Here Naess and Sessions show that they understand that a qualitatively different relationship with nature implies a qualitatively different relationship with our products. This gesture in the direction of a critique of consumerism is repeated in Naess's *Ecology, Community, and Lifestyle* when he emphasizes that "the [deep ecology] movement encourages the reduction of individual total consumption, and will through information, increased awareness, and mutual influence attempt to free the individual from the consumer pressures which make it very difficult for politicians to support better policies and a healthier society."[43] But "information, increased awareness, and mutual influence" are no match for the contemporary *compulsion* to consume. Neither Naess nor (to my knowledge) any other deep ecologist "gets" that overconsumption is a psychological and not just an ideological problem, and that the only way to stop repeating this problem is to work it through. Working it through, we shall see, is precisely what happens in twelve-step recovery programs.

Recovery

The extraordinary proliferation of self-help or mutual aid groups during the last quarter of the twentieth century is surely one of the most significant psycho-social developments of our time. According to the most comprehensive study of support groups in America, by 1994 "between 8 and 10 million people" or at least 5 percent of the adult population participated in at least 500,000 self-help groups in which they "share[d] their problems" and "receive[d] emotional support." In 1994 almost one-third of the members of these self-help groups, or between two and a half to three million people, belonged to twelve-step recovery programs,[44] or as many people as were then receiving help from professional psychotherapists.[45] Since then twelve-step membership has increased exponentially: a November 2003 report claims that "an estimated 15 million [!] Americans are currently involved in some form of recovery, making 12-steppers more numerous than Episcopalians, Jews, and Muslims combined."[46]

The largest twelve-step program is, of course, Alcoholics Anonymous, which currently claims an American membership of approximately 1 million. At one time or another, almost 10 percent of the U.S. population has attended an AA meeting.[47] But AA is only the prototype for (what were estimated in the early 1990s to be) between 120 and 260 different national recovery programs that have adopted (and in some cases adapted) its original twelve-step philosophy.[48] Thus large numbers of Americans who are addicted to a variety of different substances or activities, including alcohol, narcotics, food, sex, shopping, gambling, and codependency, increasingly seek support for their sobriety within these programs. Many of them regularly attend the meetings of two or more of these different groups. Many patronize recovery bookstores and read the recovery literature they find there or even in national chain bookstores. Monthly recovery newspapers like *Recovering* or *Sober Times* boast ever-larger circulations. In short, it is no exaggeration to claim, with Robin Room, that the original twelve-step philosophy of Alcoholics Anonymous has expanded into a "generalized twelve-step consciousness" that is shared by millions of Americans who "think of themselves as members of a . . . recovery movement."[49] In what follows I focus on the many members of this movement for whom compulsive *consumption*—of alcohol, drugs, food, clothes, or whatever—is the problem for which they seek a twelve-step solution.

The founding texts of the twelve-step movement, the so-called *Big Book* and the *Twelve Steps and Twelve Traditions*, explicitly identify *grandiosity* as the heart of the addict's problem and *humility* as the only road to his recovery.[50] Grandiosity, sometimes called "playing God,"[51] refers both to the addict's illusory effort completely to control his emotions with his "drug" of choice and to his equally sisyphean struggle to control his use of the very drug on which he (over)relies to control his emotions. Both efforts reveal that "the alcoholic [and the addict more generally] is an extreme example," the *Big Book* declares, "of self-will run riot."[52] On the one hand, the addict finds a quick fix for his anxious, empty feelings in the form of a substance that enables him to feel "connected to and participating in the world rather than in conflict with it."[53] AA cofounder Bill Wilson's description of his alcoholic high comes as close as any other to capturing in words this magical feeling of merger with the world:

> He could feel his body relaxing, a stiffness going out of his shoulders as he sensed the warm glow seeping through him into all the distant, forgotten corners of his being. . . . It was a miracle . . . a miracle that was affecting him mentally, physically, and . . . spiritually too. . . . [Nothing] ran against the overwhelming joy he was feeling. His world was all around him, young and fresh and loving, and . . . he moved easily, gracefully, as though . . . all his life he had been living in chains. Now he was free.[54]

Of course the price of this feeling of freedom is an increasing and eventually complete dependence on whatever he relies on to induce it. The irony of the addict's effort to exercise absolute control over both his emotions and the world to which they respond is that he becomes a complete slave to the substance that is its substitute.[55] And, since this slavery is as much a wound to his narcissistic pride as were the feelings of fragmentation that led him to embrace it, the denial of his dependence on the substance to which he is, in fact addicted, is his only way to restore his pride. Thus begins a "battle with the bottle"—or with whatever he is addicted to—that he can never win. "Trying to use will power," an AA leaflet warns, "is like trying to lift yourself by your bootstraps."[56] Repeated efforts to prove that he can control his drinking, drugging, eating, shopping, and so on, inevitably culminate in failures—binges—that only compound the very narcissistic injury against which he omnipotently attempts to defend.[57] Ashamed of his weakness, eventually he will drink, drug, overeat, or overspend in order to feel better, which will only make him feel more ashamed. And so on. This self-destructive cycle will continue until the addict either dies or hits bottom. If he hits bottom, he realizes that he cannot in fact control the drug he uses to control his emotions. He realizes, in other words, that his life is out of control and that he needs help.

If the addict seeks help, eventually she is likely to encounter a twelve-step program. Here she will learn that "the attainment of humility is the foundation principle of each of AA's twelve steps."[58] The first of the twelve steps affirms both her dependence on the drug she had earlier denied and her consequent *lack* of control over her life: "We admitted we were powerless over [drug of choice]—that our lives had become unmanageable." With this admission the addict begins to renounce the grandiosity that, as we have seen, all twelve-step programs locate at the heart of her addiction. She admits, in effect, that she is not God. But this admission—humbling as it may be—that her own power cannot defeat her addiction is but a prelude to her affirmation in steps two and three that faith in, and reliance on, "a Power greater than ourselves" is the only route to her sobriety.[59] Steps two and three are an even greater insult to the omnipotence of the addict than step one: it is one thing for an individual to acknowledge that she lacks the power to conquer her problem, but quite another to admit that something or someone else *has* the power she lacks.

Yet this admission, according to twelve-step thinking, is essential to her recovery. Without the first step the addict would still be "in denial" of her despair. But without steps two and three there would be no available exit from it. Having reluctantly come to the conclusion that *she* really is powerless over her addiction, the only way in which she can "keep hope alive" is to come to accept that some *other* power will help her overcome it. Given the twelve-step diagnosis of the problem, moreover, it makes sense to describe this "other" power as a "Power greater than ourselves," a "higher power" or "God as we under[stand] him."[60] If, as AA claims, addiction is a self-destructive symptom of a "soul-sickness"[61]—of "personal enslavement to the false ideals of a materialistic society"[62]—then only some sort of spirituality can save the addict's soul from that sickness.

This spirituality is defined as expansively as possible: the appeal to God *"as we understand him"* in the third step is intended to make room for people who are not religious in any traditional sense of that word. Because virtually anything, including the recovery group itself, can serve as the addict's "higher power," agnostics and even atheists can "work" the steps that are supposed to lead to their sobriety. Nonbelievers in the ordinary sense of that term can complete steps two and three by coming to the conviction that the power of the group, which after all typically includes many members with many years of sobriety, can help "restore them to sanity" if only they ask for its help and follow its (or its representative in the form of their sponsor's) advice. Whether or not the member explicitly affirms the group as the higher power to which he must "surrender," twelve-step programs understand that the support given to him by the group is indispensable to his recovery. Listening to the leads of other recovering addicts he learns just how similar his story is to theirs and thus can take heart from the sobriety that many of them have secured. Without the mutual sharing of suffering that goes on within the group, he would have been unlikely to acknowledge his own in the first place. In the group he learns, for the first time, that he does not need to hide (which is what the addict always does) but can reveal himself in all his weakness and still be accepted—indeed applauded—by the other, equally vulnerable members of the group. Thus the twelve-step group becomes, in effect, what Winnicott calls a holding environment within which a (new) sense of self can be nourished, a good-enough mother, as it were, that unconditionally supports the addict's eventual individuation.[63]

This claim that dependence on the group is essential for the *individuation* of its members deserves more attention in the light of the by-now familiar critique of twelve-step programs, namely that they substitute an addiction to the group for whatever addiction from which the addict previously suffered.[64] It is true, on the one hand, that dependence on the group (initially) takes the place of dependence on the drug. But the former kind of dependence is fundamentally different from the latter. Dependence on the drug both fueled and was fueled by an omnipotence that knows no distinction between what is and what is not within the power of a human being. Dependence on the group, in contrast, is designed to help the addict learn, and practice, the distinction between limited and unlimited power that had previously always eluded him. Thus it encourages him to take, rather than evade, responsibility for the things that *are* within his power to control.[65]

Steps four through nine make this crystal clear. The fourth step asks the addict to undertake "a searching and fearless moral inventory"[66] of himself, a painfully honest appraisal of both his defects and his assets. Here he is challenged to break the cycle of "grandiosity . . . and abjection"[67]—and thus his tendency alternately to demonize others and to demonize himself—from which he suffers in order to see himself and others as he and they really are, that is, as neither all-good nor all-bad, and therefore worthy of concern. Psychoanalytically speaking, this step signals the beginning of the end of "the splitting of the good and bad self and object representation[s]. As the previously split 'good' and 'bad' self and object representations begin to merge . . . recovering substance abusers become more tolerant of their own shortcomings and that [sic] of others."[68] In working step four, then, the recovering addict moves from shame to guilt, from the fantasy that *he* is bad (as well as the fantasies that defend against this feeling) to the reality that some of his *actions* have been bad, and thus from a position that precludes taking responsibility for those actions to one that encourages it. Thus we can say that step four is a step in the direction of a reparative response to what Klein calls the depressive position, and that the group whose support makes this step possible is like the good-enough mother whose ministrations make it possible for the child to begin to negotiate it.

Steps five through eight move him further down the road toward the righting of the wrongs identified in his moral inventory. Step five asks him to admit these wrongs to both another human being and to his higher power, and is thus at once an additional lesson in humility, the beginning of more honest relationships with others, and public protection against any denial of the defects that keeping them private might otherwise promote.[69] Steps six and seven reproduce, in effect, the logic of steps two and three: just as two and three assert that faith in, and reliance on, a higher power is required for his recovery, so six and seven proclaim that he needs help from his higher power in order to begin the difficult reparative work on which that recovery depends.

That reparations are in fact essential to recovery is spelled out in steps eight and nine, which ask members first to make "a list of all persons we have harmed, and become willing to make amends to them all" and then to make "direct amends to such people wherever possible, except where to do so would injure others."[70] Since, according to *Twelve Steps and Twelve Traditions*, "defective relations with other human beings have nearly always been the immediate cause of our [addiction],"[71] the effort to repair those relations is essential to the process of recovering from it. Since the active addict "is like a tornado roaring his way through the lives of others"[72] there is a great deal of damage he has done and many wrongs he will therefore have to try to right. He is, in short, faced with a formidable task indeed. But the recovering addict is assured that the difficulty of the task is more than matched by the rewards for undertaking it. "In nine cases out of ten" he will find that his former lovers, friends, or associates are moved to forgive him by the sincerity of his remorse over, and his willingness (where possible) to make restitution for, that harm he has caused them.[73] With forgiveness comes enormous relief. And even when forgiveness is not forthcoming, the recovering addict at least gains satisfaction from knowing that he has done what he can to "clean house" and "put [his] life in order."[74] Moreover, even when restitution to the other is impossible, in the course of reflecting on the damage he has done to him he will often become more aware of the damage he has done to *himself* as a result of that very damage.[75] Thus steps eight and nine offer recovering addicts the opportunity not only to make reparations to others but also to themselves.

If we take consistent advantage of these reparative opportunities, the *Big Book* assures them, "we are going to know a new freedom and a new happiness. We will not regret the past nor wish to shut the door on it." Thus in redeeming his past the recovering addict gives himself a (new and different) future: his compulsion to repeat gives way to "peace" and "serenity."[76] Along with this serenity comes a loss of "interest in selfish things" and a gain in "interest in our fellows." This growing interest in others is reflected in the twelfth step, which commits the recovering addict to "carry this [twelve-step] message to [other] addicts." In serving them, he is assured, he will joyfully "experience the kind of giving that asks no reward." In short, the drive to *take in* from the world is replaced by the freedom to *give back* to it. Thus recovery both requires and results in a new "outlook on material matters: money [becomes] our servant and not our master." It changes from a "symbol . . . of self-importance" to "a means of exchanging love and service with those about us."[77]

If we assume, with Freud, that "ostensibly normal people do not be-
have very differently from neurotics,"[78] then we recognize that the difference between the "neurotic" addiction to, and "normal" overconsumption
of, a wide range of stuff is merely a matter of degree.[79] This recognition
authorizes Kurtz's claim that modernity is "inherently addictive: the striv-
ing always harder for the ever more that satisfies ever less."[80] If modernity is, in that sense, "inherently addictive," then we can also say, with
Kurtz, that the twelve-step critique of addiction is a "counter-Enlighten-
ment phenomenon antithetical to the central assumptions of . . . modernity."[81] Thus twelve-step recovery programs recommend themselves as
programs for what might be called the *recovery from modernity*.

Conclusion: Toward Green Recovery

By now the depth-psychological connection between recovery and deep
ecology should be clear. But there is also, as I intimated at the outset of
this chapter, an organic (or mutually causal) connection between them. If
compulsive consumption defends us from the loss of meaning mandated
by the denial of our dependence on nature, then the recovery from compulsive consumption ultimately requires the deep ecological effort to re-
connect with a world that would no longer be an object of compulsive
production. If the insatiable search for stuff is an unconscious prop (as well
as conscious justification) for compulsive production, the deep ecological
challenge to compulsive production must eventually embrace the struggle
to recover from the addiction to stuff. Thus the fate of deep ecology and
the fate of (what might be called) deep recovery are, in fact, inextricably
intertwined.

I suspect, however, that many if not most of the supporters of both
movements are currently unaware of this fact. The anti-anthropocentrism
of deep ecology may make many of its members skeptical of, or even hostile to, the preoccupation of the partisans of deep recovery with the repair
of the self. Moreover, even those deep ecologists for whom the commitment
to biocentrism and individual self-realization go hand in hand generally fail
to recognize that the individual who is addicted to overconsumption lacks
the psychological wherewithal to realize either of these twin commitments.[82]
Unless and until this individual is able to find a supportive emotional context within which she can first "own" and then mourn her omnipotent
relationship with objects, she will continue compulsively to consume them
in order to control her emotions, and to lend support for the unlimited

production from which they issue. Thus deep ecology typically ignores or at least underestimates the deep psychological transformation essential for the realization of its goals.

On the other hand, the commitment of recovery programs to the repair of the self is generally unaccompanied by an awareness that the repair of the self requires a repair of the planet. Recovery doesn't realize that the addict's frantic but futile search for a fix for his broken emotions is the inevitable result of a broken relationship with the nonhuman world. If the contemporary epidemic of nihilism—of depression, anxiety and a general sense of meaninglessness—is the inevitable consequence of a culture whose system of production is predicated on the (manic) denial of dependence on nature, then individuals will continue to suffer these symptoms, and thus to overconsume in order to (try to) alleviate them, until they are able to form a more culturally reparative relationship with the world.

Recovery has yet to recognize, in other words, that its commitment to a transformed relationship to a "higher power" must come to include a commitment to a transformed relationship to (nonhuman) nature. Although it is true that its concept of a "higher power" is sufficiently capacious to make room for the "nature"of the deep ecologist, it is also true that explicit references to "nature" are conspicuously absent in the twelve-step literature and (it is my understanding) in twelve-step meetings. Neither are its members encouraged to include in their "searching and fearless moral inventory" their treatment of the nonhuman beings with whom they share the planet, or to make reparations to those beings whom their compulsive consumption (and the compulsive production reciprocally related to it) has harmed.[83]

Moreover, the twelve-step program proscription on discussing potentially contentious, outside issues[84] discourages its members from consciously connecting the repair of the self with the repair of the planet. The commitment to "singleness of purpose" makes it effectively impossible to explore this connection in the context of an addiction-specific twelve-step group. But the recent emergence of generalized twelve-step recovery groups suggests that a change may be in the offing. As Room points out, "ironically the search for singleness of purpose has led many in the movements to multiple memberships in 12-step organizations," and the inconvenience of multiple membership in groups dealing with related addictions has, in turn, led (at least in the Northern California Bay Area) to the formation of "unofficial 'All Anonymous' meetings where sharing on any addiction is allowed. There are unofficial Twelve Step meetings where those from many programs gather for step study and don't discuss individual diseases."[85] Similarly, a recent report on the twelve-step movement in *U.S. Catholic* magazine refers to a twelve-step program in Oregon called *Recoveries Anonymous* which, as the name implies, focuses not on individual addictions but rather on the steps necessary to recover from any of them.[86] It is not clear whether explicit attention to the need for a new relationship to nature would be ruled "out of court" in the context of these generalized recovery groups. But even if it was, nothing would prevent twelve-steppers from creating unofficial groups specifically devoted to the connection between the repair of the self and the repair of the planet. Thus there is reason to hope that *green recovery* might soon find its natural habitat.

Notes

Introduction

1. Isaac D. Balbus, *Marxism and Domination: A Neo-Hegelian, Feminist, Psychoanalytic Theory of Sexual, Political, and Technological Liberation* (Princeton, NJ: Princeton University Press, 1982).

2. Isaac D. Balbus, *Emotional Rescue: The Theory and Practice of a Feminist Father* (New York: Routledge, 1988).

3. Isaac D. Balbus, "De-Kleining Feminist Mothering Theory?" *Political Theory* 21 (1992), 817–835.

4. C. Fred Alford, *Melanie Klein and Critical Social Theory* (New Haven: Yale University Press, 1989).

5. Not previously published.

6. Nancy Chodorow, *Feminism and Psychoanalytic Theory* (New Haven: Yale University Press, 1989), p. 109.

7. Judith Butler, *Gender Trouble: Feminism and the Subversion of Identity* (New York: Routledge, 1990); Judith Butler, *Bodies That Matter: On the Discursive Limits of "Sex"* (New York: Routledge, 1993).

8. Isaac D. Balbus, "Against the Idealism of the Affects," *Political Theory* 31(6) (December 2003), 859–870.

9. Britannica.com (the online magazine of *Encyclopedia Britannica*), December 11, 2000.

10. Not previously published.

11. Isaac D. Balbus, "Mourning the Movement," *Soundings* 14 (Spring 2000), pp. 39–52.

12. Isaac D. Balbus, "The Psychodynamics of Racial Reparations," *Psychoanalysis, Culture & Society* 9(2) (August 2004), pp. 159–185.

13. Not previously published.

14. Not previously published.

15. Coparenting and cultural mourning are related both because men who have mourned stereotypical forms of masculinity are more likely to coparent and because a coparent's intimate relationship with his child is likely to evoke early, unmet needs that must be mourned.

16. Alexander and Margarete Mitscherlisch, *The Inability to Mourn* (New York: Grove Press, 1975). The qualification "post-Freudian" is necessary insofar as Freud's drive theory, as Peter Homans has argued, can itself be understood as "an epoch-specific defense against mourning." See his *The Ability to Mourn: Disillusionment and the Social Origins of Psychoanalysis* (Chicago: University of Chicago Press, 1989), p. 114. It is not until the "object" is grasped, *pace* Freud, as constitutive of (rather than incidental to) the "drive" that it becomes possible to explain what Freud acknowledges is "not at all easy to explain in terms of economics [of the libido]," namely, why the "de-cathexis" from the object in mourning is typically so "piecemeal" and painful. Sigmund Freud, "Mourning and Melancholia" [1917], *The Standard Edition of the Complete Psychological Works* (hereinafter cited as *SE*) vol. 14 (London: Hogarth Press, 1957), p. 245.

17. Homans, *The Ability to Mourn*, pp. 5, 111–112.

18. Ibid., p. 198.

19. Philip Rieff, *The Triumph of the Therapeutic* (Chicago: University of Chicago Press, 1966), pp. 12, 261. Although Rieff is principally preoccupied with the threat that a (popularized) psychoanalysis poses for a common culture, at least at one point he anticipates Homans's concerns about the effects of the common culture on psychoanalysis: "To change the dynamics of the culture, the analytic attitude would have to become a moral demand, and thus it would cease to be analytic." *The Triumph of the Therapeutic*, p. 20, n. 1.

20. Homans, *The Ability to Mourn*, pp. 5, 347.

21. Ibid., p. 199.

22. Ibid., pp. 334–335, emphasis added.

23. Ibid.

24. For this distinction, see D. W. Winnicott, *Playing and Reality* (New York: Basic Books, 1971).

25. Jean-Jacques Rousseau, *Emile, or On Education*, trans. Alan Bloom (New York: Basic Books, 1979), p. 221.

Chapter 1

1. For an account of the limits of Freudo-Marxism, see Balbus, *Marxism and Domination*, pp. 169–265.

2. The founding manifestos of feminist mothering theory were Dorothy Dinnerstein's *The Mermaid and The Minotaur* (New York: Harper & Row, 1976) and Nancy Chodorow's *The Reproduction of Mothering* (Berkeley: University of

California Press, 1978). Works of the early 1980s that draw on either Dinnerstein or Chodorow include Balbus, *Marxism and Domination*; Jessica Benjamin, "The Bonds of Love: Erotic Domination and Rational Violence," *Feminist Studies* 6/1 (Spring 1980), 144–174; Jane Flax, "Political Philosophy and the Patriarchal Unconscious: A Psychoanalytic Perspective on Epistemology and Metaphysics," in Sandra Harding and Merill B. Hintikka, eds., *Discovering Reality: Feminist Perspectives on Epistemology, Metaphysics, Methodology and the Philosophy of Science* (Boston: D. Reidel, 1983), pp. 245–281; Nancy C. M. Hartsock, *Money, Sex, and Power* (New York: Longman, 1983); and Evelyn Fox Keller, "Gender and Science," in Harding and Hintikka, *Discovering Reality*, pp. 187–205.

3. Chodorow, *The Reproduction of Mothering*, pp. 57–91.

4. Dinnerstein, *The Mermaid and The Minotaur*, pp. 95–105.

5. Janet Sayers, "Melanie Klein and Mothering: A Feminist Perspective," *International Review of Psycho-Analysis* 16 (1989), p. 363.

6. Michael Rustin, "A Socialist Consideration of Kleinian Psychoanalysis," *New Left Review* 131 (1982), 71–96; Barry Richards, ed., *Capitalism and Infancy: Essays on Psychoanalysis and Politics* (London: Free Association Books, 1984).

7. Juliet Mitchell, ed., *The Selected Melanie Klein* (Harmondsworth: Penguin, 1986); *Women: A Cultural Review* 1/2 (November 1990).

8. Christopher Lasch, *The Culture of Narcissism* (New York: Norton, 1978); Christopher Lasch, *The Minimal Self* (New York: Norton, 1984); C. Fred Alford, *Melanie Klein and Critical Social Theory* (New Haven: Yale University Press, 1989).

9. Alford, *Melanie Klein and Critical Social Theory*, p. 193.

10. Dinnerstein, *The Mermaid and The Minotaur*, p. 95.

11. Ibid., p. 97. This formulation does not properly distinguish between splitting that is the inevitable result of the cognitive immaturity of the infant and defensive splitting at a later, more developed stage. See below, pp. 60, 63–64, 95.

12. Melanie Klein, "Notes on Some Schizoid Mechanisms," in *Envy and Gratitude and Other Works, 1946–1963* (New York: Free Press, 1984), pp. 2–14; Dinnerstein, *The Mermaid and The Minotaur*, p. 97.

13. Klein, "Notes on Some Schizoid Mechanisms," pp. 14–15. Mastery of the depressive position is never complete. As Alford correctly points out, "it is a developmental achievement that must be constantly defended and regained throughout life in that stress, as well as depression itself, reinforces defenses associated with the paranoid-schizoid position." *Melanie Klein and Critical Social Theory*, p. 33.

14. Alford, *Melanie Klein and Critical Social Theory*, p. 34.

15. Ibid., pp. 34–37, 75; Melanie Klein, *Envy and Gratitude* (New York: Basic Books, 1957), pp. 89–90.

16. Dinnerstein, *The Mermaid and The Minotaur*, pp. 52–53, 69.

17. Ibid., p. 53.

18. Dinnerstein, *The Mermaid and The Minotaur*, pp. 51–52. See also Chodorow, *The Reproduction of Mothering*, pp. 122–123. According to Dinnerstein, this is the

typical, but not the only, solution available to the girl. Overidealizing the mother or projecting bad feelings onto the father are other possibilities, but these options run counter to the "traditional emotional equilibrium that is thought of as hetero-sexual 'adjustment'" (p. 52).

19. Dinnerstein, *The Mermaid and The Minotaur*, pp. 52–53.

20. Ibid., p. 52.

21. Ibid., p. 234.

22. Ibid., pp. 189, 134. Dinnerstein adds that "it is possible . . . that we will prove unable to marshal the strength for this integration" (p. 134). Thus she under-stands coparenting as a necessary but not necessarily sufficient solution to the problem of patriarchy.

23. Ibid., p. 191.

24. Alford, *Melanie Klein and Critical Social Theory*, pp. 194–195.

25. Ibid., p. 195.

26. Ibid., p. 194. Alford's claim entirely ignores Klein's own account, in *Envy and Gratitude*, of how the girl's "disappointment and grievance [toward the mother] may lead to a turning away from her; but an idealization of the second object, the father's penis and the father, may then be more successful [and] then the woman can combine some hatred against the mother and love for the father and later on for other men" (p. 37). This account clearly anticipates Dinnerstein's subsequent elaboration, which I have summarized above. Alford's critique of Dinnerstein thus relies on a "Kleinianism" that is more orthodox than Klein herself.

27. Alford, *Melanie Klein and Critical Social Theory*, p. 195.

28. Ibid.

29. Melanie Klein, "The Mutual Influences in the Development of Ego and Id," in *Envy and Gratitude and Other Works*, p. 58.

30. Melanie Klein, "The Psychogenesis of Manic Depressive States," in Mitchell, *The Selected Melanie Klein*, p. 141.

31. Stephen Robinson, "The Parent to the Child," in Richards, *Capitalism and Infancy*, p. 181.

32. Susan Isaacs, "The Nature and Function of Phantasy," in Joan Riviere, *Developments in Psycho-Analysis* (London: Hogarth Press, 1952), pp. 67–121.

33. Donald Meltzer, "The Kleinian Expansion of Freud's Metapsychology," *International Journal of Psycho-Analysis* 62 (1981), 178.

34. Alford, *Melanie Klein and Critical Social Theory*, pp. 49, 47, 50, 31.

35. Ibid., p. 53.

36. Since Dinnerstein anticipates that even the coparented child will be tempted to defend against "depressive anxiety" when she admits that "it is pos-sible . . . that we [coparented children] will prove unable to marshal the strength for this [depressive] integration" (p. 134), Alford could not dismiss the prospec-tive part of her account as an un-Kleinian repudiation of the inevitability of "psy-chological defenses" against ambivalence. And, since Klein herself argues that normal children enter and successfully negotiate the depressive position, Alford

could not claim that there is anything un-Kleinian about Dinnerstein's optimism about the overcoming of those defenses.

37. Clifford Yorke, "Some Suggestions for a Critique of Kleinian Psychology," *The Psychoanalytic Study of the Child* 26 (1971), 139.

38. Otto Kernberg, "Structural Derivatives of Object Relationships," *International Journal of Psycho-Analysis* 47 (1966), 245.

39. Chodorow, *The Reproduction of Mothering*, p. 150.

40. Susan Isaacs, "The Nature and Function of Phantasy," cited in Robinson, "The Parent to the Child," p. 177.

41. Alford, *Melanie Klein and Critical Social Theory*, pp. 44–45.

42. Beatrice Beebe, "Mother–Infant Mutual Influence and Precursors of Self- and Object Representations," in Joseph Masling, ed., *Empirical Studies of Psychoanalytic Theories*, vol. 2 (Hillsdale, NJ: Analytic Press, 1986), p. 39; Daniel Stern, *The First Relationship: Mother and Infant* (Cambridge: Harvard University Press, 1977).

43. Jean Piaget and Barbel Inhelder, *The Psychology of the Child* (New York: Basic Books, 1975).

44. F. Pine, "Libidinal Object Constancy: A Theoretical Note," cited in Margaret S. Mahler, et al., *The Psychological Birth of the Human Infant* (New York: Basic Books, 1975), p. 111.

45. Stern, *The First Relationship*, p. 96.

46. Calvin F. Settlage, "The Psychoanalytic Understanding of Narcissistic and Borderline Personality Disorders: Advances in Developmental Theory," in Ruth F. Lax, et al., *Rapprochement: The Critical Subphase of Separation-Individuation* (New York: Jason Aronson, 1980), p. 85.

47. J. B. McDevitt, "Libidinal Object Constancy: Some Developmental Considerations," cited in Mahler, et al., *The Psychological Birth of the Human Infant*, p. 111.

48. This summary has been drawn from Mahler, *The Psychological Birth of the Human Infant*, pp. 76–108, 225–230.

49. Ibid., pp. 99, 107. See also p. 108.

50. Ibid., p. 292.

51. Ibid., pp. 22, 104.

52. Ibid., pp. 104, 106.

53. Ibid., pp. 102, 106. See also Ernest L. Abelin, "Triangulation, the Role of the Father and the Origins of Core Gender Identity During the Rapprochement Subphase," in Ruth F. Lax, et al., *Rapprochement: The Critical Subphase of Separation-Individuation* (New York: Jason Aronson, 1980), pp. 151–169; and Ricki Levenson, "Intimacy, Autonomy and Gender: Developmental Differences and Their Reflection in Adult Relationships," *Journal of the American Academy of Psychoanalysis* 12 (1984), 529–544.

54. It is true, of course, that Mahler and her colleagues argue that both boys and girls normally attain "libidinal object constancy"—and thus the ability to remain in the depressive position—by the end of the third year (p. 112). They also maintain,

however, that "in some children the rapprochement crisis leads to great ambivalence and even to splitting of the object world into 'good' and 'bad,' the consequences of which may later become organized into symptoms of the narcissistic variety" (p. 229). Thus the difference between their position and Dinnerstein's is largely one of degree. They come closest to her position when they conclude that "smooth and consistently progressive personality development, even under ordinary favorable circumstances, is difficult, if not impossible. This [is] due precisely to the fact that separation and individuation derive from and are dependent upon the symbiotic origin of the human condition, upon that very symbiosis with another human being, the mother. . . . It seems inherent in the human condition that not even the most normally endowed child, with the most optimally available mother, is able to weather the separation-individuation process without developmental difficulty. . . . [The final] subphase of the separation-individuation process has no single definite permanent terminal point" (227).

55. Alford, *Melanie Klein and Critical Social Theory*, pp. 194, 195.

56. Graeme Russell, for example, found that an alarmingly high proportion (41 percent) of the Australian couples who were coparenting when he first interviewed them had reverted to a traditional division of labor by the time of his follow-up study two years later. *The Changing Role of Fathers?* (London: University of Queensland Press, 1983), p. 184.

57. Thus demands for greater participation of fathers within the home must be coupled with demands for comparable worth and other reforms that would equalize the power of women outside the home. Coparenting is as dependent on gender equality as gender equality is dependent on coparenting. On this point see Balbus, *Marxism and Domination*, pp. 382–384.

58. Diane Ehrensaft, *Parenting Together* (New York: Free Press, 1987), pp. 150–158.

Chapter 2

1. Karl Marx, *The Grundrisse*, David McLellan, ed. and trans. (New York: Harper & Row, 1971), p. 110.

2. Judith Burton and Douglas Kellner, review of *Marxism and Domination* in *The Minnesota Review* (Fall, 1984), 202–203.

3. Lawrence H. Simon, review of *Marxism and Domination, The Review of Politics* 45(2) (July 1983), 458.

4. Wolf V. Heydebrand, review of *Marxism and Domination*, in *The Insurgent Sociologist* 13:1–2 (Summer-Fall 1985), 141–142.

5. Tim Luke, "The Dreams of Deep Ecology," *Telos* 76 (Summer 1988), 80–81, 83. Henryk Skolimowski makes a similar point: " All claims made on behalf of the biotic community are made by human beings; they are filtered by human sensitivities and human compassion." "The Dogma of Anti-Anthropocentrism and Ecophilosophy," *Environmental Ethics* 6 (Fall 1984), 284.

6. Since he does not claim that an objectifying perception of nature does not also involve a projection of human needs onto nature, this conclusion cannot be explicitly attributed to Luke. But from the fact that he only accuses the proponents—and not the opponents—of "deep ecology" of projection, it can reasonably be inferred that he believes that the former suffer from a "false consciousness" to which the latter do not fall prey. If not, as I argue below, then the force of his point about projection is lost.

7. But see below, Chapter 10, for a qualification of this claim. I will argue there that a relationship that affirms our dependence on (nonhuman) nature is in fact more *realistic* than one that denies that dependence.

8. Heydebrand, op. cit., p. 141; Jurgen Habermas, *Knowledge and Human Interests* (Boston: Beacon Press, 1971), p. 33.

9. Otto Kernberg, *Borderline Conditions and Pathological Narcissism* (New York: Jason Aronson, 1975), p. 228.

10. Alford, *Melanie Klein and Critical Social Theory*, p. 31.

11. For a discussion of this and related issues, see Seyla Benhabib and Fred Dallmayr, eds., *The Communicative Ethics Controversy* (Cambridge, MA.: MIT Press, 1990).

12. Anthony Wilden, *System and Structure: Essays in Communication and Exchange* (London: Tavistock Publications, 1972).

13. Heydebrand, op. cit., p. 142.

14. Ibid.

15. Simon, op. cit., p. 459.

16. Ibid., p. 458.

17. Richard A. Watson, "A Critique of Anti-Anthropocentric Biocentrism," *Environmental Ethics* 5 (Fall 1983), 256.

18. But see the qualification of this argument in Chapter 10 of this book.

19. Robert A. Dahl, *After the Revolution?* (New Haven: Yale University Press, 1990), p. 8.

20. In fact it can be argued (under the assumptions of rational self-interest) that aggression is a more likely outcome than cooperation. Even individuals who might otherwise have come to the conclusion that a strategy of cooperation is in their self-interest would not rationally pursue that strategy unless they had good reason to *trust* that all other individuals had come to the same conclusion. But trust is precisely what must be lacking when communication among individuals does not exist. Under these conditions it would be more prudent to assume the worst and to protect oneself accordingly, that is, to act hostilely to preempt any possible hostile response. Thus aggression fueled by a universal paranoia, rather than peaceful cooperation, is the probable culmination of countless, purely private, self-interested calculi of costs and benefits. To put this another way, civil social relationships presuppose a trusting communicative context, but a trusting communicative context presupposes the transcendence of individual self-interest.

21. Dinnerstein, *The Mermaid and The Minotaur*, p. 101.

22. In *Marxism and Domination* I report that a review of some fifty cross-cultural studies concluded that "In spite of a great deal of cultural diversity, all the infants drawn from preindustrial communities shared certain experiences during the first year: membership in an extended family with many caretakers, breast-feeding on demand, day and night; constant tactile stimulation by the body of the adult caretaker who carried the infant on her back or side, and slept with him, [and] lack of set routines for feeding, sleeping, and toileting." Emmy E. Werner, "Infants Around the World: Cross-Cultural Studies of Psychomotor Development from Birth to Two Years," in Stella Chess and Alexander Thomas, *Annual Progress in Child Psychiatry and Infant Development*, vol. 6 (New York: Brunner/Mazel, 1973), pp. 84–112.

23. For a defense of Dinnerstein against exactly the *opposite* critique, namely that Dinnerstein improperly privileges *reality* over fantasy, see Chapter 1, above.

24. Patricia Elliot, *From Mastery to Analysis* (Ithaca, NY: Cornell University Press, 1991), p. 116.

25. Ibid.

26. Ibid., pp. 89–112. See also H. R. Hays, *The Dangerous Sex: The Myth of Feminine Evil* (New York: G. P. Putnam's Sons, 1964), for the more exhaustive survey of misogynist myths on which Dinnerstein relies.

27. Elliot, op. cit., p. 116.

28. Nancy J. Chodorow and Susan Contratto, "The Fantasy of the Perfect Mother," in Chodorow, *Feminism and Psychoanalytic Theory* (New Haven: Yale University Press, 1989), p. 81, emphasis in original.

29. Ibid., p. 89.

30. Chodorow and Contratto contradict this claim when they also argue that our "cultural ideology" of mothering "gains meaning from and is partially produced by infantile fantasies that are themselves the outcome of being mothered exclusively by one woman. If mothers have exclusive responsibility for infants who are totally dependent, then to the infant they are the source of all good and evil." Ibid., p. 90. This argument seems to me to be identical to the Dinnersteinian position they attack elsewhere in their essay.

31. Roger S. Gottlieb, "Mothering and the Reproduction of Power: Chodorow, Dinnerstein, and Social Theory," *Socialist Review* 77 (September-October 1984), 110.

32. Ibid., pp. 110–111.

33. Dinnerstein, op. cit., p. 60.

34. Gottlieb, op. cit., p. 100.

35. Elliot, op. cit., p. 119. See also Gottlieb, op. cit., pp. 99–100.

36. Gottlieb, op. cit., p. 109. Elliot is somewhat more cautious: "[T]he difficulty entailed in acquiring a feminine identity may have less to do with phantasies of maternal omnipotence and more to do with the social signification of sexual difference in a patriarchal society." Op. cit., p. 119.

37. Dinnerstein, op. cit., p. 166.

38. Ibid., p. 110.

39. Ibid., p. 111.

40. Margaret S. Mahler, et al., *The Psychological Birth of the Human Infant* (New York: Basic Books, 1975).

41. Gottlieb, op. cit., p. 107.

42. Balbus, *Marxism and Domination*, Chapters 2 and 5.

43. Gottlieb, op. cit., pp. 102–104.

44. Balbus, op. cit., pp. 315–322.

45. Since Gottlieb cites my book in an endnote we can assume that he is aware of the hypothesis that I derive from Dinnerstein. But it is neither evaluated nor even mentioned in the course of his critique of her theory.

46. Elliot, op. cit., p. 119.

47. Ibid.

48. In 1983 there were 600,000 single fathers in the United States raising almost one million children under the age of eighteen. Geoffrey L. Greif, *Single Fathers* (Lexington, MA: D. C. Heath and Company, 1985), p. 3.

49. For some evidence that supports this hypothesis, see Diane Ehrensaft, *Parenting Together* (New York: Free Press, 1987), pp. 183–250, as well as my *Emotional Rescue*, pp. 103–114.

50. Elliot also argues on pp. 105–107 and p. 118, that the devaluation of women is also in part a consequence of compulsory heterosexuality, that Dinnerstein's explanation of the devaluation of women presupposes rather than problematizes compulsory heterosexuality, and that her explanation is therefore, at best, incomplete. Although it *is* true that Dinnerstein takes heterosexuality for granted, and although it is also true that *secondary* aspects of her account of the differences in the paternal identification of boys and girls do indeed presuppose their heterosexuality, it is also true, as I demonstrate at length in Chapter 3 of this book, that the assumption of an initial feminine identification (with the mother) on the part of both little boys and little girls, and the assumption of a "core gender identity" that is either "male" or "female," are sufficient (without the presupposition of heterosexuality) to derive both a common devaluation of women and a gender-based difference in the way in which it is expressed. For a defense of the assumptions of a primary "feminine identification" and "core gender identity" against Judith Butler's deconstruction thereof I would refer the reader to that chapter.

51. Jean Bethke Elsthain, "Symmetry and Soporifics: A Critique of Feminist Accounts of Gender Development," in Barry Richards, ed., *Capitalism and Infancy: Essays on Psychoanalysis and Politics* (London: Free Association Books, 1984), p. 67. Elsthain also questions Dinnerstein's description of the "oral stage" itself, arguing that it is based on a problematic "notion of splitting involving not only *mechanism* but *meaning* and *content* [that is] link[ed] along gender lines to the totality of arrangements in the social and political world" (p. 67). This argument anticipates C. Fred Alford's critique of Dinnerstein and is therefore vulnerable to my critique of Alford's critique in Chapter 1 of this book.

52. Ibid., pp. 69–70.

53. Ibid., p. 69.

54. Ibid., p. 71.

55. Susan Brownmiller, *Against Our Will: Men, Women and Rape* (New York: Simon & Schuster, 1975), especially pp. 284-288. Peggy Reeves Sanday's "The Socio-Cultural Context of Rape: A Cross-Cultural Study," *Journal of Social Issues* 37(4) (1981) is often cited as a refutation of the claim that rape is culturally universal. Sanday classifies about half of the tribal societies in her sample as "rape-free." But she acknowledges in a subsequent essay that "by rape-free I do not mean to imply that rape is entirely absent." Peggy Reeves Sanday, "Rape and the Silencing of the Feminine," in Sylvana Tomaselli and Roy Porter, *Rape* (Oxford: Basil Blackwell, 1986), p. 84. She also admits that the ethnographic accounts on which she relies in her original study "may obscure the actual incidence of rape." One wonders, for example, whether the insistence of a Khalka Mongol man that "our women never resist" should be taken as evidence for the absence of male sexual assaults on women. Sanday, "The Socio-Cultural Context of Rape," p. 16.

56. Dinnerstein, op. cit., p. xii.

57. This claim does not imply the absence of reciprocal interaction between the mode of child rearing and the mode of symbolizing nature but rather merely that the former has a certain kind of causal primacy over the latter. See *Marxism and Domination*, pp. 344–352.

58. Heydebrand, op. cit., p. 142; Simon, op. cit., p. 455.

59. Simon, op. cit., p. 455.

60. Jean Piaget, *The Child's Conception of the World* (New York: Humanities Press, 1951), pp. 153–155, 236, 256, and 385. Because Piaget treats the modern Western mix of maternal gratification and deprivation as the only possible mix, his conclusion is that a sharp sense of separation from the world is both natural and inevitable. Thus he fails to acknowledge the possibility that a mix that was weighted more heavily in favor of gratification would produce persistent feelings of "participation" and "communion" that are not "outgrown." But this possibility can be inferred from his assumptions.

61. Imre Lakatos, "Falsification and the Methodology of Scientific Research Programmes," in Imre Lakatos and Alan Musgrave, eds., *Criticism and the Growth of Knowledge* (Cambridge: Cambridge University Press, 1970), pp. 155, 118.

62. Heydebrand, op. cit., p. 142; Simon, op. cit., p. 456.

63. Lakatos, op. cit., p. 118.

64. Norbert Elias, *The Civilizing Process: The History of Manners* (New York: Urizen Books, 1978).

65. Lawrence Stone, *The Family, Sex and Marriage in England: 1500–1800* (New York: Harper & Row, 1977), p. 151.

66. See for example Steven Ozment, *When Fathers Ruled* (Cambridge, MA: Harvard University Press, 1983), and Levin L. Shucking, *The Puritan Family* (New York: Schocken Books, 1970).

67. This formulation begs the question of whether my claim is that *within* the context of any given culture women are more indulgent parents than men, or that women *across* all cultures are generally more indulgent parents than men. I take up this question in *Emotional Rescue* on pp. 176 and 250–251.

68. This phrase is taken from Irving Howe, *World of Our Fathers* (New York: Harcourt Brace Jovanovich, 1976).

Chapter 3

1. Nancy Chodorow, *Feminism and Psychoanalytic Theory*, p. 109.

2. Chodorow, *The Reproduction of Mothering*, p. 150.

3. Chodorow, *Feminism and Psychoanalytic Theory*, p. 109.

4. Judith Butler, "Gender Trouble, Feminist Theory, and Psychoanalytic Discourse," in Linda J. Nicholson, ed., *Feminism/Postmodernism* (New York: Routledge, 1990), pp. 324–340; Judith Butler, *Gender Trouble: Feminism and the Subversion of Identity* (New York: Routledge, 1990); Judith Butler, *Bodies That Matter: On the Discursive Limits of "Sex"* (New York: Routledge, 1993).

5. Butler, *Gender Trouble*, p. 25.

6. Ibid., p. 16, emphasis in the original.

7. Butler, "Gender Trouble, Feminist Theory, and Psychoanalytic Discourse," p. 329.

8. Ibid., pp. 330, 339.

9. Ibid., p. 332.

10. Ibid., p. 331.

11. Ibid., pp. 330–331.

12. Ibid., p. 331.

13. Ibid., p. 337.

14. Butler, *Gender Trouble*, p. 17.

15. Butler, *Bodies That Matter*, p. 232.

16. Butler, "Gender Trouble, Feminist Theory, and Psychoanalytic Discourse," p. 335.

17. See Chapter 1, above, p. 15.

18. Cited in Paul Ricoeur, *Freud and Philosophy* (New Haven: Yale University Press, 1970), pp. 218, 223.

19. Paula Bernstein, "Gender Identity Disorder in Boys," *Journal of the American Psychoanalytic Association*, 41(3) (1993), 739. See also Richard C. Friedman, *Male Homosexuality: A Contemporary Psychoanalytic Perspective* (New Haven: Yale University Press, 1988).

20. Object-relations theory can also accommodate the apparent independence of "gender-role identity" from sexual orientation. The fact that many gay men are, and many straight men are not, stereotypically "masculine" in their affect and demeanor is entirely consistent with object-relations theory, because for that theory "gender-role identity" is no more predictive of sexual identity than is core

gender identity. The same can be said of the persistence of stereotypically masculine and feminine identities within homosexual relationships, such as the "butch" and "femme" members of lesbian couples. Thus there is no necessary connection between the object-relational assumption of masculine and feminine gender-role identities and the heterosexist assumption that the only normal love is between masculine men and feminine women.

21. Butler, "Gender Trouble, Feminist Theory, and Psychoanalytic Discourse," pp. 330–331.

22. Butler, *Gender Trouble*, p. 136, emphases in the original.

23. Ibid., p. 33.

24. Ibid., p. 6.

25. Ibid., p. 24.

26. Butler, *Bodies That Matter*, p. xi.

27. Ibid., pp. 6, 10, 93–94.

28. Ibid., p. 10.

29. Ibid.

30. Ibid., p. xi.

31. Ibid., pp. 94, xi.

32. Ibid., pp. 10–11.

33. Ibid., p. 12.

34. Robert Stoller, *Presentations of Gender* (New Haven: Yale University Press, 1985), pp. 11–14.

Chapter 4

1. Nel Noddings, *Starting at Home: Caring and Social Policy* (Berkeley: University of California Press, 2002); Kelly Oliver, *Witnessing: Beyond Recognition* (Minneapolis: University of Minnesota Press, 2001); Cynthia Willett, *The Soul of Justice: Social Bonds and Racial Hubris* (Ithaca, NY: Cornell University Press, 2001); Sonia Kruks, *Retrieving Experience: Subjectivity and Recognition in Feminist Politics* (Ithaca, NY: Cornell University Press, 2001).

2. Noddings, *Starting at Home*, pp. 31, 17, 58, 301, 29, 30.

3. Ibid., pp. 22, 48, 24.

4. Ibid., p. 121.

5. Sarah Ruddick, *Maternal Thinking: Toward a Politics of Peace* (Boston: Beacon Press, 1989).

6. Noddings, *Starting at Home*, p. 62.

7. The second claim is vulnerable to the obvious objection that many parents who would seem to be caring (in Noddings's threefold sense) are apolitical or even politically reactionary. Noddings could respond, of course, that such parents are not *really* caring, and are not because they themselves were never adequately cared for. But this brings us back to her first claim and all its attendant problems.

8. Noddings, *Starting at Home*, p. 45.

9. Ibid., p. 28, first emphasis added, second emphasis in the original.

10. Ibid., p. 168, emphasis added. As my colleague Stephen Engelmann has pointed out to me, this inconsistency could be overcome by distinguishing between a caring *inclination* and an *ethic* of care, and by arguing that the former is indeed triggered by having been *cared for* but that the latter also requires the experience of *caregiving*. But for Noddings, as far as I can tell, a "desire to care" and an "ethic of care" are synonymous terms.

11. According to Donald Winnicott, parents who are unable to calmly withstand their childrens' rage and who either attempt to suppress it or capitulate to it are unlikely to encourage the capacity to tolerate emotional ambivalence. See his "The Use of an Object and Relating Through Identifications," in D. W. Winnicott, *Playing and Reality* (New York: Basic Books, 1971), pp. 86–94.

12. Noddings, *Starting at Home*, p. 247.

13. Oliver, *Witnessing*, pp. 15, 27–28, 36, 39, 170, 189, 39, 7, 87.

14. Emmanuel Levinas, *Totality and Infinity* (Pittsburgh: Duquesne University Press, 1969), p. 46.

15. Robert R. Williams, *Recognition: Fichte and Hegel on the Other* (Albany: State University of New York Press, 1992), p. 143.

16. G. W. F. Hegel, *The Phenomenology of Mind* (New York: Harper Torchbooks, 1967), pp. 231, 236.

17. Ibid., p. 231.

18. Williams, *Recognition*, p. 155, emphasis added.

19. Jacques Derrida, *Writing and Difference* (Chicago: University of Chicago Press, 1978), p. 99. I am grateful to Bob Williams for bringing Derrida's critique of Levinas to my attention.

20. Williams, *Recognition*, p. 159. I have taken the liberty of removing Williams's italicization of "of some sort" in order to italicize the word "is."

21. At a number of points Oliver implicitly calls into question her explicit repudiation of the inevitability of conflict. For example, she tells us that "we must be able to imagine working through whatever we might find threatening in relations of otherness and difference. . . . We need a new model of subjectivity . . . that does not ground identity in hostility toward others but, rather, one that opens onto the possibility of working-through hostilities" (pp. 10–11). This formulation appears to acknowledge that witnessing, like recognition, requires a struggle against persistent hostile tendencies, but this formulation (1) is indistinguishable from the Hegelian position she rejects, and (2) (like Hegel) fails to clarify the source of those hostile tendencies. See also what Oliver says about the need for "vigilance" in the context of witnessing (pp. 133–136).

22. Oliver, *Witnessing*, pp. 196, 198.

23. Ibid., p. 80.

24. Ibid., p. 138.

25. Although Oliver objects to the "normalization" of the "neo-Hegelian model

[of abjection]," she acknowledges at one point that it is "very effective in *explaining*
the existence of war and oppression" (p. 10). But the problem is that her (ostensibly) alternative model of witnessing, which is designed to make it possible "to
imagine peaceful compassionate relations with others across or through differences" (p. 10), excludes the very possibility of "war and oppression." Thus she
leaves us with a split between the "is" and the "ought," rather than a mediation of
that split.

26. Oliver, *Witnessing*, pp. 48, 68, 80.

27. Willett, *The Soul of Justice*, p. 163.

28. Ibid., pp. 42, 41, 25, 126–127, 207–208. See also Willett's *Maternal Ethics
and Other Slave Moralities* (New York: Routledge, 1995), pp. 88–94.

29. Willett, *Maternal Ethics*, p. 88.

30. Ibid., pp. 89–90.

31. Aristotle, *Poetics* 1459 a 3–8, cited in Paul Ricoeur, *The Rule of Metaphor*
(Toronto: University of Toronto Press, 1977), p. 23.

32. Willett, *The Soul of Justice*, pp. 33, 79.

33. Ibid., pp. 183, 128, 144; see also pp. 121, 148–149, and 153.

34. Ibid., pp. 21, 165.

35. Ibid., p. 25; see also pp. 59, 61, 164, and 233. Despite this explicit repudiation of an inevitable separation from the mother, and the "emotional
trauma" (p. 62) it entails, just one page later Willett argues that "the most rele-
vant *test* for an authentic moral encounter [demonstrating maturity] under
conditions of domination (*i.e., in this world as we will ever know it*) is the experience of existential turmoil" (p. 63, second emphasis added). The difference between "emotional trauma" and "existential turmoil," if any, is unspecified and
therefore entirely unclear. Thus it would appear that Willett inadvertently calls
into question her own explicit rejection of separation and the anxiety associated with it.

36. Kruks, *Retrieving Experience*, p. 6.

37. Ibid., p. 8.

38. Ibid., pp. 51, 14, 147.

39. Ibid., pp. 144, 152, 149, 155.

40. *Sympathy and Solidarity and Other Essays* (Lanham, MD: Rowman and
Littlefield, 2001), pp. 69–89.

41. Kruks, *Retrieving Experience*, p. 175.

42. Ibid., pp. 84, 164.

43. Ibid., pp. 175, 162, 175.

44. Ibid., p. 162.

45. Dinnerstein, *The Mermaid and The Minotaur* (New York, Harper & Row,
1976).

46. Klein also emphasizes innate or constitutional sources of love and hate,
for which she has, I think, been properly criticized. See for example D. W.
Winnicott, "A Personal View of the Kleinian Contribution," in his *The Matura-*

tional Processes and the Facilitating Environment (New York: International Universities Press, 1965), p. 177.

47. There are two (related) reasons why parenting that was shared by women would not eliminate their demonization. The first follows from Dinnerstein's assumption that it is the identification with a "blameless" father or father-figure that enables boys and girls to evade the task of integrating their love and hate for the mother. On this assumption there is no reason to expect that children raised by two (or more) women, but who could identify with male adults who were uninvolved in primary child care, would be any more likely to negotiate the depressive position successfully than conventionally raised children. Second—and this reason is rather more emphasized by Chodorow than Dinnerstein—as long as boys are initially and exclusively dependent on, and identified with, one or more women, the conflict between their primary female identification and their emerging "core gender identity" will (most often) require that they dis-identify from these women, repudiating the female within them in the process. Thus not only their depressive anxiety but also what might be called their gender anxiety will encourage them (manically) to deny their dependence, first on their mother(s) and then on women as a whole. This argument, of course, presupposes that core gender identity is not, *pace* Judith Butler, a mere social construction or performative effect of "masculine" and "feminine" socialization. For a critique of Butler and a defense of the concept of core gender identity as a genuine cultural universal, see Chapter 3 of this book.

48. Neither Kruks nor Oliver even mentions the possibility of coparenting, and Willett even appears to argue against it (see her critique of Nancy Fraser's "universal care giver model" on pp. 89–93). Only Noddings—in one sentence and almost in passing—endorses this model (see p. 45).

49. In fact Dinnerstein's assumptions in no way exclude the possibility of parenting that is shared between homosexual women and men. Starting from her assumptions it is also possible to argue, as I do in *Emotional Rescue* (pp. 264–265), that coparented children are likely to be far less homophobic than conventionally raised children.

Chapter 5

1. On the political (and personal) conflicts within the British Psycho-Analytic Society, see Phyllis Grosskurth, *Melanie Klein: Her World and Her Work* (Cambridge, MA: Harvard University Press, 1987).

2. The *locus classicus* is of course Freud's *Group Psychology and the Analysis of the Ego* (New York: Bantam Books, 1965).

3. For an introduction to Kleinian group theory, see Alford, *Melanie Klein and Critical Social Theory*, especially Chapter 3, pp. 57–103.

4. Winnicott, *The Maturational Processes and the Facilitating Environment*, and *Through Paediatrics to Psycho-Analysis*.

Chapter 6

1. Christian Lenhardt, "Anamnestic Solidarity: The Proletariat and its *Manes,*" *Telos* 25 (Fall 1975), 134–154; Walter Benjamin, "Theses on the Philosophy of History," in Hannah Arendt, ed., *Illuminations* (New York: Schocken Books, 1968), p. 260.

2. Benjamin, "Theses," pp. 255, 258, 263.

3. Ibid., pp. 254–255.

4. Lenhardt, "Anamnestic Solidarity."

5. Sigmund Freud, "Remembering, Repeating, and Working Through" [1914] *SE*, vol. 12 , pp. 147–156.

6. Theodor Adorno, *Prisms* (Cambridge, MA: MIT Press, 1967), p. 230.

7. Herbert Marcuse, *Counter-Revolution and Revolt* (Boston: Beacon Press, 1972).

8. Benjamin, "Theses," p. 255.

9. Walter Benjamin, "On the Mimetic Faculty," in *Reflections* (New York: Harcourt Brace Jovanovich, 1978), p. 333.

10. Walter Benjamin, "Doctrine of the Similar," *New German Critique* 17 (Spring 1979), 65.

11. Ibid.

12. Walter Benjamin, "One Way Street," in *Reflections*, pp. 92–93.

13. Benjamin, "On the Mimetic Faculty," p. 334.

14. Walter Benjamin, "On the Program of the Coming Philosophy," in Marcus Bullock and Michael W. Jennings, eds., *Selected Writings, Volume I* (Cambridge, MA: Harvard University Press, 1996), p. 100.

15. Benjamin, "One Way Street," p. 93.

16. Ibid.

17. Irving Wohlfarth, "Walter Benjamin's Image of Interpretation," *New German Critique* 17 (Spring 1979), 76.

18. Walter Benjamin, "On Some Motifs in Baudelaire," in Arendt, ed., *Illuminations*, p. 158.

19. Walter Benjamin, "The Storyteller," in *Illuminations*, p. 91.

20. Walter Benjamin, "Images of Proust," in *Illuminations*, p. 211.

21. Benjamin, "On Some Motifs in Baudelaire," p. 159.

22. "Memory creates the chain of tradition which passes a happening on from generation to generation." Benjamin, "The Storyteller," p. 98.

23. Benjamin, "The Storyteller," p. 84; Benjamin, "On Some Motifs in Baudelaire," pp. 158–159; John McCole, *Walter Benjamin and the Antinomies of Tradition* (Ithaca, NY: Cornell University Press, 1993), p. 277.

24. Benjamin, "The Storyteller," pp. 93–94, 98.

25. Benjamin, "On Some Motifs in Baudelaire," p. 163.

26. McCole, *Walter Benjamin and the Antinomies of Tradition*, p. 283; Susan Buck-Morss, *The Dialectics of Seeing* (Cambridge, MA: MIT Press, 1989), p. 108;

Peter Osborne, "Small-Scale Victories, Large-Scale Defeats," in Andrew Benjamin and Peter Osborne, eds., *Walter Benjamin's Philosophy* (New York: Routledge, 1994), p. 83.

27. McCole, *Walter Benjamin and the Antinomies of Tradition*, pp. 272–279.

28. Benjamin, "On Some Motifs in Baudelaire," p. 159.

29. Osborne, "Small-Scale Victories, Large-Scale Defeats," pp. 83–84.

30. Benjamin, "Theses," p. 261.

31. Cited in Buck-Morss, *The Dialectics of Seeing*, p. 99, and Osborne, "Small-Scale Victories, Large-Scale Defeats," p. 83.

32. Benjamin, "Theses," p. 262.

33. Ibid., p. 256.

34. Ibid., p. 255.

35. Lenhardt, "Anamnestic Solidarity."

36. Benjamin, "Theses," p. 254; see also Andrew Benjamin, "Time and Task," in Benjamin and Osborne, *Walter Benjamin's Philosophy*, pp. 232–233.

37. Benjamin, "Theses," p. 263.

38. Cited in Margaret Cohen, *Profane Illuminations* (Berkeley: University of California Press, 1993), p. 10.

39. Benjamin, "Theses," p. 261. On Benjamin's concept of *Jetztzeit*, see Benjamin, "Time and Task," pp. 216–250, and Irving Wohlfarth, "The Messianic Structure of Walter Benjamin's Last Reflections," *Glyph 3* (Baltimore: The Johns Hopkins Press, 1978), pp. 148–212.

40. Lenhardt, "Anamnestic Solidarity"; Jurgen Habermas, *The Philosophic Discourse of Modernity* (Cambridge, MA: MIT Press, 1987), pp. 14–16.

41. Benjamin, "Theses," p. 255.

42. McCole, *Walter Benjamin and the Antinomies of Tradition*, pp. 270–272; Buck-Morss, *The Dialectics of Seeing*, pp. 110–158.

43. Richard Wolin, *Walter Benjamin: An Aesthetics of Redemption* (New York: Columbia University Press, 1982), pp. 179–180; Buck-Morss, *The Dialectics of Seeing*, pp. 120–124.

44. McCole, *Walter Benjamin and the Antinomies of Tradition*, p. 270. On the relationship between "non-sensuous similarities" and the "dialectical image," see Michael W. Jennings, *Walter Benjamin's Theory of Literary Criticism* (Ithaca, NY: Cornell University Press, 1987), pp. 118–120, and Rolf Tidemann, "Dialectics at a Standstill: Approaches to the *Passagen-Werk*," in Gary Smith, ed., *On Walter Benjamin: Critical Essays and Recollections* (Cambridge, MA: MIT Press, 1988), pp. 269–270. For an elucidation of the concept of "non-sensuous similarities," see Anson Rabinbach, "Introduction to Walter Benjamin's 'Doctrine of the Similar,'" *New German Critique* 17 (Spring 1979), 60–64.

45. Cited in Richard Wolin, "Benjamin's *Passagenwerk*," in Gary Smith, ed., *Benjamin: Philosophy, History, Aesthetics* (Chicago: University of Chicago Press, 1989), p. 222.

46. Cited in Buck-Morss, *The Dialectics of Seeing*, p. 256.

47. Buck-Morss, *The Dialectics of Seeing*, pp. 264–265.

48. Cited in Wolin, "Benjamin's *Passagenwerk*," p. 215.

49. Lenhardt, "Anamnestic Solidarity," pp. 136–138.

50. Cited in Wohlfarth, "On the Messianic Structure of Walter Benjamin's Last Reflections," p. 158.

51. Walter Benjamin, "N[Re The Theory of Knowledge, Theory of Progress]," in Smith, ed., *Benjamin: Philosophy, History, Aesthetics*, p. 64.

52. Benjamin, "Theses," p. 260.

53. Gillian Rose, "Walter Benjamin—Out of the Sources of Modern Judaism," *New Formations* 20 (Summer 1993), 81.

Chapter 7

1. The funeral orations take many forms. Richard J. Ellis, in *The Dark Side of the Left* (Lawrence, KS: University Press of Kansas, 1998) contends that the "illiberalism" or authoritarianism of the New Left was inscribed from the very beginning in its "radical egalitarian" commitments, and that a revitalized progressive movement must therefore abandon those commitments. David Burner complains in *Making Peace with the Sixties* (Princeton, NJ: Princeton University Press, 1996) that the Sixties spawned a divisive "identity politics" that obscures the common economic interests on which a majoritarian contemporary Left movement must be based. In both cases the claim is that nothing of value was lost and thus that the only thing worth learning from the Sixties is how not to repeat them. Frederic Jameson, on the other hand, argues in "Periodizing the 60s," in Sohnya Sayres, et al., *The 60s Without Apologies* (Minneapolis: University of Minnesota Press, 1984) that whatever was lost *had to be lost*: "the 60s had to happen the way [they] did" (p. 178) as they were but the inevitable effect of "the transition from one infrastructural or systemic stage of capitalism to another"(p. 208). Thus for Jameson, historical necessity recuperates any sense of regret that might otherwise exist. It also dictates that *nothing at all* can be learned from the Sixties: "nostalgic commemoration of the glories of the '60s or abject confession of the decade's many failures . . . are two errors which cannot be avoided by some middle path that threads its way in between" (p. 178). It is precisely this middle path that I attempt to chart in this chapter, which should therefore be read as a rejoinder to Jameson's argument.

2. In 1984 the *Social Text* editors of *The 60s Without Apologies* confessed that they found it "astonishing that the trashing of the '60s in the media generally should be met with so little indignation or resistance. The numbers of Americans still living today who were involved or touched in at least one political demonstration in the course of the period must be immense. Where are all those people, and what has become of the radical political culture that might normally be expected to emerge from such a tremendous wave of collective experience?" (p. 8). I believe that the claim that "those people" are *politically depressed* goes a long way

toward answering this question and thus explaining the otherwise "astonishing" absence of "indignation or resistance."

3. Sigmund Freud, "Mourning and Melancholia," *SE* vol. 14, p. 243.

4. Ibid., passim. In Freud's later writings this clear-cut opposition between mourning and melancholia is implicitly called into question, especially in "The Ego and the Id," where the ego is defined as "a precipitate of abandoned object-cathexes"; that is, identification with the "lost object" is constitutive of the sense of self. "The Ego and the Id" [1923], *SE* vol. 19 (London: Hogarth Press, 1961), p. 29. But Freud never retheorizes mourning in the light of this effort to modify his drive theory. For an interpretation of drive theory as itself a defense against mourning, see Peter Homans, *The Ability to Mourn* (Chicago: University of Chicago Press, 1989), pp. 114, 222–226.

5. In *Love, Guilt and Reparation and Other Works, 1921-1945* (New York: Free Press, 1984), pp. 344–369.

6. Ibid., p. 353.

7. Ibid., p. 344.

8. Ibid., p. 353.

9. Winnicott, *The Maturational Processes and the Facilitating Environment,* and *Through Paediatrics to Psychoanalysis.* In *Marxism and Domination* and "De-Kleining Feminist Mothering Theory?" (among other earlier works), I argued—following Dorothy Dinnerstein—that the "mother-monopolized" *structure* of early child care itself militates against the successful negotiation of the depressive position, and that it must, therefore, be replaced by coparenting. I continue to believe that this is the case. But if coparenting is *necessary,* it is *not sufficient* for depressive integration. Winnicott is helpful in identifying the (coparenting) *practices* that would facilitate this integration. For the beginnings of a synthesis of a feminist psychoanalytic focus on child-rearing structures and an object-relational focus on child-rearing practices, see my *Emotional Rescue,* especially Chapter 12.

10. This is Winnicott's summary of Klein's argument in "The Depressive Position in Normal Development," in *Through Paediatrics to Psychoanalysis,* p. 275.

11. Klein, *Mourning and Its Relation to Manic-Depressive States,* pp. 352–355.

12. Max Forman, "Two Defenses Against the Work of Mourning," in Sol Altschul, ed., *Childhood Bereavement and Its Aftermath* (Madison, CT: International Universities Press, 1988), p. 378. See also Hans W. Loewald, "Internalization, Separation, Mourning, and the Superego," *Psychoanalytic Quarterly* 3 (1962), especially pp. 485–487.

13. Klein, "Mourning and Its Relation to Manic-Depressive States, p. 360.

14. Ibid., emphasis added.

15. Vamık Volkan, *Linking Objects and Linking Phenomena* (New York: International Universities Press, 1981), pp. 13–14, 112–113. See also pp. 79–80, and S. Ritvo and A. Solnit, "Influences of Early Mother–Child Interaction on the Identification Process," *The Psychoanalytic Study of the Child* 13 (1958), pp. 64–

85; George R. Krupp, "Identification as a Defense Against Anxiety in Coping with Loss," *International Journal of Psycho-Analysis* 46 (1965), 303–314; Joseph H. Smith, "Identificatory Styles in Depression and Grief," *International Journal of Psycho-Analysis* 52 (1971), 259–266; George H. Pollock, "Mourning and Adaptation," in George H. Pollock, *The Mourning–Liberation Process* (Madison, CT: International Universities Press, 1989), pp. 3–45.

16. Joseph H. Smith, "On the Work of Mourning," in B. Schoenberg, et al., *Bereavement: Its Psychological Aspects* (New York: Columbia University Press, 1975), p. 20.

17. "Mourning and Its Relation to Manic-Depressive States," p. 360.

18. Ibid., pp. 362, 353.

19. Ibid., p. 363.

20. Ibid., p. 362.

21. For a useful summary of this literature, see Alford, *Melanie Klein and Critical Social Theory*, Chapter 3.

22. Edward P. Morgan, *The Sixties Experience: Hard Lessons About Modern America* (Philadelphia: Temple University Press, 1991), p. 10. The fact that so many New Left activists were so intensely mother-identified also testifies to the maternal origins of their identification with the Movement. See Balbus, *Marxism and Domination*, pp. 391–394.

23. Henri Lefebvre, *La Vie Quotidienne dans le Monde Moderne* (Paris: Editions Gallimard, 1968).

24. Mark Poster, *Existential Marxism in Postwar France* (Princeton, NJ: Princeton University Press, 1975), p. 288.

25. Walter Benjamin, "Doctrine of the Similar," 65.

26. Walter Benjamin, "Theses," p. 261.

27. Theodor W. Adorno, *Prisms*, p. 230.

28. Wini Breines, *Community and Organization in the New Left, 1962–68* (New York: Praeger, 1982), pp. 1-8.

29. Eric L. Santner, *Stranded Objects* (Ithaca, NY: Cornell University Press, 1990), pp. 53, 126–127, 147; Kenneth J. Doka, *Disenfranchised Grief: Recognizing Hidden Sorrow* (Lexington, MA: Lexington Books, 1989), pp. 80, 86–87, 133, 330.

30. Walter Benjamin, "Theses," p. 255.

Chapter 8

1. Tamar Lewin, "Calls for Slavery Restitution Getting Louder," *New York Times* June 4, 2001; Rachel L. Swarns, "After Much Rangling, an Accord at U.N. Race Meeting," *New York Times* September 9, 2001.

2. Boris Bitker, *The Case for Black Reparations* (New York: Random House, 1973); Randall Robinson, *The Debt: What America Owes to Blacks* (New York: Dutton, 2000); Raymond Winbush, *Should America Pay?: Slavery and the Raging Debate on Reparations* (New York: HarperCollins, 2003); Elazar Barkan, *The Guilt*

of Nations (New York: Norton, 2000); George Schedler, *Racist Symbols and Reparations* (New York: Rowman & Littlefield, 1998).

3. It should go without saying that what is in the emotional interest of whites would also be in the interest of blacks. If, as I argue below, making reparations for racism would be conducive to the emotional development of whites, reparations would also result in better treatment of blacks on the part of whites, which better treatment would undoubtedly contribute to both the material and emotional well-being of blacks as well.

4. As we shall see, the Kleinian case for depressive anxiety and guilt does not require that any given individual white person has actually harmed blacks but rather only that they have fantasied having done so. As long as whites have harbored demonizing (as well as idealizing) racial fantasies there are good Kleinian grounds for assuming that they will experience anxiety and guilt and thus the temptation to defend against them.

5. I say "in some sense" in order to emphasize that the blacks who are "loved" by whites are merely containers of the split-off parts of the selves of whites, projective entities rather than separate, whole persons. In contrast, any "love" genuinely worthy of the name presupposes the overcoming of pathological splitting. This will become clear in the second section of this chapter, on the role of reparations in individual development.

6. After working out this argument in the first draft of this chapter I discovered that a similar argument is advanced by Eric Lott in his impressive *Love and Theft: Blackface Minstrelsy and the American Working Class* (New York: Oxford University Press, 1993). Lott demonstrates that the longstanding and intense attraction of whites to blackface can only be understood if we assume that "negrophobia and negrophilia . . . are not at all contradictory" (p. 103), and that the fantasies of the "white Imaginary [are] constituted by the elements it has attempted to throw off" (p. 150).

7. Barkan, *The Guilt of Nations*, p. 288.

8. Melanie Klein, *Contributions to Psycho-Analysis, 1921–1945* (London: Hogarth Press, 1965), p. 313.

9. Jean-Michel Petot, *Melanie Klein, Volume I* (Madison, CT: International Universities Press, 1990), p. 187.

10. Jean-Michel Petot, *Melanie Klein, Volume II* (Madison, CT: International Universities Press, 1991), p. 172.

11. Melanie Klein, *Envy and Gratitude and Other Works, 1946–1963* (New York: Free Press, 1975), p. 6.

12. Of course it is only by virtue of the gradual development of the self–other distinction that the processes of introjection and projection described above become possible. Thus the relationship between introjection/projection and the formation of the distinction between self and object must be understood as mutually constitutive.

13. See Chapter 1 of this book.

14. Melanie Klein, *Love, Guilt and Reparation and Other Works, 1921–1945* (New York: Dell, 1975), p. 227.

15. Petot, *Melanie Klein, Volume I*, p. 276.

16. Klein, *Envy and Gratitude and Other Works*, pp. 35–36.

17. Klein uses the term "position" rather than "stage" in order to emphasize that depressive integration is an ongoing, lifelong task that is always haunted by the specter of paranoid-schizoid tendencies. On this point see Alford, *Melanie Klein and Critical Social Theory*, pp. 39, 43.

18. Klein, *Envy and Gratitude and Other Works*, p. 13.

19. Thus Klein notes, in Ibid., p. 7, that idealization presupposes the earlier introjection of an all-good breast.

20. Hanna Segal, *Melanie Klein* (New York: Viking, 1980), pp. 79–80.

21. Klein argues that "schizoid mechanisms . . . remain in force [after the first six months] . . . and early anxiety-situations are again experienced in the process of modification. The working through of the persecutory and depressive positions extends over the first few years of childhood." (Klein, *Envy and Gratitude and Other Works*, p. 15).

22. Petot, *Melanie Klein, Volume II*, p. 124; see also p. 72.

23. Klein, *Contributions to Psycho-Analysis*, pp. 339–390.

24. Alford, *Melanie Klein and Critical Social Theory*, pp. 31–50; Grosskurth, *Melanie Klein: Her World and Her Works*, p. 450.

25. Klein, *Contributions to Psycho-Analysis*, p. 306. See also p. 12, where she argues that "the visible mother . . . provides continual proofs of what the 'internal mother' is like, whether she is loving or angry, helpful or revengeful."

26. Klein, *Love, Guilt and Reparation and Other Works*, pp. 298, 301.

27. Alford, *Melanie Klein and Critical Social Theory*, pp. 34–37; Klein, *Envy and Gratitude and Other Works*, pp. 89–90; Klein, *Contributions to Psycho-Analysis*, pp. 311–338.

28. This argument does not imply that defensive splitting is not encouraged in non-Western or "premodern" cultures. Indeed, in *Marxism and Domination*, Chapter 9, I argue that it *is*, but that it takes a different form. The relatively indulgent child-rearing practices in these cultures typically engender predominantly idealizing defenses against depressive anxiety and guilt, whereas the more repressive child-rearing practices of the modern West tend to privilege manically denying defenses.

29. Thus I disagree with the argument, advanced for example by Volkan in *The Need to Have Enemies and Allies* (Northvale, NJ: Jason Aronson, 1994), pp. 30–33, and apparently shared by Alford, *Melanie Klein and Critical Social Theory*, pp. 68 and 75–76, that group splitting is consistent with, and even facilitates, individual integration. This argument, it seems to me, renders demonizing and idealizing racial fantasies immune to individual emotional growth and the conditions that might facilitate it, and thus effectively essentializes racism.

30. Leon F. Litwack, *Trouble in Mind: Black Southerners in the Age of Jim Crow* (New York: Vintage Books, 1999).

31. Of course it is always possible for the racist to find examples of black people who do in fact fit his or her stereotype. Indeed, we should always expect that a certain proportion of people who are debased for their alleged "dependence"—or any other demonized attribute—will come to embody the very qualities for which they are debased. A black song from the 1930s makes this point as well as it is possible to make it:

'Cause white folks expect a nigger to be lazy

Ain't no cause to worry

I wouldn't disappoints him for the world

That's why I never hurry. (Litwack, *Trouble in Mind*, p. 434.)

32. Lott, *Love and Theft*, p. 122.

33. Thus for Klein idealization and persecutory anxiety are always two sides of the same coin. See *Envy and Gratitude and Other Works*, p. 7.

34. Julia Kristeva, *Powers of Horror: An Essay on Abjection* (New York: Columbia University Press, 1982); Lott, *Love and Theft*, p. 148.

35. Winthrop Jordan, *White Over Black: American Attitudes Toward the Negro, 1550–1812* (Chapel Hill: University of North Carolina Press, 1968).

36. Mary Ellen Goodman, *Race Awareness in Young Children* (Cambridge, MA: Addison-Wesley Press, 1962); Marjorie McDonald, *Not by the Color of Their Skin* (New York: International Universities Press, 1970).

37. McDonald, Ibid., pp. 114, 161–162.

38. Klein, *Love, Guilt and Reparation and Other Works*, p. 410.

39. Joel Kovel, *White Racism: A Psychohistory* (New York: Columbia University Press, 1984), pp. 48–49, 263–272.

40. Lawrence Kubie, "Ontogeny of Racial Prejudice," *Journal of Nervous and Mental Disorders* 141(3) (1965), 265–273.

41. Sander Gilman, *Difference and Pathology* (Ithaca, NY: Cornell University Press, 1985); Noel Ignatiev, *How the Irish Became White* (New York: Routledge, 1995).

42. The problem with *this* explanation, however, is that it appears that the anal repression that is supposed to engender unresolved anal conflicts and defenses against them barely exists, if at all, in many of the premodern societies in which this cultural equation nonetheless also exists. But there may be another psychodynamic explanation for this cultural equation at which Kovel occasionally hints (on pp. 92, 95, 169, 237) but does not really develop. Perhaps the association of black with bad reflects a fear of the darkness of night that the dark skin of blacks comes to represent, a fear that can be considered a conscious expression of the anxiety of nighttime separation from the mother. Thus aversion to blackness could be the defensive consequence of rage against the mother for separations imposed well before the anal stage. My earlier account of orally based racism could thus be

expanded to include an explanation for the metaphorical association of blacks with evil and danger. Such an explanation, I believe, would be completely complementary to the anally based explanation, which would still be necessary to account for the origins of the fantasy that blacks are dirty and smelly.

43. Franz Fanon, *Black Skin, White Masks* (New York: Grove Press, 1967), p. 177.

44. John Cash, *The Mind of the South* (New York: Vintage Books, 1960); Calvin Hernton, *Sex and Racism in America* (New York: Grove Press, 1965); Jordan, *White Over Black*; Kovel, *White Racism.*

45. Lillian Smith, *Killers of the Dream* (Garden City, NY: Doubleday, 1963).

46. Litwack, *Trouble in Mind.*

47. Cited in Hernton, *Sex and Racism in America*, pp. 98–99.

48. Hernton, *Sex and Racism in America*, pp. 25, 113; see also Lott, *Love and Theft*, pp. 121–122.

49. John Dollard, *Caste and Class in a Southern Town* (New York: Doubleday, 1949).

50. Cash, *The Mind of the South*, p. 117.

51. Elizabeth Young-Bruehl, *The Anatomy of Prejudices* (Cambridge, MA: Harvard University Press, 1966).

52. Cited in Young-Bruehl, *The Anatomy of Prejudices*, p. 490.

53. Malcolm X, *The Autobiography of Malcolm X* (New York: Grove Press, 1965), pp. 119–120.

54. Hernton, *Sex and Racism in America*, pp. 89–90.

55. I hasten to add that the sexual "thing" that many whites have for blacks is not the only reason—or even the main reason—for most serious interracial relationships. There are plenty of reasons other than racialized sexual fantasies why a person who happens to be white would be attracted to a person who happens to be black.

56. But Klein also emphasizes what Freud did not, namely that the boy's oedipally based hatred of the father results in part from the boy's projection of rage against the bad breast into him. See her *Love, Guilt and Reparation and Other Works*, p. 408.

57. Of course the oedipal implications of the desire of white men for black women are even clearer in the case of white men who were either raised (during slavery) by a black mammy or (after slavery) by a black nanny. For these men sexual relations with a black woman provided (and provides) an access to the maternal body that is more direct—and perhaps even more desired—than the access available to white men who did not or do not have black primary caregivers. For a summary of the literature on this issue, see Heidi J. Nast, "Mapping the 'Unconscious': Racism and the Oedipal Family," *Annals of the Association of American Geographers* 90(2) (2000), 515–555. I am grateful to Jim Hall for alerting me to this article.

58. Dinnerstein, *The Mermaid and The Minotaur*, pp. 51–53. Here Dinnerstein echoes Klein, who concludes that the oedipalized girl "is capable of complete submission to [the] admired internalized father." *Love, Guilt and Reparation and Other Works*, p. 414.

59. Jessica Benjamin, *The Bonds of Love* (New York: Pantheon, 1988), p. 81.

60. Fanon, *Black Skin, White Masks*, p. 167.

61. To this I can relate personally. I still remember how I swelled with pride when, back in the Sixties, a *black person* actually asked *me* how I had learned to dance so well.

62. Cited in Hernton, *Sex and Racism in America*, p. 117.

63. Lawrence Kubie, "The Fantasy of Dirt," *Psychoanalytic Quarterly* 6 (1937), 382–425.

64. Kovel, *White Racism*, p. 194.

65. CNN.Com/Law Center, March 27, 2002.

66. Some of these discussions are archived in the files of the author.

67. Malcolm X, *The Autobiography of Malcolm X*, p. 204.

68. Ibid., p. 370.

69. Because the repression of those needs is normatively reinforced—since independence, control, sexual restraint, and a civilized body are central modern Western cultural values—an authentically racially reparative process would also necessarily be a countercultural process. Thus the struggle against racism is complementary to, and ultimately merges with, other central struggles against the madness of modernity.

70. James Baldwin, *The Fire Next Time* (New York: Modern Library, 1995), p. 96.

71. Cited in Young-Bruehl, *The Anatomy of Prejudices*, pp. 488–489.

72. Whereas in authentic reparation one gives in order to limit damage to the (m)other, in mock reparation one gives to limit damage to the self. But this struggle to save the self can never succeed. Because the fearful child has no reason to trust that his or her restitutive efforts have in fact propitiated the persecutor, these efforts tend to multiply compulsively and/or are often followed by a renunciation of a restitutive strategy in favor of more overt paranoid-schizoid counterattacks. On the distinction between authentic and mock reparations, see Petot, *Melanie Klein, Volume I*, pp. 281–282.

73. Juan Williams, "Get a Check? No Thanks," *Frontpage* (online) magazine, April 21, 2001.

74. Ralph Ellison, *Time* (April 6, 1970), 54–55.

75. It may now be the case that many whites—to judge from the decline in their support for affirmative action—are in fact *less* well-intentioned than they were prior to this period of neglect. If they *have* become less reparatively inclined, perhaps this is (in part) because they perceived increasing black militancy to be an ungrateful, even hostile response to the (arguably but insufficiently)

reparative efforts that preceded that period. The fact that the rhetoric of Black Power and the reality of ghetto revolts followed so closely on the heels of the major civil rights legislation of 1964 and 1965, and that what Stephen Steinberg has called the "retreat from racial justice" began almost immediately thereafter, support this interpretation. See *Turning Back: The Retreat from Racial Justice in America* (Boston: Beacon Press, 1995). So too does the fact that so many of the neoconservative intellectuals who have since led the assault on affirmative action are Jews, who were once deeply committed to and involved in the struggle for racial integration. On this interpretation, then, the assault on affirmative action looks like a resentful response to—a schizoid attack on—unrequited reparations. The properly reparative process I have called for would be obliged to acknowledge, and work through, this resentment.

76. This sense derives from discussions of this chapter with a number of African-American friends and colleagues.

Chapter 9

1. http://www.nua.com/surveys/how_many_online/index.html. February 21, 2002. Nua.com describes itself as "the authoritative online source for information on Internet demographics and trends."

2. Sherry Turkle, *Life on the Screen: Identity in the Age of the Internet* (New York: Simon & Schuster, 1995).

3. http://www.findarticles.com/p/articles/mi_m4021/is_200 . . .

4. Wysiwyg://6http://www.europemedia.net/shownews.asp?.

5. Annette N. Markham, *Life Online* (New York: Altamira Press, 1998).

6. See for example the essays in Michael Benedikt, *Cyberspace: First Steps* (Cambridge, MA: MIT Press, 1991).

7. Winnicott, *Playing and Reality*, p. 11.

8. Dinnerstein, *The Mermaid and The Minotaur*, p. 60.

9. Sigmund Freud, "On Narcissism: An Introduction," in Peter Gay, ed., *The Freud Reader* (New York: Norton, 1989), p. 556.

10. Jean Piaget, *The Construction of Reality in the Child* (New York: Basic Books, 1954), pp. 103–104.

11. Ibid., p. 348.

12. Ibid., p. 240.

13. Ibid., pp. 249, 227–228.

14. Jean Piaget, *The Child's Conception of Reality* (New York: Humanities Press, 1951), pp. 125, 153.

15. Piaget, *The Construction of Reality in the Child*, pp. 376–377.

16. Piaget, *The Child's Conception of Reality*, pp. 125, 152.

17. Ibid., p. 125.

18. At least since Klein, and especially with Winnicott, however, psychoanalysis emphasizes far more than cognitive developmental psychology the continu-

ing centrality of fantasy to a creative relationship to reality. See Winnicott's distinction between infantile omnipotence and transitional phenomena, and his discussion of the relationship between maternal "illusionment" and "disillusionment" in *Playing and Reality*, pp. 11–14.

19. It should of course go without saying that I refer here and elsewhere in this chapter to the primary caregiver as the "mother" not because I assume that mother-dominated child rearing is either desirable or inevitable, but rather simply because it is *statistically* normal. For the critique of this arrangement, see Chapters 1 through 3 of this book.

20. Dinnerstein, *The Mermaid and The Minotaur*, p. 60.

21. Ibid.

22. Otto F. Kernberg, *Borderline Conditions and Pathological Narcissism*, p. 227.

23. Grandiose narcissists do tend to attract idealizing narcissists who want to bask in their reflected glory. But even idealizing narcissists will eventually fail to supply the grandiose narcissist with the perfect mirroring he requires.

24. Kernberg, *Borderline Conditions and Pathological Narcissism*, pp. 33, 228.

25. Ibid., pp. 213–214, 229.

26. Ibid., pp. 214, 222.

27. Winnicott, *Playing and Reality*, p. 89.

28. Otto F. Kernberg, *Internal World and External Reality* (New York: Jason Aronson, 1980), p. 137.

29. Franco Ferrarotti, *Time, Memory, and Society* (New York: Greenwood Press, 1990), p. 31.

30. Kernberg, *Internal World and External Reality*, p. 140.

31. As I intimated in the introduction to this chapter, this relationship is not only parallel or analogous but is also *causal*. But the causality is reciprocal. On the one hand, modernity mandates child-rearing structures and practices that encourage individual narcissism, and on the other hand individual narcissism supplies unconscious emotional fuel for the shared fantasies of modernity. Thus modernity can be understood as (among other things) a culture of omnipotence that both engenders and is engendered by the omnipotence of the individuals who inhabit it.

32. Karl Marx, "Estranged Labour," in Robert C. Tucker, ed., *The Marx–Engels Reader* (New York: Norton, 1978), p. 76.

33. Jean Baudrillard, *For a Critique of the Political Economy of the Sign* (St. Louis, MO: Telos Press, 1981).

34. As far as I am aware, this phrase was first used by T. Hagerstrand in "Time and Culture," in G. Kirsch, P. Nijkamp, and K. Zimmermans, eds., *Time Preferences: An Interdisciplinary Theoretical and Empirical Approach* (Berlin: Wissenschaftszentrum, 1985), pp. 1–15.

35. Barbara Adam, *Time and Social Theory* (Philadelphia: Temple University Press, 1990), p. 139.

36. Ferrarotti, *Time, Memory, and Society*, pp. 74, 90.

37. Ibid., p. 91.

38. H. Nowotny, "From the Future to the Extended Present: Time in Social Systems," in G. Kirsch, et al., eds, *Time Preferences*, p. 14.

39. Norman O. Brown, *Life Against Death* (Middletown, CT: Wesleyan University Press, 1959), p. 284; Zygmunt Bauman, *Mortality, Immortality, and Other Life Strategies* (Cambridge, UK: Polity Press, 1992), p. 142.

40. Nowotny, "From the Future to the Extended Present," p. 15.

41. David Harvey, *The Condition of Postmodernity* (Cambridge, MA: Basil Blackwell, 1989), p. 229.

42. Ferrarotti, *Time, Memory, and Society*, p. 92.

43. Cited in Barbara Adam, *Time and Social Theory*, p. 140.

44. Ferrarotti, *Time, Memory, and Society*, p. 92.

45. David Holmes, "Introduction," in David Holmes, ed., *Virtual Politics* (London: Sage Publications, 1997), p. 15.

46. Ibid., p. 6.

47. Chris Chesler, "The Ontology of Digital Domains," in David Holmes, ed., *Virtual Politics*, p. 88.

48. Arthur Kroker and Michael A. Weinstein, *Data Trash: The Theory of the Virtual Class* (New York: St. Martin's Press, 1994), p. 9.

49. Cited in Albert Borgmann, *Crossing the Postmodern Divide* (Chicago: University of Chicago Press, 1992), p. 88.

50. Howard Rheingold, *Virtual Reality* (New York: Simon & Schuster, 1991), p. 386.

51. Simon Cooper, "Plenitude and Alienation: The Subject of Virtual Reality," in David Holmes, ed., *Virtual Politics*, p. 93.

52. Cited in Paul Virilio, *The Information Bomb* (London: Verso, 2000), p. 93.

53. Michael Heim, *The Metaphysics of Virtual Reality* (New York: Oxford University Press, 1993), p. 85.

54. Markham, *Life Online*, p. 124.

55. Sherry Turkle, *Life on the Screen*, p. 11.

56. Markham, *Life Online*, p. 214.

57. Ibid., pp. 135, 170.

58. Sherry Turkle, *The Second Self: Computers and the Human Spirit*, cited in Howard Rheingold, *The Virtual Community*, p. 153.

59. John Carroll, *Ego and Soul* (Sydney: HarperCollins, 1998), p. 157. See also similar descriptions in Gary Chapman, "Taming the Computer," in Mark Dery, ed., *Flame Wars: The Discourse of Cyberculture* (Durham, NC: Duke University Press, 1993), p. 832, and Albert Borgmann, *Crossing the Postmodern Divide*, p. 107.

60. Carroll, *Ego and Soul*, p. 157.

61. David Holmes, "Virtual Identity: Communities of Broadcast, Communities of Interactivity," in David Holmes, ed., *Virtual Politics*, p. 39.

62. Markham, *Life Online*, p. 186.

63. Borgmann, *Crossing the Postmodern Divide*, p. 105.

64. Michael Heim, *The Metaphysics of Virtual Reality* (New York: Oxford University Press, 1993), p. 100.

65. Markham, *Life Online*, p. 58.

66. William Gibson, *Neuromancer* (New York: Ace Books, 1984), p. 6.

67. Ibid., p. 89.

68. Margaret Wertheim, "The Pearly Gates of Cyberspace," in Nan Ellin, *Architecture of Fear* (New York: Princeton Architectural Press, 1997), p. 302.

69. Cited in Nicola Green, "Beyond Being Digital: Representation and Corporeality," in David Holmes, ed., *Virtual Politics*, p. 61.

70. Kroker and Weinstein, *Data Trash*, p. 42.

Chapter 10

1. My assumption is that there is not merely an analogical but also a *transferential* relationship between the infant's relationship to its mother and the adult's relationship to nature. See Chapter 2 of this book where I assume, following Dinnerstein, that nature inevitably inherits the explosive mixture of the infant's feelings for its mother, who is normally its first representative of the world. This assumption authorizes the hypothesis, first proposed in my *Marxism and Domination*, that the symbolization of nature is determined by the mode of child rearing. But I also argue in that work (pp. 344–352) that this causal priority of the mode of child rearing over the mode of symbolization does not prevent the latter from exercising an important influence over the former.

2. For the concepts of "holding" and "mirroring" see Winnicott, *The Maturational Processes and the Facilitating Environment*, pp. 43–55, and *Playing and Reality*, pp. 111–118. For the ecological analogues, see Harold F. Searles, *The Nonhuman Environment* (New York: International Universities Press, 1960), pp. 54–139.

3. Hegel, *The Phenomenology of Mind*, p. 238.

4. See Jonathan Lear, *The Place of Love in Nature* (New York: Farrar, Straus & Giroux, 1990), p. 154, for the concept of a "good-enough" world.

5. Winnicott, *Playing and Reality*, pp. 89, 14.

6. David Abram, *The Spell of the Sensuous* (New York: Pantheon Books, 1996), p. 22. See also Bill McKibben, *The End of Nature* (New York: Random House, 1989), pp. 47–91; Robert E. Goodin, *Green Political Theory* (Cambridge, UK: Polity Press, 1992), pp. 37–41; David W. Kinder, *Nature and Psyche* (Albany, NY: State University of New York Press, 2001), pp. 283–321; and Searles, *The Nonhuman Environment*, pp. 54–139.

7. Walter Truett Anderson, *To Govern Evolution* (New York: Harcourt Brace Jovanovich, 1987), pp. 326, 325.

8. Anderson is aware of, but ultimately underestimates, the strength of this temptation. On the one hand, he acknowledges that "the human ability to avoid

knowing the truth about its own ecological interventionism is nothing less than stunning" (p. 240), and that "it is a responsibility we greatly want to resist" (p. 327). But on the other, he argues that "as the accumulation of information overwhelms our fears" (p. 240) it eventually "becomes impossible to continue hiding the truth from ourselves" (p. 318). Thus, for Anderson, fantasy will ultimately, and automatically, be overpowered by (knowledge of) reality. But this positivist prognosis is undermined by his own semi-psychoanalytical diagnosis. From a psychoanalytic point of view, there is no reason to assume that reality will triumph over fantasy in the absence of a painful working-through of the defenses that protect us from it.

9. Harold F. Searles, "Unconscious Processes in Relation to the Environmental Crisis," *Psychoanalytic Review* 59(3) (Fall 1972), 369, 371.

10. For the "reflexive modernist" account, see Ulrich Beck, *Ecological Politics in an Age of Risk* (Cambridge, UK: Polity Press, 1995) and Anthony Giddens, *Beyond Left and Right* (Cambridge, UK: Polity Press, 1994). For a postmodernist account, see Ingoflur Bluhdorn, *Post-Ecological Politics* (New York: Routlege, 2000).

11. McKibben, *The End of Nature*, pp. 83, 59.

12. Otto Kernberg, *Borderline Conditions and Pathological Narcissism*, p. 220.

13. David Michael Levin, "Psychopathology in the Epoch of Nihilism," in David Michael Levin, ed., *Pathologies of the Modern Self* (New York: New York University Press, 1987), pp. 21–83.

14. Melanie Klein, "A Contribution to the Psychogenesis of Manic-Depressive States," in Melanie Klein, *Contributions to Psycho-Analysis*, p. 299.

15. Carroll, *Ego and Soul*, pp. 119, 127.

16. The term is from Michael Schneider, *Neurosis and Civilization* (New York: Seabury, 1975).

17. Heinz Kohut, *The Analysis of the Self* (New York: International Universities Press, 1971), p. 27. Thus the commodified images that advertising invents only give voice to, and work on, the preexisting fantasies of perfection that proliferate in modernity.

18. Arne Naess, "The Shallow and the Deep, Long-Range Ecology Movement: A Summary," *Inquiry* 16(1) (Spring 1973), 95–100.

19. Andrew McLaughlin, *Regarding Nature* (New York: State University of New York Press, 1993), p. 172.

20. Raymond Murphy, *Rationality and Nature* (Boulder, CO: Westview Press, 1994), p. 91. In 1982 a Republican Study Committee report decried deep ecology as a "revolutionary . . . threat" and thereby testified to its growing political influence. See T. M. Peckinpaugh, *The Specter of Environmentalism: The Threat of Environmental Groups* (Washington, DC: Republican Study Committee, 1982), p. 3.

21. Timothy W. Luke, *Ecocritique* (Minneapolis: University of Minnesota Press, 1997), p. 2.

22. Naess, "The Shallow and the Deep," p. 96.

23. Naess, "The Shallow and the Deep," pp. 94–98. In Naess's twin insistence on dependence and ignorance he is deeply indebted to his remarkably prescient

predecessor Aldo Leopold, who as early as the 1940s argued that "the individual is a member of a community of interdependent parts [that] includes soils, waters, plants, and animals, or collectively: the land," and that the "ability to see the cultural value of wilderness boils down . . . to a question of intellectual humility." See Leopold's *A Sand County Almanac* (New York: Oxford University Press, 1949), pp. 203–204, 200.

24. Arne Naess, *Ecology, Community, and Lifestyle* (Cambridge: Cambridge University Press, 1989), p. 187.

25. Bill Devall and George Sessions, *Deep Ecology* (Salt Lake City, UT: Gibbs M. Smith, 1985), p. 110.

26. See Chapter 2, p. 20.

27. Naess, *Ecology, Community, and Lifestyle*, pp. 181, 15, 198–199.

28. Stephan Bodian, "Simple in Means, Rich in Ends: A Conversation with Arne Naess," *The Ten Directions* (Los Angeles: Institute for Transcultural Studies, Zen Center of Los Angeles, Summer/Fall 1982).

29. Naess, *Ecology, Community, and Lifestyle*, p. 15.

30. Cited in Bill Devall and George Sessions, *Deep Ecology* (Salt Lake City, UT: Gibbs M. Smith, 1985), p. 70.

31. For a recent survey of this debate, see John Barry, *Rethinking Green Politics* (London: Sage Publications, 1999).

32. My argument in Chapter 2 that nature *should* be seen as an end in itself is vulnerable to this point.

33. Cited in Barry, *Rethinking Green Politics*, p. 30. As early as 1973, Naess maintained that "the ecological field-worker acquires a deep-seated respect, or even veneration, for [all] forms of life. He reaches an understanding from within, a kind of understanding that others reserve for fellow men." "The Shallow and the Deep," pp. 95–96.

34. Andrew McLaughlin, *Regarding Nature*, p. 172.

35. Anderson, *To Govern Evolution*, p. 323.

36. *Deep Ecology*, p. 72.

37. Naess, "The Shallow and the Deep," p. 95.

38. *Deep Ecology*, p. 70.

39. Naess, *Ecology, Community, and Lifestyle*, p. 168.

40. Ibid., p. 98.

41. Ibid., p. 30.

42. *Deep Ecology*, p. 70.

43. Naess, *Ecology, Community, and Lifestyle*, p. 91. See also pp. 24–26.

44. Robert Wuthnow, *Sharing the Journey: Support Groups and America's New Quest for Community* (New York: Free Press, 1994), pp. 70–71.

45. Robin Room, "'Healing Ourselves and Our Planet': The Emergence of a Generalized Twelve-Step Consciousness," *Contemporary Drug Problems* (Winter 1992), 737.

46. Heidi Schlumpf, "Recovering Grace," *U.S. Catholic*, 68(11) (November

2003), 12. See also Craig Reinarman, "The Twelve-Step Movement and Advanced Capitalist Culture: The Politics of Self-Control in Postmodernity," in Marcy Darnovsky, Barbara Epstein, and Richard Flacks, eds., *Cultural Politics and Social Movements* (Philadelphia: Temple University Press 1995), p. 97, which also cites the 15 million figure.

47. Thomasina Jo Borkman, *Understanding Self-Help/Mutual Aid* (New Brunswick, NJ: Rutgers University Press, 1999), p. 5.

48. The lower estimate comes from Alfred A. Katz, *Self-Help in America: A Social Movement Perspective* (New York: Twayne Publishers, 1993), p. 11; the higher is cited in Room, "'Healing Ourselves and Our Planet,'" p. 727.

49. Room, "'Healing Ourselves and Our Planet,'" pp. 717–722.

50. *Big Book*, pp. 60–71; *Twelve Steps and Twelve Traditions*, pp. 45, 70. The emphasis on "alcoholic grandiosity" as the heart of the problem of addiction incorporates the understanding of Dr. Harry Tiebout, psychiatrist of Bill Wilson (a cofounder of AA), that the addict suffers from what Freud called the narcissism of "his majesty the baby." Thus my account of compulsive consumption as a form of infantile omnipotence reproduces an interpretation that is already widely shared by the members of the twelve-step movement. On this point see Ernest Kurtz, *Not-God: A History of Alcoholics Anonymous* (Center City, MN: Hazelden Educational Services, 1979), pp. 126–127, 199–230.

51. *Big Book*, p. 62.

52. Ibid.

53. Liz Turnbull, "Narcissism and the Potential for Self-Transformation in the Twelve Steps," *Health* 1(2) (1997), 152.

54. Cited in Kurtz, *Not-God*, pp. 13–14.

55. Kurtz, *Not-God*, pp. 182, 209.

56. Cited in Gregory Bateson, "The Cybernetics of 'Self': A Theory of Alcoholism," in his *Steps to an Ecology of Mind* (New York: Ballantine Books, 1972), p. 313.

57. Bateson, "'The Cybernetics of Self': A Theory of Alcoholism," pp. 322, 327.

58. *Twelve Steps and Twelve Traditions*, p. 70.

59. Ibid., p. 5.

60. Ibid.

61. Ibid., p. 49.

62. *Alcoholics Anonymous Comes of Age* (New York: Harper, 1957), p. 279.

63. Turnbull, "Narcissism and the Potential for Self-Transformation in the Twelve Steps," pp. 157–58; Betsy Robin Spiegel, "12-Step Programs as a Treatment Modality," in Shulamith Lala Ashenberg Straussner, ed., *Clinical Work with Substance-Abusing Clients* (New York: Guilford, 1993), pp. 158–159; Shulamith Lala Ashenberg Straussner and Betsy Robin Spiegel, "An Analysis of 12-Step Programs for Substance Abusers from a Developmental Perspective," *Clinical Social Work Journal* 24(3) (Fall 1996), 299, 306.

64. See for example Stanton Peele and Archie Brodsky, *Love and Addiction*

(New York: Taplinger, 1975), p. 232, and Howard F. Stein, "Alcoholism as Meta-phor in American Culture: Ritual Desecration as Social Integration," *Ethos*, 13(3) (Fall 1985), 223–124.

65. Thus the ubiquitous twelve-step Serenity Prayer: "God grant me the se-renity to accept the things I cannot change, the courage to change the things I can, and the wisdom to know the difference."

66. *Twelve Steps and Twelve Traditions*, p. 6.

67. Turnbull, "Narcissism and the Potential for Self-Transformation in the Twelve Steps," p. 152.

68. Straussner and Spiegel, "An Analysis of 12-Step Programs for Substance Abusers from a Developmental Perspective," p. 307.

69. *Twelve Steps and Twelve Traditions*, pp. 55–62.

70. Ibid., pp. 7–8.

71. Ibid., p. 80.

72. *Big Book*, p. 82.

73. Ibid., p. 78.

74. Ibid., pp. 83, 77.

75. *Twelve Steps and Twelve Traditions*, pp. 79–80.

76. *Big Book*, pp. 83–84.

77. *Twelve Steps and Twelve Traditions*, pp. 9, 120, 122.

78. Sigmund Freud, "The Question of Lay Analysis," *SE* vol. 20, p. 207. See also "Introductory Lectures on Psycho-Analysis," *SE* vol. 16, p. 457, and *Civili-zation and Its Discontents* (New York: Norton, 1961), p. 98.

79. Anthony Giddens deserves credit for developing this insight in his *Mo-dernity and Self-Identity* (Cambridge, UK: Polity Press, 1991); *The Transformation of Intimacy* (Cambridge, UK: Polity Press, 1992); and "Living in a Post-Tradi-tional Society," in Ulrich Beck, Anthony Giddens, and Scott Lash, *Reflexive Mod-ernization* (Cambridge, UK: Polity Press, 1994). Giddens correctly captures compulsive consumption as a distinctively modern problem, but his account of modernity uncritically assumes the inevitability of the very "abolition of nature" which, according to my account, is the source of that problem. Thus his critique of modernity, it seems to me, is divided against itself.

80. Kurtz, *Not-God*, p. 171.

81. Ernest Kurtz, "Why A.A. Works: The Intellectual Significance of Alco-holics Anonymous," *Journal of Studies on Alcohol* 43(1) (1982), 39.

82. Naess's conviction that "with maturity, human beings *will* experience" [emphasis added] a nonanthropocentric relationship with nature implies the recognition that many individuals currently *lack* that maturity (see note 28, above). But how they might remedy that lack is never clarified. In his "Deep Ecology in Good Conceptual Health," *The Trumpeter* 3(4) (Fall 1986), p. 20, he claims that "just the ordinary sensitivity of a loving child" is sufficient for the realization of that relationship, but (1) this appears to contradict the

claim that this relationship depends on "maturity," and (2) Naess never considers how the "ordinary sensitivity of a loving child" can easily succumb to deadening defenses against his or her own not-so-loving impulses.

83. The one exception to this generalization of which I am aware appears in the *Twelve Steps and Twelve Traditions of Overeaters Anonymous* (Rio Rancho, NM: Overeaters Anonymous, 2001), p. 39, where members are asked whether they have "ever abused animals." But this is the *only* specifically nature-related question among more than a hundred others that are recommended for inclusion in their moral inventories.

84. *Twelve Steps and Twelve Traditions*, p. 12.

85. Room, "'Healing Ourselves and Our Planet,'" p. 727.

86. Schlumpf, "Recovering Grace," p. 15.

Index